**From America's #1 Cleaning Expert**

# CLEANING UP FOR A LIVING

## 2ⁿᵈ Edition

From America's #1 Cleaning Expert

# CLEANING UP FOR A LIVING

## 2nd Edition

**Everything you need to know to become a successful building service contractor.**

**Don A. Aslett**
**Mark L. Browning**

BETTER
WAY
BOOKS
CINCINNATI, OHIO

97  96  95  94  93     5  4  3

Cover design and principal illustrations by Kerry Otteson
Illustrations by Robert L. Betty
Typography by East Coast Typography, Inc.

**Library of Congress Cataloging-in-Publication Data**

Aslett, Don
  Cleaning up for a living : everything you need to know to become a successful building service contractor / Don Aslett and Mark Browning — 2nd ed.
    p. cm.
  Includes bibliographical references and index.
  ISBN 1-55870-206-7 (pbk.)
  1. Building cleaning industry—Management.
I. Browning, Mark.   II. Title.
HD9999.B882A85  1991
648'.5'068—dc20                          91-19202
                                              CIP

*There are very few new ideas in the world — the world of professional cleaning, or anything else. Even the most creative of us are mostly improving on existing ideas, or simply smart enough to seek out the persons and places that can best supplement what we know.*

*This book would have a lot less to offer without the contributions of our colleagues and associates — the managers, supervisors, and hands-on cleaners of Varsity Contractors and other professional cleaners elsewhere.*

*Our sincerest thanks to all of you for your advice and encouragement, as well as the technique, system, procedures, and irreplaceable experience you so freely shared.*

# Contents

# Acknowledgments

There are very few new ideas in the world — the world of professional cleaning, or anything else. Even the most creative of us are mostly improving on existing ideas, or simply smart enough to seek out the persons and places that can best supplement what *we* know.

This book would have a lot less to offer without the contributions of our colleagues and associates — the managers, supervisors, and hands-on cleaners of varsity Contractors and other professional cleaners elsewhere.

Our sincerest thanks to all of you for your advice and encouragement, as well as the technique, system, procedures, and irreplaceable experience you so freely shared.

# YOUR OWN BUSINESS

Can you really clean up in the cleaning business? Yes, in more ways than one, but don't expect it to be a "get rich quick" scheme. Success in the cleaning industry depends on a lot of hard work and persistence, and there is no guarantee that you will be one of the winners. The purpose of this book is to help you evaluate whether or not you are suited to having/building a cleaning business of your own, and to help you avoid some of the pitfalls which await the unwary.

Perhaps you have heard of my story — how Don Aslett, a struggling college student, became a millionaire in the cleaning business. It sounds romantic stated so simply, but I can tell you it took a lot of gut-wrenching hard work, and there were days when I wondered if it was all worth it! If you're cut out for the cleaning business, it can be one of the most rewarding things you'll ever do, but it's not for everyone. To help you decide if it's your cup of tea, let me spell out some of the pros and cons of the industry for you.

## ADVANTAGES

One of the big reasons why so many people get into the cleaning business is because it requires very little up-front cash to start. Cleaning is a very labor-intensive business, and you don't have to make a big investment in a plant and machinery to start up, like you would in manufacturing or some other business. You don't have to have a big warehouse full of expensive products, or dump trucks or backhoes or anything like that. If you start small, and do most or all of the labor yourself, all you need is a business phone and a desk in your home, a floor polisher and a few pieces of inexpensive equipment, and you're in business. Many people start out with an existing family vehicle and an office in their home, and keep their capital investment for start-up under $1,000! When you consider the low up-front investment, you can see why janitorial work has one of the best **return on investment** ratios of any kind of business.

**Opportunities** for cleaning are everywhere. Each town is full of buildings and homes that require cleaning every day, and there is plenty of work out there for a sharp operator who knows how to hustle. Add to this the fact that almost everyone has had some kind of experience in cleaning, at home, in the military, etc., and it becomes clear why so many people look to the cleaning business for a quick start-up with minimal training and learning expense. Another great advantage in this business is that you get to come and go on your **own schedule**. Most of your work is done at off-peak times; you never have to fight traffic or stand in line for lunch. You can schedule yourself to work and play at times that are convenient to you, and that fit your own needs. If this all sounds too good to be true, don't forget that the cleaning industry also has some significant challenges, and not everyone will want to pay the price to succeed as a contract cleaner. Remember, though, that where the greatest challenge lies, there also will be the greatest opportunity, because many people will be scared off by the tough going.

## CHALLENGES

Just as working at odd hours can be a real boon, it can also turn out to be a royal pain, especially if you're the kind of person who has a hard time adjusting to an off-shift schedule. For some of us, it's nice to be whizzing around town at 2:00 A.M. with the streets all to ourselves, but for others **working nights** is the worst thing that could happen. Because of your late-night work time, you usually end up doing your recreation and socializing at times when others are working. I enjoy having the use of uncrowded facilities, but it also means that your golfing or fishing or bowling buddy may be at work during the only time you have for recreation.

**Turnover** is another bugaboo you will have to face. The average turnover rate for employees of North American contract cleaners is 300% per year. That means that your average employee will last only four months before you have to find a replacement. That makes for a lot of recruiting, screening and training costs, to say nothing of the mistakes that new employees make. High turnover is part of the territory in the cleaning game, but you will have to find ways to get yours down to around 100% per year or less unless you want to spend most of your time solving employee problems.

Of all the challenges in the cleaning industry, probably the one that washes out more people than any other is **image**. The custodial profession in our society has come to be known as a dead-end job, often low-paying, and regarded by many only as something to do until "something better comes along." I have known contractors who have been quite successful in the field, but who still hang their head and scuff their toes in the dirt when their neighbors ask them what they do for a living! Personally, I love being a janitor and think it's a great field. I've been in the business for over thirty years, I own one of the premium cleaning companies in the country, and I have been successful not only at making money, but in changing people's lives, raising a good family, and keeping healthy all through it. The cleaning business has been super good to me, and **I LOVE IT**! It is a great field, and it will make a great person out of you if you commit to it, stick it out, and succeed.

One of the challenges in this or any field is simply the **responsibility** of being self-employed. For me, working for myself is the only way to go, but I recognize that it's not for everyone. When you are self-employed, you work for yourself, and there is no one there to take care of you when things get tough. There are no employee benefits, no sick-leave, no health insurance, no paid vacation, no job security, and no benefits of any kind you don't make for yourself. There is no corporate slush fund to draw on if your cash flow goes bad, no ready-made credit, and no loan guarantees. Buddy, you're on your own!

Self-employment is not for everyone. To many people, the security and benefits inherent in working for someone else outweigh the advantages of having a business of their own. For me, though, it's the only way to go! The freedom, flexibility, self-confidence, and personal growth are like the breath of life to me. But if you are going to consider a business of your own, be sure you understand the price you will have to pay, and be prepared to make the necessary sacrifices along the way.

## WHAT IT TAKES

If you're tough enough and confident enough to give up the security of working for someone else and to risk everything you have based solely on your own abilities, here's what it will take to make you a successful contract cleaner:

1. **Willingness to work** — There is no way you can make it in this business by just sitting back and letting others do the work for you. You will have to get in and do a lot of the work yourself, and learn the ins and outs of the business, in order to be able to lead others as your business grows. When you're starting up, you had better plan on some long days and longer nights, and probably on giving up a great deal of your social and recreational pursuits for awhile. In almost any rewarding enterprise, hard work and risk are involved, and you have to be prepared for both. If it was easy, everyone would be doing it.

2. **Persistence** — Anything can be accomplished by the persistent person. If you just get up each time you are knocked down and keep plugging away at it, eventually you will get to your goal. In an industry where customers have learned to expect the positive and report the negative, I guarantee that you will get knocked down a few times. Don't expect a lot of pats on the back, but be prepared for a few complaints. You can't get discouraged and drop out at the first sign of trouble. When you stumble, no one will be there to help pick you up but yourself. You have to be tough to make it in this business.

3. **Public relations ability** — If you think that just keeping a building clean will make you a success, you're wrong. Half the battle in this game is P.R. — public relations: the ability to get people to like you personally and to be on your side. If you can't get others pulling for you, the cleanest buildings in the world won't help. If you have a hard time getting along with people and getting others to like you, you'll have a difficult time in any service business.

4. **Service Orientation** — This is a service business, and if you aren't dedicated to giving good service, you don't have a product to sell. At a big restaurant grand opening, our company was there making sure that everything was going right with the cleaning. A tipsy customer spilled his drink and sandwich on the floor right in front of us and, turning to my supervisor, said, "Clean that up, boy!" My supervisor, on the verge of slugging the guy, didn't budge. I, the president of the corporation, dressed in my best suit, whipped out my monogrammed handkerchief and instantly fell to my knees and cleaned up the mess. **That's service!**

I had learned long before that we are in the business of providing a service, and we must provide it effectively and cheerfully to be successful, whether people acknowledge and appreciate our efforts or not. Sometimes we do high-class cleaning in swank areas, and sometimes we are called upon to clean up a phone booth that's been used as an emergency rest room by an unparticular passerby. A lot of it isn't very glamorous. If you plan to make it in the cleaning business, you must be committed to service.

## A TYPICAL SCENARIO

Almost daily I meet or get calls from people who are in their first year of glory. Often it's a couple who have just started a cleaning business, picked up a few accounts, and are really going strong. They can't believe how good it is. Sure they are doing well; they are doing all the work themselves, which means the quality is good and the customers are happy and paying their bills. Since they do all the work, they don't have any payroll or employee problems, and they're working so hard they don't have time to go out and spend money. They work out of their home with no overhead, and the financial picture looks great. They are flushed with the initial success of their fledgling business, and they really feel good about it.

Because their work is good, they get recommendations for more accounts, and they work more hours, and make more money. Soon, however, they get more work than they can handle themselves, so they get a second vehicle, split up the work and get a couple of part-time employees to help out. But the employees aren't as dedicated to the business as the owners are; they get sick, they sometimes get tired and do sloppy work, and they don't always show up on time. The owners compensate by using their time to cover for the employees, to train, to teach, to call on customers when service difficulties arise. And they take themselves out of the productive roles for several hours a day. As they get more and more work, they can do less and less of the actual production themselves, and must rely on employees to do most of the actual cleaning. They find themselves spending more and more time resolving complaints and solving problems, and the needs of their expanding business force them to rent an office and warehouse, increasing their overhead expenses. Now the owners can't be just good workers, they have to be good managers too, or the staff problems and expenses will eat them alive. By the end of the second year they call back tired, discouraged, in debt, and on the verge of divorce, trying to figure out what happened. What happened to this couple is typical of the experience we all go through when we make the move from a "mom and pop" operation to a full-fledged business venture. This is a crucial but difficult hurdle to get over, and failure to clear it accounts for most of the small cleaning businesses that go down the tubes in the first year or two. A large part of the material I give you in this book is designed to help you get past some of these critical points as you build your own contract cleaning business.

## SUMMARY

Every year, there are hundreds of thousands of small business start-ups, and over 90% of them fail within the first few years. If you look at this year's yellow pages under **janitorial service,** then go back and look at last year's directory, you'll notice that there have been a lot of changes. Probably half the firms listed last year are no longer there, and this year's directory offers a whole crop of new hopefuls to replace the ones who have dropped out.

If you think you're tough enough, smart enough, and committed enough to jump in and start up your own cleaning business, you will find that the rewards are there. I guarantee that it will make you one of the sharpest people in your town. You'll become knowledgeable and capable in many different fields. You will learn to be an ace public relations person, as well as a super sales person, bookkeeper, trainer, administrator, mechanic, and more. Learning all the skills and abilities required to be successful in this business will make you into an exceptional human being, capable of doing almost anything you want to do.

The material I'm giving you in this book is condensed, direct, and designed to shoot straight to the heart of how to succeed in cleaning. I've tried to sum up all of the bugaboos that caused me the lawsuits, problems, and sleepless nights during my thirty-year experience, and help you avoid them. I have also summed up the things I did which gave me the thrill of accomplishment and the sweet taste of success, both in an economic sense and in that much more important realm of human relationships and personal development. Notice I don't lead you by the hand and tell you every specific move to make. I assume you are an intelligent being, so I just give you the central kernel of information, and expect you to draw your own conclusions.

If you are ready to launch into this exciting and fun adventure, let's move on to the nuts-and-bolts of how to get started!

# GETTING STARTED

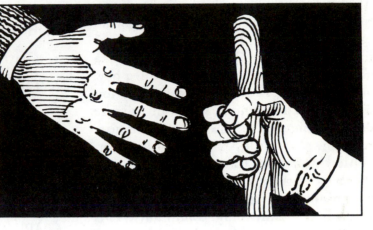

## THE JANITOR IMAGE

Before you finish this book you'll be well aware of what you're getting involved in, as far as a business or way of life goes, but, as I touched on in Chapter 1, **the status** you'll be inheriting may catch you off guard.

In the enthusiasm and newness of starting your own cleaning business, little do you notice or care about the image of the business you're in. People will chuckle that you've finally made it to being a janitor and you joke back, but in time it will be clear to you that you are in a business with a different image-level than others. I know it shouldn't be that way; how you do a job is more important than what you do, but you'll gradually notice that when your children go to school and put their father's or mother's occupation (**janitor**) on the line, the school will offers you subsidized lunches. Or people stutter when they introduce you at PTA, or have to tell others what you do for a living. The image of the "janitor" imbedded in the minds of most Americans (and even most janitors, sad to say)

is that of an unfortunate end-of-the-line individual, barely able to read or afford a razor to shave. Notice how most people leave the janitor alone! They all feel he has enough trouble just being a cleaning person, so why burden him further? People may even hesitate to shake your hand (who knows, you might just have cleaned a toilet).

You also notice that you are in a business where people expect the positive and report the negative. In other words, you can do a super job of cleaning, leave the wastebasket just right for 300 days, clean the restrooms flawlessly for two years, keep the heat perfect for a whole winter, and no one will thank you or even acknowledge it. But one time, just once, you forget to put the wastebasket on the right side of the desk or let the heat go three degrees off, and the tenants and clients will scream their heads off. You'd think you had burned their building down. Suddenly you'll have a struggle with the way people treat most cleaning professionals. Most of us do all sorts of things to compensate, such as change our title to "environmental engineer" or buy a

15

Mercedes or a condo in Hawaii to show the gang that we indeed are equal to them in stature.

I call all this the **image fight** and it's the single biggest problem in the industry. It may be one of your biggest struggles, even if you are making $100,000 profit a year, have independence and security, and enjoy your work immensely. I've seen the image fight put some good people out of the ranks of the cleaning business. If you think you are going to have a problem, better get it resolved now and be ready for it. I've become a national celebrity, joking about being a "**janitor**," and it's always interesting to see how many people are extremely ill at ease when you introduce yourself as a janitor. Generally, they're speechless. People don't know what to say to a janitor: "How's your dust mop, Shirley?" or, "How's the bathroom tile, Jackson?" If you intend to be a cleaner and a good one, you're going to have to live it and be ready to proclaim it on all fronts — to family and community. **This image problem isn't psychological, it's real!** I don't beat around the bush; my business card is embossed in the shape of a toilet (see below). You don't have to be so flagrant about it, but be prepared to stick up for what you do. You'll have to do it as long as you are in the business. Images are part of any profession and professional cleaners should leave no doubt as to what theirs is.

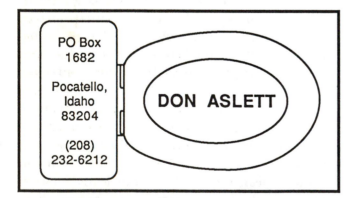

PO Box 1682

Pocatello, Idaho 83204

(208) 232-6212

DON ASLETT

## ALL THOSE RULES AND REGULATIONS

Don't be overwhelmed. The Equal Opportunity Act, fair labor practices, and all those volumes of rules fall into place and are really quite simple once you get going. Generally, when you are small with only a few employees, a lot of the rules don't apply and no one gets hung up on the few that do. When you grow into them, they will be explained to you by governing

agencies, insurance people, etc. This is one distinct benefit of being and staying small, no one bothers a small cleaning company. You can just about run things the way you want. It's when you get big and important and have lots of money that Uncle Sam and all the do-gooders in the country descend on you for every tax rule, donation, etc.

## THE COMMITMENT

You have four options to choose from:

1. You can walk down to the local paper, put an ad in the classified section, get your business cards printed (for less than $20), buy a bucket and squeegee and simply go to work. That's what I did. People will hire you, and if you've half a wit, you'll have fun and make money and start growing. This is the first, and I think, the best choice.

2. You can work for some other cleaning company for a while and learn the business. You can decide what and where and how you are going to do your operation, and then announce to the world that you are breaking off to do your own thing. Don't be a sneak, be upfront when you go to work and tell your employer that you intend to start your own business someday. He'll probably congratulate and encourage you, and maybe even sell you his business. You can learn a lot from an existing, successful company, and there's plenty of work to go around! This plan gives you a more gradual leap into what may be a lifelong career!

3. You can buy an existing cleaning company — but if you don't know the cleaning business yet, this is the worst thing you can do. Businesses are for sale all over the place, just watch the paper. Some of the owners are tired of working, some are retiring, some are caught up in divorces or family squabbles, some are going into something that interests them more, and some are sinking fast and want to bail out while they still have an account or two left. Unless you find a super-stable deal, I'd really be careful. Good, successful moneymaking companies **rarely sell!** There is a reason, maybe several reasons, for selling; be sure you know them. Buying a business which had a strong dynamic leader, for example, could be a disaster unless you can fill his shoes.

Remember, when you buy a cleaning company, you are buying names, accounts, and good will. If you lose an account or fail to run it right, your purchase money is gone for good. Businesses where the owner or boss promises to hang around and be a consultant should raise a giant red flag; sellers soon lose their interest in the business once it changes hands. If the continued success of the business depends on the outgoing owner, watch out!

4. You can buy a franchise from someone who supposedly has all the answers and can get you going fast. If you want your own business and want to be good at it and make money, I'd advise you, in 90% of the cases, to stick to starting from scratch yourself. There is no way you can learn this business without experience. This is a hands-on business, not a manipulate-from-afar type. The high rollers in cleaning usually suffer instant death. At first, much of the work is done with your head in the toilet, making the bid and the like. The less you have invested, the better off you are, because if you find you can't handle the little stuff and don't learn how before your company gets bigger, it'll flush you down the drain fast!

There are a lot of cleaning franchises available. The good ones are an acceptable way to go for someone who needs considerable help and support, but there is a price to pay. For a fee, maybe $10,000 or $15,000, the franchise gives you a name, some forms, a few gallons of cleaner, some advertising info. and some secrets of success. In three months, with a little hustle, a sharp operator can accomplish the same thing independently. In my bestselling book, *Is There Life After Housework?,* I included a chapter on going into your own business, which is addressed primarily to housewives who might want to clean part-time. I have gotten many calls on the subject, but one in particular said that the one chapter in my $7.95 book gave them more help than the whole franchise training package they had purchased. Most franchises don't give that much help after things are rolling, but the royalties you pay go on and on. What can they really give you after you've learned the basics? If you're the independent type, and are willing to hustle, you're probably better off to go it on your own. You'll likely learn a few lessons the hard way, but overall you'll be happier.

Most people don't have that hard a time learning how to clean. The two big questions that most people struggle with are: "How do I get the business?" and, "How do I know how much to charge?" The inability to deal with these two topics is what motivates most would-be contractors to buy franchises. While it is true that most franchises give you assistance in selling and in pricing your work, **they don't do it for you!** It is still up to you to sell and to bid, after they have taught you how. Since it's going to be up to you anyway, I think you can learn how to advertise, sell and bid just as easily from this book as you could by buying a franchise. You'll have to spend a little time and money developing your own forms and promotional material, but you'll save thousands of dollars in franchise fees and royalties. Contrary to what franchisers tell you, most business owners you sell to won't be the least bit impressed with your franchise affiliation, and the ongoing royalties will tend to make your pricing less competitive.

How hard is hard? People who buy into service franchises are always bawling back when things get bad, saying, "You didn't tell me how hard this was!"

## YOUR FIELD

Don't be afraid to start small, even part-time for a while as you learn. Remember, of course, part-time isn't enough of the commitment you'll eventually need to be a top banana in the business.

You don't need psychological testing and rating to find out if you're qualified or not. You might be surprised to know that most people with good common sense and an entrepreneurial spirit have enough savvy to run a business. There are lots of fields you can work in besides floors and toilets. Under the chapter on "Targeting" I've outlined a lot of them. You don't have to have an office that looks like "Dynasty" or "Knots Landing" — almost everyone has a false image of the businessman. He's just a self-employed worker, and offices have little to do with success. It's a person's ability to get the job done efficiently and make a profit **that is the measure of success.**

## COURSES, SCHOOLS, SEMINARS, AND PROFESSIONAL HELP

In the last several years the cleaning management market has been flooded with courses, seminars, classes, videos and books telling how to be a one-minute janitor. Cleaning consultants are appearing all over, all of these people and sources claiming to be the wellspring of secrets of cleaning success. You can get information from such sources, but it may be of limited usefulness. Lots of consultants and advisors are people who didn't make it; they dropped out and never did — or don't now — own or run a cleaning business.

Through national organizations I'm affiliated with, I've participated in and attended lots of seminars and have seen many of my fellow class members die of boredom as speaker after speaker explains the philosophies of glue-down, jute backing, and the chemical adhesion of floor protons with hard water. Paying several hundred dollars to hear philosophies, mingle at alcoholic gatherings, get a badge and a certificate isn't a wise way to start. Go to those who are actually doing it, not the preachers. The actual practitioners often will help you for one-fifth the cost (if not for free) and you'll get solid information. Double-check before you send in money and fly off somewhere for a seminar. Who is teaching, and are they qualified? There are a few good professional speakers, but there are also scads of ex-wax salesmen trying to counsel and organize your business. If it were me I'd go find a person respected by the real practitioners (the best) and approach him or her personally. Successful people are generally busy being successful at what they do and making plenty of money at it, not teaching seminars. Tap them first, they're all around you! If you need technical training, my Facility Care Course (F.C.C.) is taught at a number of vocational schools, and through corporations (write me for locations, if you're interested). It teaches not only "how to clean" skills, but important other aspects of the business such as public relations and personal development.

## YOUR COMPANY NAME

This is the fun part! What will you call your very own business? Ideally it should be unique, simple, powerful, and easy to remember. Believe it or not, name is all important. Your name is the tag people will associate with your service, your business and the work you do. If it's a hard name to pronounce or spell or has a negative connotation, it'll do you no good. If my last name was Allbright, I might use it in my company

name, but if my handle was Sigfried Darkenhauser or Joe Black, I'd call it Sunshine Services or Accent Cleaners or something. Come up with a good name for your company and remember: it doesn't matter if it thrills you deep inside or compliments someone in your family or some cherished personal memory. If it doesn't work to get work it will be a liability to your success. The basic purpose of a business name isn't magic, or even music — it's simply easy identification and memorable association. The final test is when someone hears it or sees it — will they remember it and associate it with cleaning? And with you? And with a positive image?

Remember you have to (1) put the thing on a business card and stationery, (2) letter it on equipment and vehicles, and (3) fit it into classified and other advertising. If it is Gobberestukekstienbergs Cleaners, you'll be hurting.

Molly Maid (a Canadian Franchise) for example, is an excellent name. The MM just rolls out, "Molly" lets you know that the workers are female, and "Maid" tells you exactly what they do. The words are also the same length so it makes a nice layout and lettering.

I knew a couple of sharp young men who started a cleaning business and used a name with a deep scriptural meaning, "Shiblon Industries." When I told them that the name was too obscure and would mean nothing at all to a good part of the public, they were crushed. Others have taken their first or last names and combined them, like George and Harry calling themselves Georry Cleaners. Names like these are unfamiliar and confusing for the public. And even Connie's Cleaners is not so good. **People want to identify a company by image, not an individual.** Personal names also hurt you if you expand or ever sell. What if automobiles came off the line named after executives or the guy who designed them? Instead of a Firebird, it would be a Herman, or instead of a Bel Aire, a Beulah. (Don't forget those great "name" cars, the *Edsel* and the *Delorean* — *Delorean* or *DeLorean*?) Stick to names that give an image or association and also be careful with city names. What if I had used Pocatello Cleaners instead of Varsity Contractors? In the phone book there are 400 companies starting with Pocatello, so watch that, too.

And as good a name as Varsity has been for us, it does have one drawback. We never thought about it until one day the nicest, newest building in Pocatello (the Federal Courthouse) went up for bid and we (the biggest and best in town) were not even called to bid it. I was furious, and found out the simple answer: lots of companies (including the government) are required to solicit five bidders for a contract. There were six companies in town at the time and, you guessed it, where does "V" for Varsity come in the telephone listing? **Last!** We found out we'd lost numerous other jobs over this and so corrected it by adding "Aslett's" (got that "A" in there) to the beginning of our listing. Why do you think all those ABM's and ABC's and Acme Cleaners and AAA Cleaners are in there? Those boys are smarter than I was.

Don't lock your name into a town or region. Twin City Cleaners, or Spokane Scrubbers — what if you want to expand into other towns or states? The people of Louisville (especially the Chamber of Commerce) aren't going to flock to Cincinnati Cleaners to have them clean the town hall, even if they are better and bid lower than Louisville Likenew Cleaners.

Keep in mind, too, that the public is always attracted to prestigious names. Would a customer be more likely to name-drop Podunk Cleaners or Crown Contractors? If you were bidding the World Trade Center in New York and the name of your company was Bashed In Skull Cleaners (true story, that's a name of a town and company in Canada), I doubt the high rise tenants would select you. Whether you should use your last name for the company depends entirely on what your last name is. If it fits and is smooth, you have the best of all worlds, but if your name is Pete Stinks or Jack Crumb, forget the vanity of having it named after you; call it Fragrant, Inc. If your name is Chief White Cloud or Willie Whistle you might consider incorporating your name with a clever logo — just use your head.

Name your boat or your dog after your wife or sweetheart, but name your cleaning business something short and zippy.

Once you get a name you like, and before you register it and print 10,000 business cards, brochures and a full set of stationery, take it to a professional artist and get some good logo ideas. This logo should be simple, memorable, and colorful, as it will be on your vehicles, advertisements, and checks for a long time. The best way to do this is to have the artist work up several "roughs" of different possible approaches before he does any of them in finished art. **If nothing** seems to work well with your name — go for a new name!

Now check to make sure you haven't duplicated someone else's name — even if it isn't a cleaning company. It would be a shame to call your company Pure White Cleaners and have a nearby dairy called Purewhite! Breeze through the phone book business listings for your immediate area to make sure you're not duplicating or encroaching on someone else's name. It's also a good idea to check with your secretary of state on registering your trademark. You have to actually have it in use to register it, but they can tell you ahead of time if anyone else is using your name or something close to it.

## YOUR OFFICE

Forget those dreams of a penthouse office! It's not necessary in the cleaning business. None of your customers care what your office looks like! They just want a clean building and happy tenants. You can have your office in a tent or your basement, wherever; your customers just want to be able to get in touch with you when they need to, not at your convenience. You can work out of your home when you start. I think it's actually a better place than a downtown office — even if you could get the office for free. Starting a cleaning business calls for **being available.** Pipes break in the middle of the night and flood the rug, and they need it taken care of **now** (it's nice extra work if they can find you). If the phone is in your home, you'll get the job, the profit, the gratitude, and consideration for more work and future contracts. You can and should put a business phone in your house, separate from your private phone. If your three-year-old answers the phone when Mr. Snarltooth calls, or the line is busy on a gossip call when Harry Hasbucks calls, it's sure not going to benefit you. Having your business mail, phone, etc., right in your home will make you tremendously efficient and available when you're first starting out. When you grow and need a secretary, or have a supervisor or two, and the city won't let you park your four rug cleaning vans in the street anymore, it'll be time to move.

## LOCATION

Thousands of little offices are available, preferably in the center of your work area. Don't save a hundred dollars on rent and lose $5,000 driving a distance daily to get to your jobs. **Use your head!**

In any case, equip your office frugally. I've used a 35-inch army surplus desk for years now (though my secretary went first cabin a few months ago and has a 48-inch one), and I'm the Chairman of the Board of a big company. I ran the first four months of my business out of a motel apartment, the next year out of a two-room basement college dormitory apartment, and the next three years from a plain old house and garage!

## THE PHONE-ANSWERING MACHINE

I immensely dislike telephone answering services, both machines and the hired human kind. I haven't figured out if they're better than nothing yet, or not. I think it's still a toss-up. Try to have your phone answered by a live, interested person as much of the time as possible, at least during regular business hours. You, your spouse, or your secretary will be much better informed, more interested, and more able to help a customer than any answering service clerk or machine could be. Use answering services and machines only for after-hours and emergency backup, and make sure you set it up so that you are reachable for emergencies.

**Now you:**
- **Have committed yourself to doing it!**
- **Have a legal and workable name!**
- **Have a place for your business!**

There is one more thing: **your spouse or mate.** If someone else's life is going to be involved, is that person with you or not? If not, you'd better pack it in. The first three years of a cleaning business is tougher on the mate than it is on the principal — without your partner's help, and support in the face of demoralizing or unfair complaints, inhuman schedules, etc., you'll never cut it.

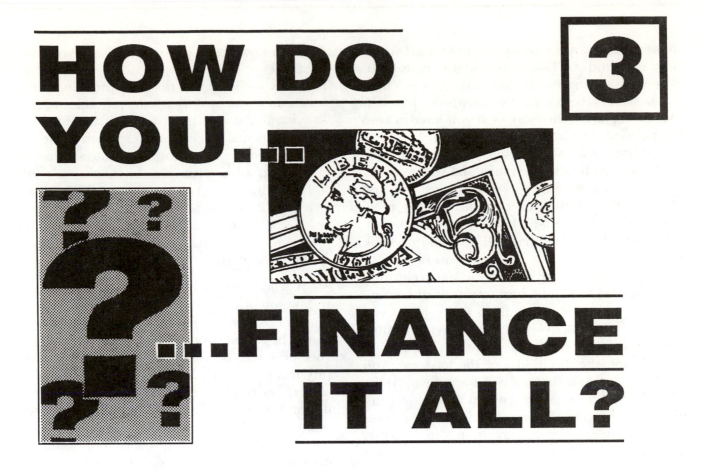

# HOW DO YOU... ...FINANCE IT ALL?

## 3

I'm really going to pound on you in this chapter. I want to save you fifteen to twenty years of gut wrenching, beating your head on the wall, and hating the banker. Listen hard to what I say. You'll be 80% more successful in your operation and 600% happier in your personal life.

The cleaning business is a low capital business.
The cleaning business is a low capital business.
The cleaning business is a low capital business.
**The cleaning business is a low capital business.**
**THE CLEANING BUSINESS IS A
LOW CAPITAL BUSINESS.**

This can be your lifesaver slogan when you're going into your own business. It does **not** take much money to get started. You don't **need** much money to get started, and that's exactly why five million people try the cleaning business out every year. Let this be an inspiration to you. You might be able to borrow huge sums of money to start your cleaning business, but if you do, you're probably not going to make it. The generally low profit margins in this business just won't support a high debt load. The return on investment is very high in the cleaning industry, because of the low up-front capital requirements. If you

borrow heavily to start, though, you neutralize this otherwise great asset. It's a low profit, on-the-job type business, not a manipulatory one, where you set it up and then sit back and rake in the profits. That will never happen, and if you hear stories about it, or know someone fat-catting it in the cleaning business, wait just a little while and I'll show you a person in trouble.

## YOUR MONEY

Again, **listen** to me in this chapter and follow the counsel and direction I give you. I know what I'm talking about. I've been through all the agony myself in thirty years of small and large business management. I've watched hundreds of cleaning businesses keel over in despair, because of poor management and use of money. It doesn't have to be that way. It can be simple, positive, and fun, and you can make a good living and be relaxed about it all. Or you can alienate yourself from your family and friends, and tie yourself up in ulcer knots. The minute you go in business (or even announce that you're going in business) you will have advice from everyone and every source imaginable telling you how to handle your money and run your business, how to get it and how to spend it. The best way still is, **earn it!** If you can't earn it in the business, then you have no basis for being in the business. **It's self-consuming any other way — if you have to keep financing a cleaning business, get out!**

When it comes to starting a business everyone pictures rounding up investors and selling stock, or borrowing a chunk of venture capital and going out and buying everything they need, lining up an accountant, lawyer, secretary, board, and then going at it. That's all TV and storybook stuff. You don't run a business, you operate it. First, you need very little money to start a cleaning business and that's the best way to start because limited money, especially if it's yours, forces you to perform productively to exist. Having limited money gets you on the job where you belong and teaches you the mechanics of the business. You could drop me in the middle of any town in the U.S. without a dime and without going to a bank or begging I could have a fat cleaning business going in three weeks and have money in the bank. I'd have to break my fanny, but that's the best way to begin. Tax yourself and your own production to the limit in the beginning, and earn the money you need. There are some real fallacies in borrowing money.

Borrowed money doesn't **take care of the bills.** It just stacks them in a different pile. Borrowed money doesn't **buy things for you to own.** It just gives you temporary possession. Borrowed money isn't **free** — it always comes with heavy interest or personal ties. You can't borrow yourself out of debt.

Here is the order in which I personally would seek financing:

1. **Myself** — If you are capable of succeeding in the cleaning business, you should be able to lay your hands on some personal money. Sell something you have, if necessary: a house, an expensive collection, a boat, etc. If you're stone broke and owe everyone because you can't or haven't managed in the past, stay out of the business, you won't make it.

2. **Mortgage** — If you have or own something of worth, a house, land, insurance, etc., use it. If you won't because you want it for security, you are only half-committed. You'd borrow from a bank or friend, asking them to take a risk for your business, when you won't even lay your own assets on the line? This is a good test of how much you want to have your own business.

3. **Banks** — They are there to provide or rent out their money — that's the sole value of their existence. If you must borrow, a bank keeps you personally accountable, which is the way it should be. But borrowing money for the start-up of a cleaning business isn't like financing a car. You're asking a bank to take a risk on an uncollateralized intangible with all the ability to pay back based on your performance. That's risky, and they will be hard to convince.

I would never, never tap a friend, relative, in-law, or other close source for financing the janitor business. It will be a mistake in the long run. The minute you do it, you're surrendering your personal control of things, emotionally and physically. Anyone who has their money in something has the right to ask, peek, seek, and demand answers. When you get someone else's money, you have an instant ever-present ghost partner, forever looking over your shoulder, questioning and advising you. If you don't follow Daddy-in-law's advice while you're using his money, you'll lose some real notches in life. Keep yourself unencumbered.

You don't need much money; work with your own vehicle, use your house or apartment, and use your own phones. Business cards will cost under $20.00, (skip a meal or two and you'll have the money). Collect the money for your first job and keep it! Collect the money for your second job and keep it. The mistake many cleaning people make is, the minute the money rolls in (and it will, when you're on the job), they think they are drunk-sailor rich and take all their buddies and the whole family out for dinner ($80 down the drain). Don't do it! The janitor business isn't a big profit business like some of you may read about. You have to sacrifice and hang onto your money. If you do need some equipment, like a $400 floor machine, then go down to the supply store. Buy it and they will give you thirty, maybe sixty days to pay for it. You can earn that easily in a week **if you are out on the job,** and pay for it; then you own it forever – no bookwork, no payments every month, no late-payment notices, it's yours hassle-free!

If you're a hustler (which you'd better be), watch the papers. Janitors who have over-borrowed and poorly handled their money are

going broke every day and selling their stuff for ten cents on the dollar. I skim the paper and get some real deals. I bought a $600 buffer and a $1,200 extractor, both new, for $250 once from a grocery store which had taken them over from an indebted contractor they fired. Some of the accounts you pick up will have all the equipment and supplies you need to do the job and you won't have to buy even a can of cleaner! Keep your eyes open for deals on used equipment at auctions, garage sales, in the classifieds, etc., as you go along.

## VANITY COSTS

The biggest financial danger you face as you start up your business is in thinking you're suddenly a big self-employed businessman, and trying to flaunt it by making donations, buying dinners and lunches, loaning money or advancing it to employees who can't manage their own money.

This will kill you! Having money when you need it in a cleaning business is your lifeline. You don't need tons of money, but you do need good cash flow. Fighting and muddling with finances is the surest destroyer of a cleaning business because it keeps **you** off the job! Running around like a chicken with your head cut off trying to meet your payroll, collect accounts, etc., because you are out of money is sure death.

Every cleaner, the second they get a thousand or two ahead, wants to show everyone that they're just as good as the next guy and they do something really dumb like buying a fancy new car or getting into a house with a mortgage way over their head. Or worse yet, buying a van with more horsepower than horse sense.

Let's take that as a good example. You'll need a vehicle to keep supplies in and lock them up, and a van acts as a perfect traveling billboard with your name lettered on it. Think of how many miles you put on a van in a year in a city — very few. It does five or ten miles to a job and sits there three hours while you're doing the work. You don't need a $20,000 deluxe *Sierra Cruiser* chrome critter for that. All vans look alike, a $2,500 late-model van, with a new $300 paint job looks exactly the same and will do the same job and not one in 400 people will know the difference. You can pack less insurance on it, too, and think about the $13,000 you still don't owe and aren't paying interest on. You are in a low-profit cleaning business, not a cost-plus government job (or wasting contest) like many other businesses are. You can buy good, used equipment and keep it up and, by the way, you don't need all the fancy gorgeous stuff that gleams in the ad pages of the cleaning magazines. If you presently have a pickup you could put a topper on, or a station wagon, the existing vehicle will probably do just fine to get started, with little cash outlay.

**Keep money ahead,** not in a savings account necessarily, but to buy and grow with. Every time you get a new building to clean, you'll need some bucks, not always for equipment and supplies, but for payroll. It's simple: the phone rings, the Federal building downtown just fired their six janitors for drug dealing and they know of your good work and stable reputation, and want you to bid their building. You run down and give them a bid of $15,000 per month and in five days they call back and say, "You got it, baby!" You are exuberant, and hire eight good hustling part-time people and start the job and do it right on your bid. Everything goes perfect and at the end of the month your payroll runs a total of $8,000, overhead is $3,000, supplies $1,000, and that means a sparkling $3,000 profit the first month and forever.

You ought to be exuberant, you're doing it

right all the way, except the Federal Building gets your $15,000 bill at the end of the month and, of course, has thirty days to process it and get it paid. In fact the first one might take forty to sixty days. You've got an $8,000 payroll to pay out today! Where do you get it? Run down to the bank and borrow it? Listen friend, if you think bankers are fishy and squirmy when it comes to loans, wait until you approach them as a janitor in your own business. They will become deaf mutes! Yes, the way they'll treat you is awful, but can you blame them? Janitorial companies have a 90% failure rate! If you have the $8,000 in the bank, it takes no time or hassle. Then, save the $4,000 profit in case the next month they don't get the check out. **Keep your money!**

Let me save you fifteen years of agony. I had to learn a simple principle the hard way: you need operating money. Once you begin to operate on a bigger scale, don't fool yourself like I did. When I was a janitor in college, things were good. I was making money, and spending my profits in over-expansion, a bigger house, etc. I had an illusion, a false one, that you will have! I had $50,000 on the books (in other words, people owed me that much money) — insurance companies, telephone companies, the government, all good money, too. That was my receivables, and the nice part of life was that my payables, or the bills that I owed, were only $20,000. Now simple arithmetic said that I had $30,000 of good money there, and I lived (for fifteen years) in the illusion that one day all of the $30,000 would come rolling in. I would run down and pay up my creditors and have $30,000 in the bank. Guess what? That day never came. Twenty-five years later, I now have $1,000,000 out on the books and owe $200,000. That $800,000 is working capital. I fought and fought to keep my bills paid up, dreaming of the salvation of the $800,000 profit that was mine. It was mine, all right, and it's like owning the pony express horse. You make money delivering the mail and the horse is your working capital. You have to have this money invested, or worth tied up in him, the vehicle, or there is no income! Don't kill the goose that lays the golden egg by trying to pull out and consume your operating money. **Don't try to spend your working capital. You'll never get that money!**

Lots of little cleaning companies, after they've made forty bad financial decisions, cry to the banks for help. The banks shudder when they see you coming and hear you out and then pawn you off on a small business administrator (SBA). You don't need SBA money in a janitor company to make it go. This is a low-capital business, you don't need capital, you need management! If a friend or family was running a cleaning business and had lots of accounts and was going in the hole and needed money to get out, would you lend him the money? Not on your life! Your money would go right down the same hole and be gone. People do incredibly stupid things with borrowed money. If the company isn't making enough money to sustain itself, how will more money help? It won't! Discipline yourself, use your own money, it makes you flexible and powerful!

## YOUR BILLS

There's another key to financial survival in the cleaning business. Keep your money collected. You are not a bank! When you finish a job, get the check. It saves billing and waiting. On your monthly accounts, talk to all of them up front and find out when they pay. Some can pay five days after billing, some can set you up on an immediate revolving payment and pay you automatically by computer right at the end of the month. We recently lost $15,000 on a health club account. Each month they stalled their $3,000 bill and bang, three months were gone and they owed us $9,000. We bawled and griped, and another month zipped by and they owed us $12,000. We put the collection pressure on them (too late, of course) and they went out of business owing us that $12,000 plus $3,000 more in setup equipment and collection costs. How would you like someone to lift $15,000 cash out of your wallet or bank account some morning? It'll happen if you let it. Collect your money, be tough; you have it coming. Ask for it, nothing is wrong with that, and then if the company is going broke, at least you won't waste three more months of energy before you realize they aren't going to pay. If you are Mr. Nice Guy too long, they will pay all the hardnoses first, and since you're Casper Milktoast, you will get yours last, if you get it at all! I'll give you lists of bewares and cautions (health spas are at the head of the list). Contrary to what you've experienced when it comes to people collecting from you — bad money isn't easy to collect. You may get 20% if you're lucky.

## THE INTERNAL REVENUE SERVICE

Don't use IRS money to finance your operation. Everyone will hold out a few thousand dollars of payroll deductions and have to send them in at the end of the quarter or monthly period. There that pile of green sits, tempting you to use it. We've all done it, often with disastrous or near disastrous results. It's not your money; make your deposits and **leave it alone!**

## BUSINESS AND PERSONAL ACCOUNTS

Keep your business and personal accounts separate. I know that it's all your money anyway, but the resulting bookkeeping and audits (they *will* come) at the end of the year will hang you up in the office for days trying to unscramble things. What is personal and deductible and what is not?

Use three-copy loose checks so that after writing one you have a copy for the accountant and one to clip to the bill you've paid and file it away. Don't pay for milk and eggs, spouse's presents, etc., out of your business checkbook or credit card. **Keep it all clean and legal!**

## INVESTMENTS

As your business gets going well (and it will) the temptation to become a big wheel will loom in front of you daily. Other pursuits and investments in real estate, land deals, ski resorts, condos, and the such will come along and con men and high rollers (relatives, too) will appear out of the woodwork. You fall for them for two reasons: (1) Greed — enough is never enough; (2) Ego — you want to show the investor that even though you are just a janitor, by cracky, you can lay the cash on the barrelhead too!

Remember, you're already in a business that

makes money and you're getting better! Do you have more faith in others than you do in yourself? Janitors buy a bunch of apartments and say, "Wow, this is a deal. I can clean those buggers cheaper, and use my crew. Why, this goes right along with my business." It doesn't! Landlording is lots different than laying wax on a floor. Be careful with the long-term investments. **Make sure you are solid** in your own business, and that you aren't investing in something that will dilute your interests.

If and when you do grow and diversify, and lose interest in the cleaning business (it can happen — some people just don't like the demands of a service business), there are ways to sell or get rid of your business profitably. That is great and honorable, but don't piddle it away or withdraw. In the cleaning business you either stick to the knitting or you are going to come unraveled and all the years of goodwill and reputation, which is your biggest asset, can be gone in a few months.

**Listen. Please listen** to what I've said in this chapter, or struggling, fighting, and juggling money problems will take all the drive and the fun out of your business.

## A FINAL WORD ON BANKRUPTCY

Going bankrupt is simply using a legal maneuver to avoid an honest debt. It's stealing money from others because of your poor management. It's dumping your problems on some trusting, undeserving person or persons. Don't consider it; sell your soul first. **Bankruptcy is an escape hatch for failure.** It's a crooked, immoral move to welch on an honest debt.

# MAKING IT ALL LEGAL

## 4

**Jail mopping isn't fun, or profitable!** Making it legal is the easiest part of getting your own business going, yet lots of good would-be toilet cleaners chicken out at this point. They just can't face up to all the legal requirements, tax setups, documents, permits and licenses. If you made it out of the sixth grade, though, you should be able to handle it and do it right. The only people who will really get confused are the bureaucrats who thought up all the forms in the first place. **They** may thrash a bit on their end but that's their job and they will eventually get it done. Lots of people starting their own business (of any kind) never file one permit, one tax form, get a license, or register anywhere. They just go out and go to work and a lot of them get away with it — for a while. Doing the "beginning" any way but the right way is a real mistake. Pour the foundation firmly, get everything legal, fair, and clean, and you will be respected forever. You will feel and be treated legally, fairly, and cleanly. Besides that, it's a good experience to set up a business and see what all the tax-paying people are doing in the world, and find out what all the government workers do who consume those tax dollars. Besides, no matter how smart and careful you think you're being, you may overlook

something. Last year, a couple of scavengers almost stole my Varsity name in one state because it wasn't technically copyrighted correctly. So don't try to skip it all and play dumb. When you get caught by the IRS or the county tax commission or the insurance company, you'll be nailed to the wall.

Remember: the government and legal people go after us honest working people when we fail to do it right because they can beat money out of us. They let the crooks and the deadbeats go swindling along because when they catch them, what can they do? Kill them? Why spend $30,000 chasing and catching a bad, non-paying bum when with a little notice in an envelope they can squeeze $3,000 out of you, Mr. Honest John, in seconds? Before you fill out anything, forms or such, you do need a name and tax I.D. number. Be sure to get one! This is the order I would follow.

## YOUR NAME AND LOGO

As I mentioned earlier, as soon as you've chosen a name, have an artist do a logo or service mark as we call it, and put it in use. Then submit the name and register your trademark with the

Secretary of State in your state capitol. If you decide to operate in a number of states, file with each state, and also on a Federal basis with the U.S. Patent Office in Washington D.C. Once they have registered the trademark or service mark (logo) to you, no one else can legally steal it or use it. If McDonald's hadn't done this, there would be all kinds of people calling themselves McDonald's and skimming the advantage of the advertising and the name off old Ronald and the franchises. We registered our Varsity name in all states in the United States, and it's a good thing we did, because we now operate in thirteen of them. Had we not filed and had moved into Texas, and there was already a Varsity Contractors, we would have been out the use of the name and its value. The Secretary of State's office will also be able to tell you if any other cleaners are using the name you've chosen, which saves you getting sued down the road. Some filings have a ten-year expiration date, and then you have to renew, some have a longer one, so if you have any questions a simple twenty-nine-cent letter of inquiry will be well worth it.

Rules, licenses, and laws are all part of the rat race, so leap in with all the rest of us rats. It really is pretty exciting! And by the way, on all of the various licenses, permits, and registrations, you might have to call for information, but write out every formal request to government agencies for information as to what you are expected to have by way of licenses, forms, permits and the like. Have it in writing and you won't forget it, and if they don't respond, you have something that shows you requested it — it might save your hide at some point.

## UNCLE SAM

Uncle Sam is next. Walk or drive down to the local IRS office, sit down with an agent and tell him or her you are starting a business and want a federal Employer's Identification number and the forms for your quarterly report (941) and payroll deposits. This is mainly for the day when you have employees and make a payroll. They will tell you exactly how to handle deductions (they have little charts, and the forms to send in, and it's simple). Lots of forms and applications will call for that little tax identification number that they give you. They will give you an instruction book on how to do it all; it is

free and simple. These are the people for whom you deduct FICA tax, match it with your own money and send it in. These are the people to fear if you don't do it right. A fifth grader can do the books if you keep a decent check register. Simple computer programs now make this even simpler and more accurate (so a third grader could probably run it).

## YOUR STATE

Do exactly the same thing that you did with the Feds. The state guys are a cinch, you'll have the confidence by now, and should be able to breeze right through their requirements. They'll show you how to hold out State Withholding, and in most states you also have an unemployment tax payable to the state. If so, they'll let you know, and if not they will send you down to the Department of Employment where you will get all the forms for free! If your business requires collection of sales tax, they can also help you get your sales tax number.

## DEPARTMENT OF EMPLOYMENT

These guys may give you a separate state employer's number and they will give you the guidelines for unemployment deposits. **Yes,** I think it's all wrong and I hated it for years, even wrote the government about it, but a percent of your payroll (2.5% or so) is sent to the Department of Employment every quarter to pay the people who draw unemployment. If lots of people draw unemployment on you, your rate goes up in some states. If they don't, you get a thing called an experience rating, and the rate goes down. All this encourages you not to fire deadbeats or to be careful not to hire them in the first place. They have a little instruction book to help you understand all the requirements.

## WORKMAN'S COMPENSATION

It's a bugger too, brother. Either your state or your insurance company will carry this for you. This is an insurance you pay, based on payroll, to compensate your employees in case of an accident or injury on the job. The premium rate is based on the type of job an employee does. Be sure to look this baby over, as Workman's Comp on a plain old floor cleaner may be $6.50

per hundred dollars of payroll, but on a window washer it's $15.00 to $50.00 per hundred, and on a roofer it's $30. If you have different jobs, make sure they get in the right category, so you will pay minimum Workman's Comp. Have only one person do the windows, instead of all eight of your floor cleaners doing one hour of windows each. It will save you a bundle, and your window person will become an expert at windows, giving you a competitive edge (see, there are all sorts of neat management things to learn). If your compensation premium goes down and your payroll gets big, it can make a $10,000 difference in what you keep at the end of the year. You get Workman's Comp from your insurance agent, or in some states it's a state fund. Your insurance person will know immediately.

## CITY LICENSE

There are many different kinds of these and different requirements for same, but for the most part they don't cost much. Call and get the name and address of the proper department, then write a letter to the city introducing yourself. Explain your desire to be operating completely legally in the area. Tell them you want information on all the permits and licenses that they deem necessary to operate in the city. This is easy and cheap and fast, and you'll get a little document with a seal to pin up on your wall. You'll never hear a word again from them. I've never figured out why we need these things, but it's the law, so I do it and smile. Keep your request letter so if five years from now they announce that they forgot to have you get a corrosive substance permit or something, they can't make it retroactive back five years.

## COUNTY

Ah, yes! Cities are in counties and county government is separate from city, state, and Federal government. This isn't as complicated as it seems; it's been this way all along, you just never noticed it before. Write the same letter (changing the names and titles, of course) to the county that you did to the city and ask them what you need. They will respond if licenses or permits are necessary. Remember, you'll be doing work out in the county — there are lots of good jobs out there — so make it **legal.**

That's it. Most of the requirements are simple, really, and take little time. People in the departments involved are experienced and helpful. There might be some unique requirements in your locality, so ask around. Repenting is always more costly than getting permission in the first place, even though many do it this way.

## CONTRACTOR'S LICENSE

This is not mandatory and you might not need one — at least not for a while. Basically, this is a license issued by each state to qualified contractors. There are indeed in this world crooked fly-by-nights who rip through town putting motor oil on old ladies' worn wood-shingled roofs instead of pure linseed oil. In order to keep these characters in check, schools and lots of other public agencies won't let you work for them unless you have a contractor's license. They issue the license after you fill out a rather complicated form citing the jobs you've done, get a number of your accounts to vouch for you, take a competency test, etc. In other words, you have to prove that you're a legitimate firm, accountable, dependable, and worthy of trust. I did all kinds of painting, building, repairing, etc., without a license for the first couple of years, then it finally caught up with me on a big roof-painting job for the Idaho Falls School District. I knew how to paint a roof — I'd done hundreds of them on homes, but Idaho law required a contractor's license to do work on a school, so I got one. I'd suggest you apply for the forms now and look them over and start collecting the information you need. In a year or so you'll have it filled out and, if you need it, you can shoot it right in and get your contracting license.

## VEHICLE LICENSE

Some states require a truck permit for any van or pickup doing commercial work in their state. This may not affect you, but be aware of it and check, in case you do need one for your locality.

## UNION OR NON-UNION?

This is your choice, but personally I would avoid unions like the plague. I feel they deprive you of the essential ability to control your own business according to your own desires. Anything that can establish control over you and limit your freedom, I would avoid. Many of the clients you deal with will feel the same way. Some companies with strong union ties will require you to be union to work for them. There are contractors who maintain both a union and a non-union shop, so they can work both sides of the street. The unions will have a difficult time trying to unionize you, if you decide to go non-union, because of the diverse locations your people work at, and the small numbers of employees the average cleaning company has. Personally I don't want business bad enough to have another hand in my pocket or in the pocket of my employees.

## ETHICS

Right now, before you go on to the glory of your own business, you ought to reach a decision as to what laws you're going to operate under: legal, moral, or both. As your business grows, you'll run into lots of situations where things are legal, but not moral. For example, you'll find that in money matters, due to technicalities of the law, you can sometimes beat people out of what you owe them, such as by declaring bankruptcy. Legally no one can touch you, but morally you owe the debt. There are also ways to sue legally, but it's not moral and you know it deep inside. You can build your whole business — and your whole life — on a foundation of integrity or dishonesty. Lots of things can be legal but wrong or immoral. Make a decision up front about how you'll operate, a decision that you'll feel good about the rest of your life.

# INSURANCE?

## 5

# YES!

Insurance isn't something new to you. For your business, the same principles apply as for your life, house, or car. Now you just need a little different brand. As for finding a place to get insurance, just make the announcement somewhere that you're going into business and you'll be like a piece of raw meat slung into a kennel of starving dogs. We are blessed with plenty of insurance companies and agents (only lawyers outnumber them). Call them when you're ready, they'll come a-running.

Now I'll tell you how to save a bundle of time and keep from looking stupid when they shoot all those abracadabra insurance words at you. You can't reply because you have no idea what they're talking about, but feel you'd better buy because it all sounds pretty scary. If I were you, I'd find out who the good, sound contractors of your type are in the city and call them and ask who has their insurance, and are they satisfied. They will tell you and then just call the agent and explain that you are new and want an insurance plan, and to bring a proposal similar to the one Acme Attic Cleaners is using. Acme

probably has everything in their policy that you need in the area, and you only have to adapt it to your size; then the agent won't know how dumb you are about business insurance. Insurance in business is for one reason: to protect you from any big problem and possible lawsuit or claim that would wipe you out forever. What kinds of things are we concerned about here? We've had a window cleaner fall from a twenty-story building to his death. We've had scrubbing machines come loose from our pickup and spear through the door of an automobile just after the person got out. Machines get loose and break windows, knock over mannequins with $15,000 mink coats on, or the wrong chemicals are used to do a cleaning job and the contents of a room or building are ruined, and like every other cleaning company we've been accused of minor and major thefts. We've had our vehicles stolen and stripped down, and I could produce pages of employee claims for injuries and the like. Insurance protects you from the unexpected and the unforeseen liabilities. Since cleaning is such a physical business, there's even more than the usual number of possible risks and damages and unforeseen hazards. Policies are simple, but there are a few hidden knuckleballs here and there that can bean you. Insurance costs have tripled in the last few years, and now insurance is a staggering cost in your business where once it was only pennies. The following are different types of coverage you'll want to consider.

## PERSONAL INSURANCE

You might already have some personal insurance, but it may need to be augmented to cover the needs of your business. Make sure you have money available in case you stick an iron mop handle in a 220-volt electrical socket. Money to provide for your family and money for your wife or husband to do something with the business after you're gone is a necessity, because at the time of death everyone wants their money. If you have $20,000 in payables (money owed by you) and $50,000 in receivables (money owed to you) and are in good shape financially, your family will find it slow going to get the $50,000 but everyone will want the $20,000 immediately. I've always used Term Life Insurance for this. I'm not sold on Whole Life Insurance. Insurance doesn't make you money, you have a business to do that, go cheap term. As you build your business and acquire significant net worth in it, you may need some estate planning help to make sure your insurance is set up to protect that worth for your survivors in the event of your death.

## PUBLIC LIABILITY AND PROPERTY DAMAGE

This is the big one! If your crew or company injures or damages a customer or a bystander or the property of others and they make a claim against you, this insurance will pay it, including any legal costs involved. If you're sued or accused, the insurance company will defend you. Most of your customers will require that you have this kind of insurance, and will ask for a certificate of insurance proving your coverage. Even if your customers don't require it, I wouldn't work one day without PL/PD coverage. Without liability coverage it's businessman's Russian roulette. Your insurance company will provide you with thirty copies of a little printed certificate you can give with your bids to show you do have this insurance. Some companies require $100,000 to $300,000 coverage, some want $300,000 to $500,000, and some require up to a million dollars umbrella coverage. Now here's a catch the other "How To Go Into Your Own Business" books miss because of inexperience: **Liability is what it says — liability. Liability doesn't insure your workmanship.**

If you are cleaning a couch and overwet it and ruin it, you pay — even if it has a $3,000 replacement cost. If you're painting a ceiling and the ladder falls over and paint sprays all over the couch and the ladder goes through the window, both are covered as an accident. If you forget to put a dropcloth over the couch and drip paint on it, **you** pay! In short, you're insured for liability, not for stupidity. My crew used an abrasive cleaning pad on the bathroom fixtures in a large telephone building once and ruined the chrome. We ended up replacing all the chrome fixtures at our own cost. **Remember that!** Liability doesn't insure you for sloppy work, or damages caused by lack of experience on the job. So you still have to be careful, insured or not. Insurance is a big expense these days. So shop around and get bids from three different agents and then choose the person you want to work with, based on price and personality. Be sure to pick an agent you can trust, even if he's a few percent higher in cost initially.

## WORKER'S COMPENSATION

Worker's Comp is another mandatory insurance. If you have employees, you are legally required to carry "comp" on them in almost all instances. Even when it's not legally required, I would still carry it. This coverage compensates your workers for any on-the-job injuries. In most cases, your best bet will be to buy this coverage as part of a business package, from the same agent you have your PL/PD and other insurance with. Some states have a mandatory state fund, which requires you to buy your Worker's Comp from the state. Like unemployment, Comp develops an experience rating based on your claims. If you can hold down on-the-job injuries and accidents, your premium goes down. Make sure your Comp carrier will help you implement a good employee safety program — it really pays!

## VEHICLE INSURANCE

Generally the same agent can and will give you a good price on the insurance on your business vehicles. I carry liability only on the old clunkers and collision and comprehensive with a high deductible on the others, and take my chances. On new, financed vehicles, the banks require you to carry comprehensive and collision insurance. Tie the liability on your vehicles in with your other business liability insurance to lessen the cost.

## HEALTH INSURANCE

You probably already have health insurance on yourself and family through the place you work or have worked. Health insurance pays for hospital bills and other medical and sometimes dental expenses. Its costs have risen considerably in the last few years (mine was once $10 for a family and now is $150 a month for just my wife and me). Health insurance is almost a necessity as one hospital stay or major surgery expense could wipe you out. Because so many jobs now have health insurance included, you'll be expected to have it for your employees. You can pay for it or they can. We are in a spoiled "take-care-of-us" society these days so you'll probably get stuck with it. The usual health insurance policy will pay justifiable claims, about 80% of the first couple thousand and everything after that. There will probably be a deductible on it. Remember, when you use lots of part-time people they will most likely have health insurance at their main job so you won't need it for them. A real savings of money and administrative hassle.

Health insurance is offered as group plans and you can have your own or join another related group. I was with the National Cattleman's Association once and didn't even own a cow! Remember, group health insurance for employees is an option. I wouldn't worry about it for a while, but the need should be tucked away in the "gonna-have-to" corner of your mind. Whether or not you carry personal health insurance for you and your family is your decision. I wouldn't be without it myself.

## DISABILITY INCOME INSURANCE

Your workman's compensation insurance will cover you personally for work-related disabilities; however, in case you are paranoid about being sick or injured or disabled from non-work causes, you can get insurance coverage to pay you while you're out of commission. This too is optional. I never liked it and never got it. You'll find that the excitement of your own business develops a drive and toughness in you, and you'll seldom be sick. In thirty years I've missed five or six days for an appendectomy and a cut hand tendon. I don't think my General Manager, Arlo Luke, has missed even one day of work in twenty-eight years for sickness, injury, or anything else. You'll find that when you don't have "sick leave" or have anyone else to do the work, you seldom or never are too sick to work.

## TAKING RISKS

Life has its risks, and I think you can be insured too much, but don't try to beat the odds by gambling on someone else's life or property. Running a business, you have a real responsibility to others and their property, and if something falls off your truck and hurts someone or destroys someone's carefully tended flower bed, you should make it right and should be prepared to do so. The big, big companies and institutions are sometimes self-insured, but don't you try it. And remember, don't rook your insurance company by turning in claims for every little thing because you have insurance. It's smart to carry fairly large deductibles and just insure the larger risks — losses that would be catastrophic if you were not insured. For smaller risks, or losses you could handle without undue strain, it's smarter just to insure yourself (take the risk). This not only saves you paying an insurance premium, it makes you more careful!

## BONDING

Bonding is not a free ticket to let you off the hook in case of stealing or job failure. Most of the people who deal in bonds (especially those who sell them) don't provide you with this fact. Bonding is not an insurance. Bonding looks like insurance and you pay for it like insurance, but a bond does not provide someone to foot the bill in your stead when things go bad. They still come after you in the end. There are three basic types of bonds you'll need to worry about.

### Bid Bond

Sometimes when you bid a job, the owner will require a bid bond. In simple terms, this says "Mr. Owner, here is my bid. If I am the successful bidder, I guarantee that I will sign a contract to perform the work for the bid price. If I back out because I discover my bid is too low or for some other reason, the bonding company will reimburse you for any expense you incur in getting the next higher bidder to sign a contract (make up the difference between the two bids)." You get a bid bond from your insurance agent, and there is usually no charge. The insurance company gets their pound of flesh if you get the job, because then they can write the performance bond for you.

### Performance Bond

Many big companies require you to have a performance bond before you start a job for them. This is essentially a written and financially-backed promise that you will indeed, as a company, do the job right and finish it as your contract states. If you fail by leaving or quitting or going out of business because you're losing money, then the bonding company steps in and finishes the job or otherwise arranges to honor your promises to the claimant. Lots of government and larger jobs require a performance bond. The catch on bonding is that the bonding company does come in and pay it up, but then it comes after you for the money. They only promise that it will be paid, but you are eventually going to pay it. They can take your car, your kid's motorcycle, the wife's diamond rings, and anything else to honor the commitment. It's kind of like you guaranteeing someone's loan at the bank — if they don't pay, then you pay it for

them, but you can be sure you're going to go after the guy who defaulted on you and get your money back if you can.

### Fidelity Bond

This is a bond that you buy to insure your clients against the possibility of employee thievery. In our business this is an expensive problem. Any theft (or **possible** theft) that ever occurs in a building will usually be blamed first on the cleaning people. Fidelity bonding was something we never had for the first twenty years in our business, but now many companies require it. You especially need it if your company works in banks or other money-related places. Now everyone is going fidelity bond happy. I don't like it, and don't think we professional cleaners should have to carry it, but sometimes it acts as a selling point when you're trying to get work because you can tell people "Hey, we and our people are bonded." It may sound good to them, but to me it says, "I've got protection on my thieves that are going to work for you."

Whether you like fidelity bonding or not, you will have to have it to do certain kinds of work. If you have a dishonest employee who is found guilty of stealing, the bonding company will make good your customer's loss, and then they go after the employee for reimbursement. Very few employee dishonesty cases end up being reimbursed by a bonding company, though, because they won't pay without a criminal conviction, and most cases don't end up being prosecuted. Without a conviction and reimbursement by the bonding company, the customer will be looking to you for redress. Your best defense is to carefully screen potential employees, and try to weed out any potential dishonesty.

## SUMMARY

You can get bonding from your insurance agent if it is required. I personally think that bonds are an unfair expense for the privilege of bidding a building. We have insurance and a reputation — that should be enough. I will often refuse to even bid a job that requires some ridiculous, over-priced bonding. Remember, all of these extras cost money, not only the cash for the bond itself, but the time for you or your staff to arrange and go pick it up, etc. If you get enough

INSURANCE — WHAT YOU NEED 35

of the dingy little things, soon all you are doing in your business is thrashing around in the office. You never get on the job, and you have to bid your work so high, because of all the little extras that you have to cover, that you're uncompetitive and never get any work. Question the people who want the bonds and make sure they know what they're asking. Lots of people have waived them for me. I tell them, hey, I just add the cost of the bond onto your bill, why don't we just forget it. It doesn't do either of us any good!

All insurance is simple if you have a good agent; they get paid to take care of these things, you just pay the bill. I'd suggest you get an agent who you know you can trust, and leave it up to him to recommend the best and cheapest coverage to you. If you choose an agent you don't have faith in just to get a cheap price, you'll have to become an insurance expert just to make sure he's keeping you out of trouble and not over-charging you. The few dollars you save are not worth the hassle. Ask other businessmen you trust to recommend a good agent, and go with the one you feel best about personally. Don't be afraid to change agents until you get one you are comfortable with. Again, remember, insurance is now a significant cost — it can run anywhere from 6-15 percent of your total sales dollar, depending on your location and the size of your payroll.

# TARGETING 6
# THE MARKET

## THE 'GRASS IS GREENER' SYNDROME

As soon as you get into the flow of the business, you won't believe the number of possible "jobs" relating to cleaning. Starting out you'll probably think of floors, walls, carpets, restrooms, and a few structurally-related things, but as you work on the job, parking lots, vehicles, and hundreds more will pop up. Angles and ideas will pour in, as will stories of imagined fortunes. You'll never make it if you chase every opportunity that comes along. Every new thing will look more attractive and interesting than what you're doing now. The old **grass is greener** syndrome. This chapter is here to help you make sure you target your efforts and focus your energies.

I was a high school and college athlete, a fierce competitor, and deeply dedicated to training. Night after night, day after day, I practiced. I'd work for months on one tough shot in basketball that might win the game. I became an accurate shooter in basketball, and a controlled pitcher in baseball, but for all my years on the court and on the diamond, I knew nothing about targeting. This lesson, which since has been a byword for me in business, came at the start of a practice well along in my playing career. We arrived in the gym that day and noticed a stepladder up to the basket. When we all assembled, the coach took two basketballs, walked up the ladder and held the balls side by side, and lowered them through the basket at the same time. We all gasped in awe. We had no idea the hoop was that much larger than the ball. He then told us that the biggest problem of shooting at something is that we aim "in the direction of," rather than at the actual bull's-eye. Instead of aiming at the basket in general, he said, aim at the exact center of the hoop. What happened after that was truly amazing: my accuracy went up 20% as I began shooting for the exact center of the bucket instead of the basket as a whole.

Targeting can do just as much for a cleaning business. Cleaning businesses have hundreds of offshoots. **Where** you shoot can make the difference between winning and losing the whole game. I will provide a long list of jobs, a menu that you'll lick your chops over. To help you not have eyes bigger than your stomach, here are a few solid guidelines for deciding where to concentrate.

## LOVE OR HATE?

**Do you like to do it?** No matter how profitable it is, or how needed a certain type of job is, if you really hate it, if it doesn't suit your personal tastes, inclinations and desires, then do something else. Remember, you're going to spend a lot of mental, emotional and physical effort on the activities you choose, so picking times, places, and procedures you feel good about is super important. For example, I could qualify to hold a building trade card in seven professions. I can do sheetrocking and taping but I hate it; it emotionally unnerves me, and even if I could make $600 an hour doing it, I'd refuse. On the other hand, painting is my favorite. I'm fast, and I love to see the dramatic change and improvement in what I'm working on. I hate parking lot sweeping and never made a dime in it, but others do well at it and hate to paint. I prefer outside work and physical work over inside and office work. The things I'm enthused about and enjoy, I do better at and work longer hours at, and I'm more contented, creative, and productive. You'll find that the same is true with you. You can't have it all (all the money, all the food, all the sex in the world), nor can you have all of the cleaning skills in your operation.

## A JACK OF ALL TRADES

When we started our business, most of the principals were "hands-on, do-it-all" handyman types. We knew how to do most everything from sheetrocking to cleaning carpets to refinishing graphite roofs. We could include the little line "and what have you" in our ads and not be lying. We were even a state-licensed painting contractor.

Today, we've reduced the number of services we offer and are staying strictly in the field we know best — cleaning — and know we can do a superior job at it. As we grew and hired more people and got further away from our original work force, our people didn't have the versatile backgrounds we had and so we were forced to stay in the specialized fields we'd trained our staff in.

**I started out doing everything:**
- Office cleaning
- Carpet cleaning
- Windows
- Parking lot sweeping and striping
- Wallpaper hanging
- Tree care
- Lawns
- Fire damage
- Construction cleanup
- Painting
- Carpentry

**Now I only do:**
- Office cleaning
- Carpets
- Windows
- Floor care
- Construction cleanup

Lots of other companies are doing just the opposite. They started cleaning carpet only, then went to walls, windows, automobiles, and now they do everything from guard service to baby tending.

**They start out specialized:**
- Painting
- Housecleaning
- Office cleaning
- Window washing

**Now they do:**
- Fire damage
- Appliance repair
- Drapery cleaning
- Ceiling repair
- Carpet cleaning
- Wall cleaning
- Chimney cleaning
- Construction cleanup
- Termite control
- Plant service
- Baby tending
- Cat grooming and hairball removal

Watch yourself that you don't try to offer so much that you're not good at anything. Note that this is the day of the expert, the specialist.

Very few doctors are general practitioners and the same is true of lawyers and other professionals. They specialize in one field of related services: eyes, ears, nose, and throat; real estate contracts, etc. When you need an eye operation, you don't call a general practitioner to do it — you call an eye specialist. Your banker isn't likely to have you come and clean his expensive oriental screens if he knows you've made your reputation steaming sewer grates and garbage dumpsters.

One of the biggest troublemakers in life, especially for new businesses, is that old haunting feeling that "the thing the other guy has is better than mine." No matter how good you have it at home, at work, or at play, you constantly yearn for their greener grass, better property, job, health, car, spouse, kids — everything looks better than yours. Their barbecue smells better, their laundry is whiter, even their pets are better behaved. If the truth were known, they're thinking the same about you! If you let this "better than me" idea plague you for long, you'll probably get into trouble. No matter how well you're doing cleaning houses, the commercial work must be better; if you're into hard floors there seems to be nothing but carpet jobs. To get down to cases, your yearning for the other side can make you diversify too soon and cause you to make some bad choices. It's just like buying a Swiss army knife that will enable you to do everything. So why doesn't everyone have one of these knives, and why aren't you carrying the one you bought? Just like getting into too many different jobs, the big, do-all Swiss army knife can't do a real job of anything. All its gadgets only partly work on only some things. The only thing it does truly well is wear out your pants pocket, just like too much variation before you have experience will wear thin your profits.

A friend of mine in the business, Jim Abdo, started his cleaning business specializing in furniture (couches, chairs, desks, etc.). You have to clean a lot of furniture to keep a company going, so after he had furniture down pat, he was tempted to move on to lights, walls, and floors. After all, he was already at the home or business, so it was a natural to do more than just furniture. It wouldn't cost him much more, as he wouldn't have to pay additional travel time, etc. But he didn't do it. Instead, he stuck with what he knew and expanded to different kinds, types, and amounts of furniture, like learning to clean an expensive leather couch, an imported

velvet settee, a brocade curtain, a cherry wood rolltop desk. He figured people who owned pieces costing thousands of dollars would pay several hundred a year to have them serviced and kept in sharp condition. He was right. He has been in the cleaning business for years and years, is the best at his specialty, and has plenty of profitable business. By perfecting his interest, he eliminated his competition and strengthened his clients' confidence.

I know another contractor who concentrated on hard floors in supermarkets and grocery stores; he became an expert at it and did even better. Soon customers were asking him to do carpets, clean carts, meat lockers, stripe parking lots, and train their Halloween hobgoblins. The new line of work was tempting, but the reason for his success had been staying in his own specialty. He's still just doing floors and is still a great success. I can think of fifty others who faced the same crossroad and leaped unknowingly into new ventures with dollar signs flashing in their eyes, but who ended up with nothing. Maid services are popping up across the country and many are franchising. Many are failing because they couldn't keep up with the needed training, motivation, capital, and growth (and still have any home life left). The owner of the most successful maid service in the world told me his or her key secret was "stick to the knitting." In other words do the simple thing better and better and better, then if you get bored or blessed with too much, carefully move one notch. But jumping up to a five thousand-dollar parking lot sweeper which you have no knowledge of and few accounts for is suicide. The money would have been better spent to upgrade and perfect your presently profitable and familiar part of the business.

Over-diversifying will be a constant temptation to you. Right when you get a good selection of services under your belt and develop a couple of really good specialties that are rolling along, you hear that there's a new thing: cleaning arc lights at the local ballparks. Your competitor or some fly-by-night is getting $40 a light to clean them, and he's a jerk, so you know you can make at least $50 a light. All you need is a lift truck and, because you're terrified of heights, a pole monkey to go up the hundred-foot ladder to the lights. **Don't touch things like this!** If you can't handle them or don't know the business, beware. I've seen thousands of cleaning and other businesses fail yearly because they jump into hot new markets and offshoots trying to make a quick buck. For years, I bit my lip wanting to set up a large truckwashing unit for the dirty eighteen-wheelers that tool through my town. It looked so easy, so profitable, all the brochures made it sound like such a sure thing, so I called and talked to all the truck washers I could find. They were all nice people, but far from rich; even the best in the business had closed up half their units. No way could they profit. Some of them even added a truck stop to see if residual business could help them make it, and it still didn't. If I'd done it, I'd be out $100,000 now. There just wasn't enough demand there to justify the large capital investment required. Keep your business simple and easy, learn what you do well and keep your energies focused so you can service perfectly what you do. Instead of instituting four hundred auxiliary services, get better at what you do and expand that; it costs less and makes more profit!

## DECISIONS, DECISIONS

**What to take and what to turn down?** Instead of ten pages of philosophies and preaching, I've made you a checklist of 16 items (on page 62). Take five minutes when you get the chance and rate each new opportunity you have in mind, using these criteria. This will keep you objective. For example, say everything is a plus except #5 and #6. It is far away and the owner or boss you answer to is a fishy character. There's no way, even if you are good, knowledgeable, etc., that you'll win. Don't touch it. **You don't have to take every job that comes along.** You don't wear clothes that don't fit, you don't eat food you don't like, and you don't hang around with people you don't enjoy. Why? Because you aren't happy or productive with them, and it's the same with business. Some contracts are great, the profits look nice, but you'll need to have twelve large carpet machines to do the job and you'll have to buy them up front. You can't do that, so you say no thanks.

Run off a few copies of the chart (on page 44) and carry it in your bid book when you go to a bid. Run down the list on each of your bids before you make a proposal, and you'll be surprised how many things you overlooked in your zeal to have more.

One loose rivet won't cause an airplane to drop from the sky nor will one leaky mop bucket

cause your business to fail, unless that bucket leaks and ruins the chairman-of-the-board's Persian rug. Generally though, it won't be the one or two isolated problems that wreck your business, it will be the repeat disasters. Likewise one black mark on the considerations chart shouldn't cause you to scratch off an otherwise attractive job. If it gets up to two or three "baddies" though, (especially if they're big ones, like the person you work with,) I'd really have second thoughts.

## A MENU OF SERVICES

### Carpet Cleaning

There are 25,000 carpet cleaners I know of nationwide, so that tells you that this is a good field. It's a little oversaturated (that's a pun), but if you become a real carpet specialist and know your stuff, you'll even be able to beat out the bounders with a giant truck setup they bought with their daddy-in-law's money.

### Ceiling Cleaning

Chemical cleaning of acoustic-type ceilings is a nice sideline for a janitorial service, or it can stand on its own as a specialty business. You can work up your own set of equipment and chemicals, or you can buy one of the many packages available from ceiling cleaning distributors.

### Chimney Cleaning

This specialty recently swept the nation, so to speak; therefore it's oversaturated in some areas. But wood burning is even more popular, leaving a lot of chimneys and stovepipes dirty. I know the King of the American chimney sweeps, David Stoll of the Chicago area, and he convinces me a well-trained and certified sweep can do well. (All of the fly-by-the-roof ones soon fall by the wayside.) David runs a school that can officially certify you as a professional sweep. (See appendix.)

### Concrete Floor Sealing

This is a good one! It requires very little investment and does real service for the customer. Looks great and there are new seals now that are much less smelly and unpleasant than the old resin products. Sealing makes a building or surface a lot easier to clean, and one or two people can do a huge job.

## Construction Cleanup

This is a big one for us. It means going in behind a contractor as he completes a building or house, cleaning all the tubs, windows, floors, etc., and making it ready to turn over to the new occupant.

## Disaster Cleanup

These kinds of jobs are done for insurance companies and they're good if you learn the ropes. Going in after a fire or flood entails cleaning and deodorizing, repairing, drying out, and restoring the structure to its original beauty. This is a real science, and there are complete manuals available for this sort of service. It has tough hours and unpredictable availability, but it's very profitable and sure money.

## Drapery Cleaning

In-place drape cleaning is the latest angle: you show up with a magic machine and dry clean drapes without unhooking them, right on location. The equipment does a good job and is getting better. This is a new field and a good place for a small specialty operator to jump in.

## Floor Care

Ironically, there are very few good floor care people out there. Stripping and waxing, and all the other daily, weekly, etc., care of hard surface floors is and always will be a good area, but you have to be a mover.

## Furniture Cleaning

You can choose from many specialties, in addition to general office furniture cleaning:
- Office furniture touchup and repair
- Complete furniture refinishing
- Complete re-upholstering services
- Electrostatic painting of metal furniture
- Fabricating of formica for desks, credenzas, file cabinets, countertops, etc.
- Shampoo and Scotchgard services for fabric furniture

- Cleaning of vinyl or fabric modular panels
- Re-upholstering fabric modular paneling, flippers and tack boards
- Cleaning under raised floors in computer rooms
- Cleaning tape drives, disc packs, air handling units, keypunch machines, CRT terminals, etc.

## Home Repair and Handyman Services

There are lots of us aging senior citizens around, our kids have grown up and are gone, and we need someone to haul or move things for us or fix a leaky faucet or cracked cement. This is a good one if you have a natural knowledge and skill of repair. If not, and you can't even fix things at home, move to the next one, because you'll put yourself out of business.

## Housecleaning

This means showing up with a crew and cleaning the whole house — walls, ceiling, carpets, windows, upholstery, etc. — in one big attack. This was my big item when I started out; it was fun and profitable and was always growing. As we grew, my crews grew scared of the finicky homemakers, and we do mostly commercial work now as a big contractor.

## Lawn Maintenance

Good work, but there are lots of kids competing for $5 an hour. You need good equipment and lean and hungry crews. This type of work is generally seasonal, so you have to gear up and down constantly.

## Maid Service

They're multiplying so fast, business must be good. Maid services are appearing everywhere and the franchises still seem to be holding up. Nowadays in most households both the man and woman work, which means more of a need for maid service. Do it faster and better and you'll get the work.

## Matron or Porter Service

We often furnish people as day porters or matrons for four hours a day or all day in different kinds of buildings. We bill the customer by the hour, saving them the cost of carrying an employee on their payroll. It's kind of a labor-brokering thing, but it works! We also provide maids this way for restaurants or big hotels; it saves them hiring and holding extras.

## Metal Cleaning

Here is another one that's getting to be more in demand. Brass and luminous chrome and aluminum lobbies and building faces are all over the place these days. Who cleans them? For the exterior building facings, this requires some specialized equipment and training, but there's a lot of call for it.

## Painting

There are fewer big painting contractors today, so small individuals can get some good jobs. It does require a license, bonding, and has its union pressure, but I like it. A good moneymaker, and it's easy to leave a satisfied customer who sees real results!

## Parking Lot Striping

Fast, fun, profitable. You run out of parking lots fast, so it isn't a full time forever job. You can do this by hand or use a spray rig, which is simple to operate. The first-time layout is the only tough part of it. Re-striping is easy!

## Parking Lot Sweeping

There are lots of parking lots around. The hours are tough by the time the lots are vacated, but there's some good vacuum equipment out now to speed the job. You need a series of these jobs to come out ahead (because of the cost of the equipment), but they're easy to do.

## Pest Extermination

Don't let this bug you. It fits in neatly with other cleaning services and can be a nice supplement. It usually takes a license, not to mention a little training to outsmart termites, but it's worth it.

## Plant Maintenance

A job for a specialist, but you can easily become one if you have a touch of the old green thumb. Your job here is to provide and take care of the live plants and plantings in large buildings and hotels and malls. You water, prune, fertilize, etc. A new field and a thriving one, and a lot of women are entering this field.

## Roof Painting

Spraying roofs made of wood shingles (with graphite and linseed oil or paint) to maintain and preserve them has been a good profitable business. It's dirty and a little scary but it's worth it. The newer composition and tile roofs are gradually phasing this out, but you can do it by hand or use an airless sprayer.

## Sandblasting

Nice way to clean fireplaces, building exteriors, bridges, machinery, and other masonry, tough surfaces, or hard-to-reach areas. A little hard on the lungs. It's easy to learn, and you can buy or rent the equipment.

## Snow Removal

You do need snow for this one! Lots of it! It's unpredictable and hard on equipment, but for a real hustler it can be a good job. And it gets your foot in the door for other bids; the scope of this work spans all the way from the old hand shovel to tractor and truck removal.

## Stone Cleaning

There's lots of rock work around, and who knows anything about it? I lay rocks and own a block plant and yet don't know as much as I'd like to about how to actually clean the stuff. Try as I may, I can't seem to find anyone who really knows this field and can teach it. This is a good, open field and will get better as fancy hotels and office building interiors multiply. This may have to be a learn-as-you-earn project — there aren't too many master stone cleaners around to study under.

TARGETING, OR PICK FROM THE MENU   43

## Substitute Janitorial Work

Ah, here's a beauty I almost forgot about. When companies have their own in-house cleaning people, they need relief when those people leave for vacation. This is a perfect way for you to get jobs. The clients get a good look at you. You know how long the job takes before you ever bid it, you really have a foot in the door for future takeovers, and you're paid for it all!

## Swimming Pool Maintenance

If you live in a warm climate, this can be a profitable business. The seasonal aspect makes caring for pools in Idaho, Minnesota, Alaska, or North Dakota not much of a paying proposition.

## Wall Covering Installation

Paperhanging about died out for a while, but it's now back in demand and not many do it well. There are all sorts of nice wall coverings on the market today, and a lot of places and individuals who want to see it on their walls. Factories will train you and there are some good profits. I think this is a hot one for the future.

## Windows

The old standby! Ultra-competitive, but always there and always getting dirty. Just figure a way to be faster and better and you'll eat regularly. High windows and staging are a specialized field, and you should make sure you fully understand the requirements for safety, insurance, and training before launching into high window work.

## OPTIONAL JOBS

When you go to the Jones building to bid a cleaning job, you find that the establishment badly needs painting. The yard requires some attention, too; the rugs are badly worn and two doors need repair. Your first impulse is to size all this up and make one gigantic and beautiful presentation. For one thing, you're concerned that if this isn't all done immediately, the customer may get someone else to do it — and you may be right. However, in spite of all the problems you've identified, the one your customer has contacted you for (janitorial maintenance) is foremost in his mind at the moment. Mr. Jones wants the janitorial job taken care of first, and

he wants someone new to do it, or he wouldn't have called you. He's also interested in saving some money, so he probably isn't interested in a bunch of unanticipated new expenses at this time. It's generally best to make a note of the necessary extra work and suggest to Mr. Jones that you could perhaps give him a bid on some or all of it at a later date.

## COMMERCIAL VS. RESIDENTIAL WORK

Bigger isn't better in the cleaning business, unless you love complication, risk and no-margin-for-error work. Yet after cleaning a few homes and a little bank or office, "big time thoughts" pop into our heads. We say to ourselves, "Gee, if I am making $40 profit a day on this little housecleaning job, that office building is ten times bigger, so if I land it, I'll be making $400 a day."

While residential work generally offers smaller-sized jobs, it also offers higher profit margins, lower overhead and insurance, and an added plus we often overlook. All of those decision makers who work and manage the big businesses have to live somewhere, and those homes you clean are owned by these people! Talk about a way to sell for the big one if you want them. A number of my big janitorial contracts have started out as a small housecleaning job for the plant manager's wife! If I didn't have this cleaning empire now and was starting out again, I'd stick to cleaning homes and do some extra jobs for the owners of businesses. Do that and you'll take lots of jobs daily away from all the big giant contracts at 30% profit while they are laboring in the massive buildings at 3% profit.

Maid service and housecleaning contractors are different. The maids stick to just coming in regularly to dust, vacuum, straighten up, and spruce up — the quick visit style. Contract housecleaners generally come in and wash walls, strip and wax floors, clean rugs and carpets, wash windows, etc., (the once or twice a year job). You can combine them or specialize. Personally, I like to do the jobs that homeowners cannot do themselves and I just plain like the more challenging jobs. This of course will vary with the town and country and with your personal preferences.

# Contract Maintenance Services Offered

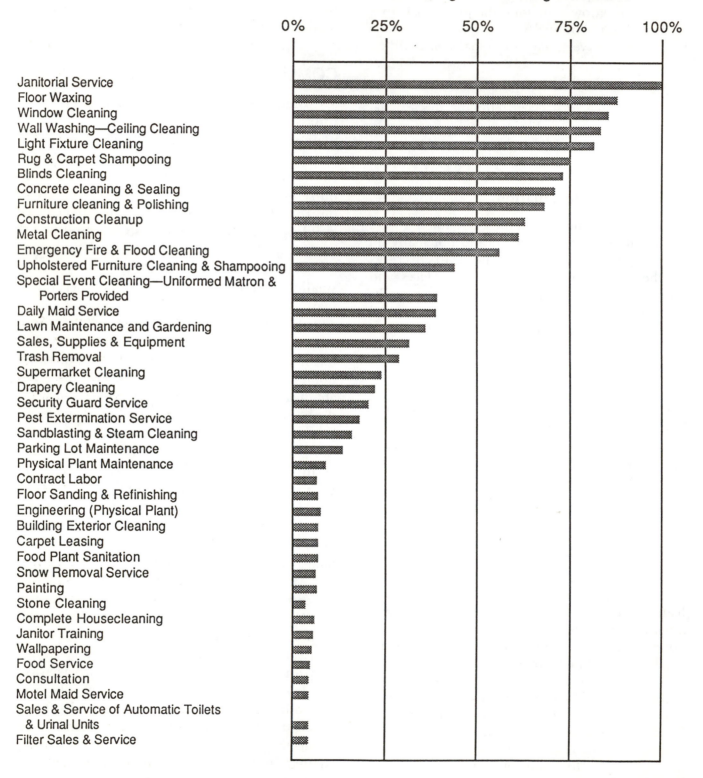

Percent of cleaning firms offering the service

| | 0% | 25% | 50% | 75% | 100% |

Janitorial Service
Floor Waxing
Window Cleaning
Wall Washing—Ceiling Cleaning
Light Fixture Cleaning
Rug & Carpet Shampooing
Blinds Cleaning
Concrete cleaning & Sealing
Furniture cleaning & Polishing
Construction Cleanup
Metal Cleaning
Emergency Fire & Flood Cleaning
Upholstered Furniture Cleaning & Shampooing
Special Event Cleaning—Uniformed Matron & Porters Provided
Daily Maid Service
Lawn Maintenance and Gardening
Sales, Supplies & Equipment
Trash Removal
Supermarket Cleaning
Drapery Cleaning
Security Guard Service
Pest Extermination Service
Sandblasting & Steam Cleaning
Parking Lot Maintenance
Physical Plant Maintenance
Contract Labor
Floor Sanding & Refinishing
Engineering (Physical Plant)
Building Exterior Cleaning
Carpet Leasing
Food Plant Sanitation
Snow Removal Service
Painting
Stone Cleaning
Complete Housecleaning
Janitor Training
Wallpapering
Food Service
Consultation
Motel Maid Service
Sales & Service of Automatic Toilets & Urinal Units
Filter Sales & Service

## CAREERS AND JOBS IN CLEANING

To help you visualize the different duties in cleaning, here are some brief job descriptions. These are jobs you can work in yourself, or can hire people to fill, either now or in the future.

### Maid

Here's a versatile position with lots of opportunity either in homes or commercial work. You can work as a maid for yourself, or for a company. The flexible hours and duty assignments make this great for part-time work or work that has to be woven in with the demands of a family.

### Executive Housekeeper

The executive housekeeper manages the entire housekeeping department of a facility like a hospital, hotel, or college. A very active and educational position, it provides lots of personal contact and life-building experience. It is challenging and interesting, with very good pay and promotion prospects for high performance. No age or other restrictions.

### Janitors

There are 7,000,000 of us! Good ones get paid well and enjoy education, exercise, and handy hours — plus you can work anywhere if you are good.

### Property Manager

Lots of investors buy property and, to make it productive, need to retain someone to look after it, keep it rented, and repaired. You manage all aspects of the interior and exterior of the property: administer contracts, leases, and maintenance. You'll spend most of your time on various kinds of maintenance, but it's all exciting and challenging. These days the majority of property managers are women, where twenty years ago it was all men! Malls, commercial offices, condos, and apartments are the most common properties. This career is well worth going after.

### Salesperson

Who sells all the contract business and all those cleaning maintenance supplies and equipment? What about you? Once you obtain a knowledge of what they cost and how they perform, you are valuable to both janitorial firms and cleaning supply companies. If you know or think you can learn how to sell, look into this. Salespeople get to travel, meet lots of people, make bids, presentations, do training and demonstrations. There are commission or salary setups, and there are almost no bounds.

### Cleaning Foreman/Supervisor

Who bosses, organizes and outlines all the crews that clean the buildings and care for grounds and parking lots? Supervisory spots are always open for above-average, ambitious cleaners who can direct and motivate people. The pay is upgraded and there's lots of rewards and action.

### Building Manager

Notice all the big buildings around. Well, just as a train needs an engineer, all of these need a manager to direct cleaning, air conditioning, landscaping, decorating, food service, etc. You have your own office and a job where you learn to be a superb P.R. and management person.

### Trainer/Teacher

Trained people in cleaning are in great demand by thousands of companies. Where do they come from? Someone with experience needs to teach them. You can set up your own private company or school and offer to run an in-house training program for them. Once you are good and get results, you will make lots of friends and money, as well as have a lot of personally enriching experiences.

### Consultant

After succeeding at any of these careers, you can do consulting for others, help them solve their cleaning problems, and increase their efficiency through design. You can earn over $100 per hour. All careers in cleaning can lead to this if you're interested in it.

# GETTING...  7
# ...THE
# BUSINESS

The little sign hanging in my office, **Get The Business**, espouses the philosophy I've always used and found most effective. Once you've chosen your business name, you have a location, and it's all legal and insured, you open the door for customers to come rolling in. If you soon find that business isn't rolling in, well, going into business on your own is no guarantee that anyone will buy from you or even hire you. A few accounts might dribble in on their own, but never enough, so now you have to go out and get some business. Don't make this hard for yourself. I get ill looking at and reading the piles of marketing concepts and strategies and money spent to round up a few jobs. Keep it simple; all you're doing is convincing some people to let you clean their toilets, windows, and floors. That's pretty humble, and all you basically have to do is:

1. Convince them that it's better to have someone clean it than to do it themselves.
2. Convince them that you're better than the forty other cleaners who have called on them in the past week.
3. Convince them it does need to be done, and they can afford your price.

Selling is that simple. I've watched cleaning companies tackle customers with such a barrage of brilliant and expensive marketing techniques that the customer gave his work to someone else because he figured anyone who could afford all those expensive frills must be a rip-off. Getting work is easy and self-perpetuating if you are good enough to deliver the goods. In the cleaning business getting enough work to have it backlogged and waiting is the best position in the world to be in. Then you can be effective and efficient and profitable. Waiting and hunting and selling costs you a bundle and pays you nothing. On-the-job production, getting the cleaning job done, is the only way you make money. **Remember that** — selling and advertising doesn't count until you are doing the job. The job is the actual goal, not the marketing program. Too many white-shirt MBAs and bankers and lawyers and accountants advise and discuss and think you get paid as easy as they do for giving bids and advising and looking over buildings and having meetings about dirty buildings. It pays nothing, **you can only bill for work accomplished.**

The key to selling in this business is to treat people right and do good work. When you do that, you get a lot of word-of-mouth advertising, and can give good references. You also feel good about yourself and the job you're doing and have confidence you can deliver the goods for your prospective customers. This makes it natural and easy for you to convince them to do business with you.

In truth, lots of you already have an account or two staked out before launching into the cleaning business, so you aren't starting out completely from scratch. You'll need more work fast, especially if you drop your other job and go full-time. Remember, other income, insurance, perks, bonuses and vacation time are now gone forever. **You are your own boss — you're on your own!** My directions to you remain the same. Keep it simple and start small. The first work-finding investment I would make is in some good business cards. They will cost you $20 or so. Print a lot of them, because after three hundred they are almost free to print. Right now you have nothing to really brag about in a brochure so hold off for a while. Print some stationery at the same time, and by the way, put both your **home phone and business phone on the card.** The out-to-lunch attitude or "don't call me after work or on Saturday" is future failure talking. When you're starting, you take business whenever and wherever you can get it. The furnace never blows up, the house never floods, and the dog never wets on the carpet at a good time. I've taken numerous accounts away from good competition because I was on the job and available at night and at 3:00 A.M. on Saturday morning, while my competitors were "not available."

## PERSONAL CONTACT

**Be available and be visible.** This is the first law of cleaning marketing. You don't have to push your manure-picking wheelbarrow down Main Street yet, but you had better push your body down there and get out on the street with a handful of business cards. Some call it door-to-door, I call it personal contact. I'll tell you a little secret that none of us big contractors or medium contractors will admit to, but 98% of the doors you knock on, the customers will not be satisfied entirely with the cleaning service they have. No one is ever totally satisfied. They will tell you that they are and might even turn you away, but even my ten best accounts, that have kept my company for ten years, in some way are not completely satisfied. And the same goes for the other cleaning companies, too. This gives you a real opportunity to get in and bid the job. Remember that when and if you get the account — even if you think everything's going fine — they won't be 100% happy with you. Don't ever rest on your laurels.

## A NEED AT EVERY DOOR

And that thin little business card can open up a million-dollar account for you. Nothing beats personal contact and personal commitment. A good little conscientious contractor like you can beat me and the other big boys every way imaginable because of your personal closeness, even to big business. The largest company's door you knock on is still run by an ordinary person, with kids and a wife at home, who has good and bad days, and you can get close to him. Remember that, make lots of personal calls. You aren't spending any money doing it, and right off you won't get many offers. After all, you're new, green, inexperienced, unconfident — why should they trust or hire you? But once that card is in their hand and you've given them a handshake and a personal commitment of good service, they won't forget you. I constantly get calls, even from cards I've dropped off over three years ago. Then start taking what you can get, at whatever hours, place, and time available — you need experience and a track record and to go on the job yourself. I'll repeat this a dozen times more: this business is a "hands-on" business, not a manipulatory one. There is no way in the beginning of the business that you will succeed by going and hustling the work and then sending a bunch of "help" to do it. You do it yourself and you do it right and you clean the corners! If you don't go yourself, you won't last long. Once you've learned the job and have got it going smoothly, and have trained someone to do it right, then you may be able to back off a bit, but not at first. If you need help, take help with you. Learn and do, get fast and sure; once done, go to the boss of the account and thank him and give him another card and lick your chops and beg for more work anywhere.

That guy will go home thinking about you and end up looking for work to give you. Lots of my crews of college kids would kid me about selling the customer all through the jobs we did; to them each job was an end in itself. Wrong, dead wrong! If we do a good job there and leave a couple of cards, that person can't stand it until she is over to the neighbors and telling all of them about us. Building managers are the same breed of cat, they get together often and talk about us, the good and the bad. In the cleaning business, your first and best advertisement and endorsement comes from . . .

## WORD OF MOUTH

You can sell all day on radio, TV, and in the papers, you can "ad" yourself to death and not even touch the value of one client saying to another potential client, "Hey, you know I hired old Sam Smith and Company, and he did a marvelous job at a good price." If word of mouth gets you a nice job, find out where it came from and drop some inexpensive little item in the mail to them with a thank-you note. You won't believe what that will do. Cleaning businesses are a lot like doctors, barbers, and beauticians — a personal experience. You don't want just anyone milling in and cleaning your personal effects and your desk and your home, do you? No! You want the good Sam Smith guys, the same as Ace Motor Company hired.

Let me give you a vivid example of this from my own experience. I got a call from a married couple moving into a new home. The job was a bunch of piddly chores like removing the manufacturer's stickers from the new bathtub, and other ding-work which I wasn't too excited about, but remember what I told you. This is a service business! You don't always choose your morsel to chew. I cleaned well, treated them well, and did some extras for a modest price. Little did I know then her husband was an executive for the Bell System, then the world's largest company, and Bell System had just built a new building in our town, with the Western Electric company installing the new telephone switching equipment. I was a freshman in college then, and my wife and I lived in a little basement apartment. It was Saturday, I believe, when the phone rang and the Western Electric supervisor said he'd heard we do good work and would we come down and see him. I got the job of sweeping up the bolts and wire snippings following installation, a good $125-a-month job. We were there and available and got another job, while they were wiring the building. In eight months the new phone building was ready to go on-line and Bell System, which was all in-house (meaning they have their own janitors) considered moving us in and their own janitors out. We had done a good job and the staff janitors had a hard time following us. The manager asked me for a bid on the maintenance of the new building. Our bid was one-third the price he was paying for his janitors, so amid a lot of union hollering, we got the job. This was the first of the 30,000 Bell buildings in the U.S. ever to be contracted. We have that building still, and thousands more, and it all started with a little word-of-mouth advertising for a job well done. I was instrumental in converting the entire Bell System nationally to contract maintenance (they are 70% contracted today). My company ended up bidding whole states for Bell and getting them. In some areas, where Bell buildings doubled and tripled in size, we doubled and tripled with them. The better we did, the more they called their buddies and complimented us, and the more buildings and states we went into. **Do you get the message?** Pour your heart and soul and commitment into your work. Yes, you'll come up against people who will treat you inconsiderately, even bad-mouth you while you're doing good work. Eventually, though, the white-coveralled janitor triumphs, and those people you never stop treating well are the best and most effective advertisement you have going for you, **and they are free!**

Marketing a cleaning business, especially a small one starting up, isn't a difficult job. Just keep all the big ideas and big spending out of your head for a while, at least until you have some money to lose. Keep yourself visible and your business cards circulating, and do good work. I get most jobs while I'm travelling, at church, ball games, restaurants, making speaking appearances, shopping, etc. Keep your business cards handy all the time, and give them out whenever you can. Secretly, everyone wants you, "the poor cleaner," to make it. Give them a chance to help you, and keep arming them with your name.

## VISIBILITY

### Vehicle Lettering

Decide on a company logo and get your vehicle lettered professionally. It might cost you $200 to do it, but it's a travelling billboard. When parked in front of the fanciest bank in town (even if it's just to open a savings account) four hundred people will see it and say, WOW, if they work in that fancy place they must be good. I have a city where I only have one sharp lettered van, but people constantly say that they see my trucks all over town. That's the value of a memorable logo!

Get the job done well — sloppy lettering projects a sloppy image, the last thing you want! Do a rough design of what you want to see, and have a good, reputable truck or sign lettering firm do it for you. Sketch the proportions and design accurately enough for them to use as a guideline, and if you have an existing logo or letterhead, bring it along for them to use. A few guidelines from my own experience:

1. Don't fall into the common trap of putting too much printing on your vehicles. If it ends up looking like a mobile dictionary, it won't get read. Put your identification on both sides as well as the rear of the vehicle, with a byline of what you do, such as "Contract Cleaner," etc. On the next line, put three to four jobs that you do, such as "Floors, Walls, Carpets, Ceilings," etc. Lengthy cute slogans don't really add anything when you consider that this is a moving vehicle, not the Yellow Pages. Keep it short and concise. If you add your telephone number, remember to also include the area code, and it's a good idea to also include your city and state in smaller letters.

2. Consider your colors, and have the artist match them correctly. Choose non-fading paints, since a vehicle is exposed to weather constantly.

3. Don't allow other "decoration" (bumper stickers, swinging dashboard bangles) and other clutter on or in your vehicles. Most people think negatively of them and it will hurt your business.

4. Don't use magnetic signs. We tried it at our company for years on all types of vehicles and surfaces. They tend to look tacky, they blow off or get stolen, plus there's a subtle feeling that magnetic signs lack commitment and permanence, which can lower your company's image in the eyes of the public.

5. Investigate the use of decal stick-ons. We've been using them for about ten years, and find them cost-efficient if you have a number of vans or trucks in operation. They are economical, last a long time, and can be applied in about 45 minutes.

What all this accomplishes is the projection of a competent and professional image for your cleaning service. It may seem expensive to you now, but when people begin to recognize your vehicles and familiarize themselves with your name, it will begin to pay off in job references and new clients.

### Yellow Pages

They are effective — somewhat! Remember, there are twenty other people with big ads and the reader has a smorgasbord of "truth stretching" companies in front of him all exaggerating their prowess of bufferhood. All starting companies make the same mistake, they **buy too big an ad.** One hundred fifty dollars a month for a Yellow Page ad sounds cheap the evening after you've done the big profitable job, but month after month it eats you alive. I've gone three months in an area with $200 a month in Yellow Pages ads without a call from it. Be super conservative, but do have your name listed so they can find it and remember it from your personal sales call. Count on your personal calls to get you most of your business, though, especially in the commercial field. Let everyone else buy the half-page ads; when you're starting out they just don't pay. Remember, the price of the Yellow Pages is a **monthly,** not a one-time cost. For sample ads, open your phone book to the janitorial section and behold!

On the other hand, if you're doing residential work, big bucks for "mass media" ads such as the Yellow Pages may be a good investment. If you're targeting only the biggest fifty commercial buildings in town, it would be much cheaper and better to just contact the fifty decision makers personally.

## Radio

For a commercial cleaning service, I don't consider radio a strong media. I think for lots of things it's actually better than TV, but for the janitorial business, you pay too much for the number of commercial decision makers your message reaches. Almost all new companies get roped into a deal with the local station for forty spots in return for cleaning their building. You'll never or, at least, seldom come out on the deal. I never did on five different stations. I love radio and think it can be a good media for residential services, but janitorial cleaning just doesn't sell that well on it.

## Television

This can work for big-time residential carpet cleaners, etc., but it has the same drawbacks as radio for commercial services, with much higher costs.

## Newspaper

Classified ads are best! We get results from the classifieds. I've spent thousands in newspaper advertising in half-page ads and gotten nothing. I mean nothing. And yet a cheap little classified under the "services" section will bring calls like you can't believe. You'll have to play around with various formats and wording until you hit upon an ad that works for you.

## Local Tabloids

Lots of basketball tournaments, county fair programs, Jr. Miss contests, etc., will approach you to buy a half- or quarter-page ad in their program. This is just a donation; if you feel you can afford it, do it. If you think it is doing you good advertising, **forget it!** I bought one in the

Law Enforcement Gazette or something and found out the only place it was distributed was in the driver's license office where each citizen only came in three times in ten years, **almost zero benefit!**

## Handbills

They work OK, but don't put them on windshields at ball games or church meetings or the public will hate you (this is a cleaning company?). They don't get a strong response, but are usually read before they're crumpled up and thrown away, so they do have some long-range recognition value.

## Phone Soliciting

Phone calls are not too effective in getting work cold turkey. Reminders or followups, on the other hand, are fine! It's great — and often effective — to call a past customer and thank them and say, "By the way, we have a special on carpets this month." As far as cold-call telephone soliciting — I don't enjoy being a target of solicitors, and I don't think my customers will, either.

## Coupons

These can work well for residential services. When you go with one of the "coupon advertising" companies, you share in the cost of mailing with other advertisers, and your per-piece cost is very reasonable.

## Uniforms

With your name, emblem, etc., on them they are great! You are a live, moving advertisement, especially if you and your people look sharp. On the other hand, if your people are unshaven, smoking, filthy-mouthing around, uniforms will associate your company name with something negative. Keep your uniforms and people looking sharp, and you'll get a lot of good advertising value out of this simple tactic.

## Project Quality

When you get art or brochures or layout work done, get a professional artist to do it. I can't believe some of the booklets and brochures that hit the market. Companies will spend $5,000 to print something and be too tight to spend $75 to have something designed by an artist and typeset. Printing this art will be your cheapest — and your most beneficial — expenditure. Look at the example below:

I found out a long time ago that hand-drawn stick men, and the most brilliant page typed by my grey-slacked, blue-eyed secretary just doesn't project the image of someone offering a snappy cleaning service.

Take your brochure or advertising idea to a good commercial printer (not an instant printer) for this first one and ask for advice, including where you might find a layout artist. They will know and maybe even have one on staff or may have a piece of "clip art" ready-made for your use.

## Trinkets and Novelties

Keychains, imprinted pens and pencils and other promotional novelties convey a feeling of goodwill and stimulate smiles, but should not be what you lean upon for serious sales. Suppose a cheap pen saying "Varsity Contractors, Inc." quits writing; the user will probably think "just like their operation." Buttons and badges and such get tossed in the trash fast and will never leave the lasting impression that a professional sales call will. Some people call these marketing aids, I call them trinkets. (I do use novelty gifts like toilet earrings, etc., for comic awards, laughs, and creating a little positive P.R., but don't try to actually sell yourself with trinkets.)

## Friends (Unpaid Salespeople)

I love 'em. Tell your friends what you are doing. People love to help each other out, just for the sake of brother and sisterhood. Don't pay them or it will ruin everything. Let your friends know you're one hungry hombre, desperate for work, and they'll all be out there hunting for you. You and I have helped **our** friends get customers when they've started their service stations, clothing boutiques, and dog grooming services, etc., and now they'll do the same for us.

## Salespeople

A few big companies do this successfully (I think). That is, they hire a full-time person to drive and walk around and make sales calls for them. I never could make it work out the way I wanted. Others (our sneaky competitors) hire some Mr. Hunko or babe with breathtaking legs and they get some interest for a while, but not in the long run, not for the company's good. The biggest problem with salespeople is that they often promise the customers grandiose worlds of sparkling restrooms, and when your crews try to reach the brag level and can't, lots of friction results. I'd suggest you do it yourself until you get to about $12,000,000 in sales a year, then try a professional salesperson for a month or two, but don't go the legs bit.

**Remember the two simple sales techniques that will outsell all other ways combined: (1) Personal sales calls, (2) Word-of-mouth from super service. And these two cost nothing!**

You can't sit around waiting for the world's opportunities to beat a path to your door — you have to go out and get them!

# YOUR MARKETPLACE

- Office buildings
- Nursing homes
- Government facilities
- Schools and universities
- Private homes
- Utility companies
- Military bases
- Motels/Hotels
- Grocery stores and supermarkets
- Stadiums
- Factories
- Airports
- Resorts
- Parks
- Hundreds more

# THE RIGHT PRICE...

# ...IT HELPS

# 8

## BIDS AND ESTIMATES

How much should I charge? How do I know how much to bid? What if I bid too much and they laugh at me? What if I don't charge enough and go broke or have to work free for a time?

Relax . . . bidding jobs seems to be the big bugaboo that causes beginners to fear and tremble, but it's actually one of the easier business skills to master, once you get a grasp of the basics. With the information in this chapter and a little practice, you'll soon be figuring accurate and fair bids with ease, even if you've never done it before. Looking back, I just wish I'd had someone to teach me the ropes.

When I first started out in my own little cleaning business in 1958, I knew nothing about bidding, so I advertised my services by the hour — $1.25 per hour. That was a little better than minimum wage at the time. The first call I got was to clean some windows five miles away. I had no car, so carrying my ladder and bucket and cake of Bon Ami (that's what Mom always used), I walked all the way. I really hustled on the windows, and did them in two hours. The lady gave me a check for $2.50, and I walked the

five miles back home. I was just a dumb farm kid at the time, but I was smart enough to realize that I wouldn't be getting rich at that rate. I learned the first big lesson of success in the cleaning business: it is hard to charge enough by the hour to do well. You have to bid your work to make a decent profit.

The next job I bid at $15.00, did it in three hours, and thought I was really on my way to fame and fortune. The big lesson came when I bid to clean the walls and ceilings in twelve big offices and hallways for the Grimm School of Business — a staggering big job for me at the time. I bid the job at $125, and confidently marched in with a three-man crew to make my killing. Three weeks later, we were still there, trying to finish the job, and I was the one getting killed. The lesson: bidding is the way to go, but you have to have some system to make your estimates accurate and consistent. Over the years, I have learned systems and methods which enable just about anyone to put out consistently accurate bids on cleaning work, and that is the information I will share with you in this chapter. The systems approach I explain here applies mainly to bidding contract cleaning services (janitorial contracts). For maid work and residential services, you will end up using a mix of pricing methods. You may figure carpet cleaning and wall washing by the square foot, but will probably use a "per unit" price for shampooing a couch or cleaning blinds. For many residential cleaning jobs, you will simply use a "time and materials" method. Before we get into actually figuring the bid, however, there are some basic ground rules and precautions I want you to think about.

## SOME BASIC ETHICS AND PRECAUTIONS

1. Always go to the area and look at what you bid for — sets of plans and oral descriptions never tell much or anything about textures or building condition, surfaces, climate, working conditions, places, or people. The size of the building and frequency of service do not provide enough information to bid accurately.

2. Always write your bid and description of work out in enough detail to have a record so there is absolutely no misunderstanding at some later date about the amount, terms, time, or services.

3. Make any necessary adjustments before you start the work, if you discover you have miscalculated a bid. Even the experts sometimes make an error in figuring a job and find out they bid much too low or too high. Present this to the client, and either reduce, increase or withdraw upfront, not after you're into the job. Some contractors will start a job on an unreasonably low bid, planning to negotiate an increase once they're in and accepted by the owner. This practice does not inspire long-range trust and good business relationships. You will do a lot better by being honest and straightforward up front.

4. Keep pricing and other information confidential. Never reveal, peddle, or discuss pricing with outside parties after a formal quote is submitted. Don't collaborate or price-fix bids with your competitors. Such underhanded shortcuts to success may look appealing to the uninitiated, but practices like this lead to nothing but trouble in the long haul.

5. Plan to subcontract only to bonafide subcontractors. Some contractors will bid a job, and then go out and try to find someone else to sub the job out to, who will do it cheaper and leave them the difference. There is nothing wrong with this, except that the subcontractors are often times little more than glorified hourly workers, and are not bonafide contractors. Some contractors set up hourly workers as "subcontractors" to avoid paying payroll taxes. This practice is blatantly illegal, and is potentially very dangerous. Government labor auditors will assess back taxes for several years when they discover such a situation, and the contractor is held liable for any on-the-job accidents suffered by uninsured "subs."

Make sure before you start that your bidding ethics and value structure are in harmony with good honest business practices. There are a lot of traps out there which threaten to compromise your integrity if you are not prepared for them. These principles are a lot more important and far-reaching that the arithmetic of figuring the bid.

## THE STEP-BY-STEP BID PROCESS

1. Gather all the information you will need to figure the job. This includes specifications, sizes and types of areas covered, any available history on the buildings and on the people you'll be dealing with, any potential problems or particular challenges, etc.

2. Go to the job site and look it over. Measure, confirm the figures quoted in the specs, get a feel for the use and density of the various areas, and estimate production times. Gather any information available on special work conditions, job requirements, people involved. Steps 1 and 2 are referred to as the survey, or information-gathering phase.

3. Sit down and put together the information you have collected and, using the production rate tables (see page 65), come up with an estimate of the labor required to do the job. Figure in materials and other job-related costs, mark up for overhead and profit, and compute the bid price.

4. Apply any qualifying factors for any special circumstances on the job, and weigh your computed price against your pre-determined comparatives to see how it stacks up with competitive market prices and production rates for comparable buildings.

5. Work up a detailed proposal, including all

pertinent specifications (or specs), prices, and your qualifications. Include a contract document which can be signed to formalize the agreement.

6. Set up a meeting in which you can personally present your proposal and sell the decision makers on the merits of working with you and your company. Always push for a personal presentation whenever possible, as it carries a much greater chance for success than a mailed-in proposal.

## A WALK-THROUGH

To see how the process works, let's just walk through the bidding of a typical job. Since we cover how to solicit work elsewhere in the text, we won't go into how to hustle an invitation to bid here. We'll just assume that you have an invitation to bid, either from cold-calling or a mail solicitation or something, from the ABC Company. They have sent you a bid packet containing blueprints, specifications for the job, and an invitation to a bidwalk for one day next week. This initiates what we call the survey, or the information-gathering phase of the bid process.

### The Homework

The first thing you want to do is gather information on the company and the people you'll be dealing with, and familiarize yourself with the specs. Nothing makes you look more unprofessional than to show up at a bidwalk and ask a lot of stupid questions because you haven't done your homework. At various bidwalks I've been on, I have heard questions like these:
"Well, Mr. Company representative, I'm sure glad to be asked to bid your building here today. Just what is it ABC company does, anyway?" (What a lack of interest on the part of the contractor this question betrays! Never go on a bidwalk without first doing some homework on the company, and the people you'll be working with if possible. This is not only good manners, it is good business.)

Or, you might hear someone ask: "Mr. company rep, is carpet cleaning included as part of the contract price, or is it to be figured as an extra-cost item?" A question like this is safe only if you don't have specifications for the job already in hand, or are certain that the information is not covered in the packet material. Nothing

makes you feel and look more foolish than to ask a question on a bidwalk that is already spelled out in the bid packet. I have found that it suits my purposes best to just keep mum, look wise, and let others ask the questions. This way, you get the answers to most questions you might have, and you don't risk asking something painfully obvious. Then, at carefully chosen moments, you can insert some piercingly perceptive question or comment that sets you apart as a true professional in the mind of the company rep. Other than this, I try to keep my mouth shut except to ask needed questions that no one else has come up with.

Before the bidwalk, gather all the information you can about the people you'll be dealing with, and review the plans and specs so you will be familiar with the facility and the job requirements when you actually tour the building. Knowing the precise location of the meeting is important, too. You don't want to show up late because you couldn't find the place!

### Contract Specifications

Thirty years ago, when I first began bidding buildings and houses, a thing called specifications (the whereas and wherefores performance list) did not exist. Owners of huge buildings would take me through, without a slip of paper or written or, for that matter, oral direction, and say "give me a bid on cleaning this." I'd submit a bid that said we would clean their five-story building for $2,000 and they would accept it and I would clean it. Thanks to the thousands of lawyers looking for work, most bids today have a twenty- to two hundred-page set of contracting documents, requirements, and a set of cleaning specs that cover every conceivable speck of dust in every corner.

It's hard, if not impossible, to specify how clean is clean. The government has tried, with the amendments and addendums they attach to a bid for a government maintenance contract. I've been to college for ten years and I've written documents for the world's biggest companies and I tell you I couldn't figure the first set of government plans and requirements I saw. I gave up and didn't bid it. Some specs are ridiculous; in fact most of them are. Most building owners agree but are so paranoid about contractors putting the screws to them that the owners carry the specs around like a gun and draw on you at every hint of a problem, along with threats of cancellation.

Owners are frustrated because they don't know how to get a building clean, and many contractors look for devious ways to beat the specs. Specs are a necessary evil, read them and bid the building accordingly. If the specs don't include enough or specify too much, write a polite formal letter asking for clarification or spec something out yourself. I'll admit that it's possible to get away with ignoring specs, but the time will come when you'll be required to live the letter of the specs you agreed to and in many cases you'll face bankruptcy or destruction. If you can't live with the specs, if you think they're petty and troublesome, don't bid the job. The best way to cushion spec problems is to give such good service that the owner doesn't care whether you're cleaning to the specs or not. Your and their only purpose is to get the building clean, keep the tenants happy, and do it at a fair price. If you do these things well and keep your speed and brilliance always before their eyes, most owners won't care if you're dusting daily or weekly.

The simple bottom line on specifications is that they're a road map to get the job done properly; the owners furnish the "map" to tell you what they want. The specs tell you where to go. If the "map" isn't complete, both of you are in trouble — they don't get the job done the way they wanted it and you're lost somewhere, doing it. If the specs (or the maps) are too complicated and detailed, you can't understand them, so half the time you won't read it all and you end up lost again. It only takes minutes when you're looking at the specs to say, "I don't understand this" or to get a point or two clarified so you can read and follow the map. It sure is cheaper for both parties than an arbitrative argument over an overlooked or misunderstood assignment. For example, if you're told to "clean the floors," "clean" has thirty different meanings to thirty different people. So you clarify: does it include sweeping, mopping, scrubbing, stripping, or waxing — and how many coats of wax? BINGO! You've covered everything in a quick and easy minute of conversation and ironed out the problems. If the customer is unsure of what he wants, then you (the professional) make suggestions on what you feel it needs. Generally they'll agree and love you for it!

I like to spec out the job duties on the "Detailed Contract Work Schedule" (page 57) and make it part of the contract agreement, so that both parties understand exactly what is expected.

## The Bidwalk

Assuming you've done your homework, the bidwalk will be your opportunity to view the facilities, draw judgments, and gather as much information as you can about the job and the people involved. Knowing what kind of information to gather is critical. One of my early learning experiences illustrates this.

For my first ten years in business, I did smaller jobs, often on a very informal basis, for local people. The owner would say, "Don, how much would you charge to keep my offices clean?" It would be up to me to decide how often the offices required cleaning, draw up adequate specs, and make a bid. If the owner accepted it, he would often just tell me "Fine, why don't you start at the first of the month." We would do the job, send in our bills and get paid, all without a contract. We figured our bids strictly by looking over an area and estimating the amount of time we thought it would take on an "eyeball appraisal" method. Sometimes we guessed right, sometimes wrong, so our bidding was unsure and inconsistent, but we managed to average out alright. We were hardworking and persistent enough to overcome the inherent weaknesses of our "by gosh and by golly" bidding system, and as our company grew, we found ourselves being invited to bid on larger properties.

Boise Cascade Corporation built a national headquarters building in Boise, Idaho on a full city block. Because of our strong local reputation, the general contractor hired my firm on a cost-plus basis to do all of the construction cleanup and final polishing of the building before occupancy. Because they liked our work, the owners invited us to submit a bid for the ongoing maintenance, but of course, they also invited other bidders, including one large national janitorial company. We were ecstatic over the chance to bid the huge building, which dwarfed anything we had done previously, but we were also somewhat awed by the task. We knew we couldn't afford to be off very far on the bid. We wanted to be high enough to make money, but not so high as to not get the bid. We knew that underbidding by very much on such a large job could easily sink our whole ship, so we geared up for the

# Detailed Contract
# Work Schedule

For

    ABC BUILDING
    101 Sunshine Way
    Anytown, U.S.A.

Days of Service **Mon. - Fri.**
Time Service is performed **6:00 pm - 11:00 pm**
Building Representative **Hal Hardnose**

## Work to be Performed

| GENERAL CLEANING | TIMES PER WEEK | TIMES PER MONTH | TIMES PER YEAR |
|---|---|---|---|
| Empty and Damp-wipe AshTrays & Urns | 5 | | |
| Empty Wastebaskets | 5 | | |
| Dust Tops of Desks, Furniture, Counters | 5 | | |
| Dust Telephones | 5 | | |
| Dust Tops of Cabinets, Picture Frames | 5 | | |
| Dust Partitions and Ledges | 5 | | |
| Spot-clean or Damp-wipe Desk Tops | 5 | | |
| Spot-clean Doors, Light Switches | 5 | | |
| Spot-clean Walls, Partitions | 5 | | |
| | | | |
| Clean Drinking Fountains | 5 | | |
| Clean Sinks | 5 | | |
| Damp-wipe Furniture In Eating Areas | 5 | | |
| Dry clean Chalkboards (if erased) | No | | |
| | | | |
| **PERIODIC GENERAL CLEANING** | | | |
| High Dusting | | 1 | |
| Dust Venetian Blinds | | 1 | |
| Polish or clean Kick Plates and Handrails | 1 | | |
| Replace Burned-Out Bulbs and Lamps | No | | |
| Dust or clean Vents and Grills | | 1 | |
| Vacuum Window Draperies | | | 4 |
| | | | |
| **FLOOR MAINTENANCE** | | | |
| Vacuum Carpeting - General Offices | 5 | | |
| Vacuum Carpeting - Executive Offices | 5 | | |
| Vacuum Carpeting - Lobbies and Hallways | 5 | | |
| Vacuum Mats and Runners | 5 | | |
| Dust-mop or sweep Hard Surface Floors | 5 | | |
| Dust-mop or sweep Stairs & Landings | | 1 | |
| Damp-mop or spot-mop Floors | 5 | | |
| Spot-clean Carpet | 5 | | |
| Buff or spray-buff Resilient Floors - Offices | | 1 | |
| Buff or spray-buff Resilient Floors - Hallways | 2 | | |
| Buff or spray-buff Resilient Floors - Entrance | 5 | | |
| Surface Scrub Carpet | | 1 | |
| | | | |
| Scrub and Wax Resilient Floors | As needed to maintain a clean, | | |
| Strip, Seal, and Wax Resilient Floors | attractive appearance | | |
| Shampoo and/or Extract Carpeting | | | 1 |
| | | | |

## Varsity Detailed Contract Work Schedule (Continued)

| Work to be Performed | TIMES PER WEEK | TIMES PER MONTH | TIMES PER YEAR |
|---|---|---|---|
| **REST ROOM CLEANING** | | | |
| Empty Trash and Waste Containers | 5 | | |
| Re-fill Dispensers (Paper, Soap, Etc.) | 5 | | |
| Clean Mirrors and Bright Work | 5 | | |
| Clean and Sanitize Sink and Fixtures | 5 | | |
| Clean and Sanitize Toilets and Urinals | 5 | | |
| Dust Partitions and Furnishings | 5 | | |
| Spot Clean Partitions and Walls | 5 | | |
| Sweep and damp-mop Floors | 5 | | |
| Check Time-mist dispensers | 5 | | |
| **MECHANICAL EQUIPMENT AND POWER ROOMS** | | | |
| Sweep Floors | No | | |
| Change Filters | No | | |
| Dust Low Flat Surfaces (Wall Fixtures, Etc.) | No | | |
| Dust upper Cable Racks | No | | |
| Dust Tops of Equipment | No | | |
| Wax Floors | No | | |
| **EXTERIOR MAINTENANCE** | | | |
| Sweep Walks | 5 | | |
| Sweep Entranceway | 5 | | |
| Police Grounds for Trash and Debris | 5 | | |
| Cut and Trim Lawns | No | | |
| Remove Weeds | No | | |
| Water Lawns | No | | |
| Sweep Parking Lot | No | | |
| Remove Snow from Walks | No | | |
| **GARAGE AREA** | | | |
| Remove Grease Spots | No | | |
| Sweep Floor Area | No | | |
| Hose Down Floor Area | No | | |
| Low Dust Wall Fixtures | No | | |
| **WINDOW CLEANING** | | | |
| Exterior Windows | Extra | | |
| Interior Windows | Extra | | |
| Lobby Glass | Extra | | |
| **CLOSING INSTRUCTIONS** | | | |
| Arrange Furniture | 5 | | |
| Clean Janitor Closet | 5 | | |
| Report any Damage or unusual Circumstances | 5 | | |
| Secure Exterior Doors and Windows | 5 | | |
| Turn off Lights | 5 | | |
| Turn on Night Lights | 5 | | |
| Set Alarm System | 5 | | |

| EQUIPMENT AND SUPPLIES | FURNISHED BY CONTRACTOR | FURNISHED BY OWNER |
|---|---|---|
| Buffers - Vacuums | x | |
| Cleaning Equipment (Carts, Buckets, Pails) | x | |
| Restroom Soap, Paper, Napkins | | x |
| Cleaning Chemicals and Compounds | x | |
| Light Bulbs and Fluorescent Lamps | | x |
| Dust Mops | x | |
| Cleaning Rags - Cloths | x | |
| Plastic Bags | x | |

most careful bid we had ever figured. At that time, we sometimes used unit costs for things like cleaning light fixtures and windows, so we tried to unit cost that huge building. We spent hours and hours counting how many water fountains, toilets, desks, and windows there were in the building, and then practice-cleaned these items and timed ourselves to see how long each would take. We multiplied unit times out, haggled, re-counted, sweated and pored over figures for three days prior to the bid deadline, and finally came up with a price of $15,271 per month.

The bids were due in by 5:00 P.M. on Thursday, and at 2:00 that afternoon, we were exultant. The big national company had not submitted a bid, and we knew there was no way they could do it in the short time remaining. The owners loved us because of the super job we had done on the move-in, and we were sure we had the contract in the bag. At 3:00 P.M., a tall, sport-jacketed representative of the national company rolled up to the building in a taxi from the airport. He hesitated a few minutes out in front, eyeing the building, and then casually strolled through the facility, not even looking at the whole thing. He wrote a few things down in a little notebook, and left. We learned that he went to his local office, figured the bid and had it typed up, and had it back in to Boise Cascade by the deadline. As he enjoyed his steak in a local restaurant that evening, we scoffed. How did he think he could bid a big project like that with such a casual walk-through? Why, it had taken three of the finest janitorial minds in Idaho almost three days to come up with our bid. We were sure he would be totally out of the ballpark.

As it turned out, he was right on the money! His bid of $8,760 was less than 60% of our figure, but was within ten minutes of what it actually took to clean the building in labor per day. We had missed it by over twenty hours! We were mortally wounded. He not only got the bid on this fat plum right in our own back yard and made good money on it, he made us look amateurish in the process. How did he do it? He did it by employing the production rate method of bidding, which I soon learned and which I will teach you. He knew the production rates for certain area types, and all he had to do was compute from the plans how many square feet of each type of area existed in the building, then multiply it out. For instance, if there was 8,000 square feet of restroom space in the building, he

knew that his crews could clean typical restrooms at, say, 500 feet per hour. All he had to do was inspect a couple of restrooms to see that they were typical, with no surprises, and get out his calculator. Eight thousand square feet divided by five hundred square feet per hour is sixteen hours per night cleaning restrooms. He quickly did this with office space, corridors, lobby, conference room, etc., and came up with a total daily labor figure for the building. From that, computing the bid was a piece of cake.

This story points out how important it is to gather the right kind of information on the bidwalk. While we were wasting our time counting toilets, this gentleman was looking at the things that matter. You will find the production rate tables later on in this chapter, but you won't use them until you get back to your desk to figure the bid. At this point, on the bidwalk, you'll be looking for the same kinds of things that the estimator at Boise Cascade did. If you have blueprints or engineer's estimates of square footages for the various area types, you will want to verify them on the bidwalk, if only roughly, to make sure they appear to be accurate. Even engineers make mistakes, and I have often found gross errors in engineers' estimates of square footages. If you use erroneous figures in computing your bid, there is usually no recourse; it is up to you to look at the job and verify the figures. If you have no prints or engineering estimates, you may have to measure the building yourself to get the square footages. You don't have to actually get out your tape measure and detail out every room. Just a close estimate as you go through will suffice. Quick size estimates of large rooms can be made by counting ceiling tiles, floor tiles, distances between pillars, etc., and multi-plying it out. As you get experience, you will be able to quickly and accurately estimate small rooms with just a quick glance. Sometimes sketching out a rough floor plan (see ABC Building Plan, page 60) as you go through helps you remember the areas and their sizes, and keeps things in perspective. If you jot dimensions on your sketch, you'll have no trouble figuring footages when you get back to your office. When you measure a building, figure inside wall to inside wall, and don't include dead space such as elevator shafts and mechanical chases. You are trying to get just "cleanable" space. I usually don't try to eliminate such statistically insignif-icant areas as the space covered by interior

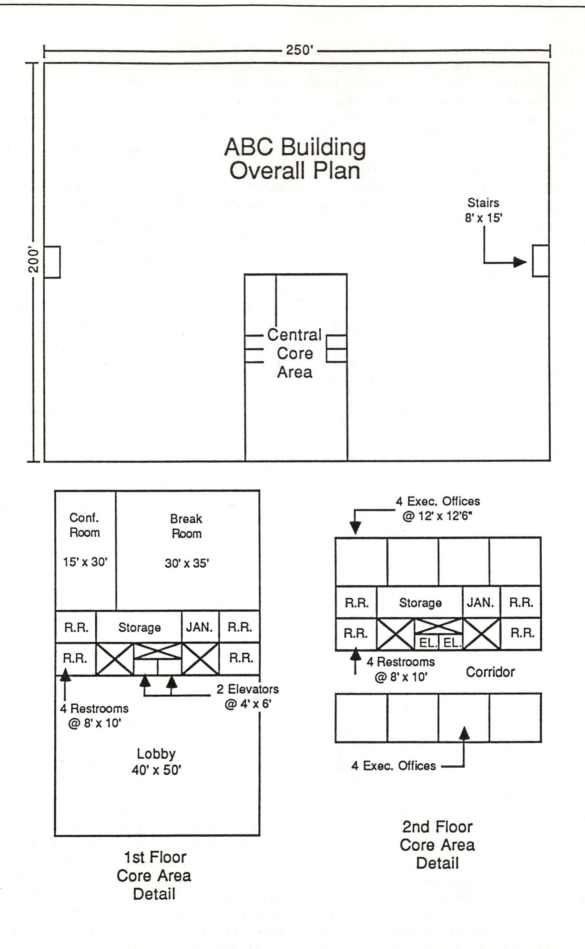

**ABC Building Overall Plan**

250'

200'

Stairs
8' x 15'

Central
Core
Area

**1st Floor Core Area Detail**

Conf. Room

15' x 30'

Break Room

30' x 35'

R.R. | Storage | JAN. | R.R.

R.R. | | R.R.

2 Elevators
@ 4' x 6'

4 Restrooms
@ 8' x 10'

Lobby
40' x 50'

**2nd Floor Core Area Detail**

4 Exec. Offices
@ 12' x 12'6"

R.R. | Storage | JAN. | R.R.

R.R. | EL. | EL. | R.R.

4 Restrooms
@ 8' x 10'

Corridor

4 Exec. Offices

partitions, pillars, etc. It usually takes just as much time to clean around this type of obstruction as it would to clean the floor area it covers up, so I include such space in my figures.

As in the Boise Cascade story, you will want to be looking to see if the use of the various areas is consistent with the production rates you normally use. As you become expert at bidding, you will learn to assign production rates based on your own experience as you walk through and look at various areas. At first, the average rates given in the tables will be sufficient to get you started and will enable you to make quite accurate bids. You will learn to fine-tune the production rates as you gain experience. You also will want to gather the information necessary to help you make decisions on the basic control factors shown in the Bidding Considerations chart on page 62. These factors play an important part in how you bid a building, and you will need to see if any of them affect this particular facility while you are at the job site, before you sit down to figure the bid.

You will find that it is also necessary to count some units, such as windows, blinds, or light fixtures to be cleaned, in order to figure an accurate bid, if such units are not already listed in the bid packet specs.

## The Survey Form

I have included a copy of the Survey form I use on page 63. You will notice that I have filled this one out for our "ABC Company" example, to show you how it works. You can find a blank copy of this form, along with the others I use, in the back of the book. There's no magic in a form, it just gives you an organized format in which to record your information, and it prompts you to remember to gather all the necessary data. A blank piece of paper is just as good, if you remember to get all the information on it, and put it down in a way that it is easy to retrieve. You will notice that the top of the form prompts you to get the needed information on the facility: the contact person's name and phone number, the days and times the building is to be cleaned, whether there are any special alarm or security requirements, etc., etc. It is important to get a good idea of the present condition of the building, and whether or not any initial work is required to bring it up to an acceptable level before you start your maintenance

program. You will notice, too, that the form prompts you to get answers to such questions as, "Who supplies the materials and equipment?", "Is there any exterior maintenance involved, such as groundskeeping or parking lot maintenance?"

The bottom of the form (and the back) give you space to list the various area types and their dimensions or footages, what kind of floor exists in each area, spaces to count units such as windows, blinds, and light fixtures, and places to make notes. One important column I like to use is the "Estimated Time" area. As I go through a lot of the areas, I will jot down an "eyeball" estimate of the time I think the area will take to clean, based on my experience and judgment. When I figure the production times from the tables, I will then compare the production table results to my on-site estimates to see how closely they agree. If off very far, it alerts me to take another look, as something isn't adding up. I call this comparative estimating, and this is just one of the points at which I like to make a comparison. I'll point out some other comparisons later in this chapter which I use to help me insure that my bid is accurate. After you have gathered all the information on the bidwalk that you need, you can retire to your office to actually figure the bid.

## The Production Rate Tables

When you look at the Production Rate Table on page 65, you will notice that it gives a rate for each area type, listed in square feet per hour, for both carpeted and waxed floors, and for three levels of cleaning difficulty. This means that if you see a production rate of 3,000, the typical worker should be able to clean, on average, 3,000 square feet of that type of floor space in one hour. **Remember:** The rates include periodic tasks, such as high dusting, light fixture cleaning, floor waxing and carpet cleaning. The actual daily production times of your general cleaners will have to be a shade faster than the table figures, because a part of the production time has to be allotted to the floor/carpet work, and any periodic tasks not handled by the general cleaners. The janitorial production table lists rates for overall cleaning, including common periodic tasks, for simplicity of use. The "Extra Work" tables list times for specific tasks. If you are figuring a job which does not include certain periodic tasks, you

# Bidding Considerations

| Considerations | Good | Marginal | Bad |
|---|---|---|---|
| 1. Condition of the building | | | |
| 2. Company stability | | | |
| 3. How secure will the job be? | | | |
| 4. My past experience with this company and this type of contract | | | |
| 5. The person I will have to work with on the job | | | |
| 6. Distance from my center of operations | | | |
| 7. Working hours | | | |
| 8. Do I have the personnel available to do the job? | | | |
| 9. Duration of the job | | | |
| 10. Equipment needed | | | |
| 11. Potential for additional work | | | |
| 12. Initial investment required | | | |
| 13. Area growth potential | | | |
| 14. How much of my time will it take? | | | |
| 15. Potential harm of job failure | | | |
| 16. What is my knowledge of this particular job? | | | |

# Building Survey

Surveyed By: __JOHN JANITOR__   Date: __ANY OL' DAY__
Account: __ABC COMPANY__   Contact: __HAL HARDNOSE__
Address: __101 SUNSHINE WAY__   Zip: __ZZZZZ__ Phone: __123-4567__
Frequency: __5/WK.__ Work Days: __M-F__   Work Time: __6P—11P__ Alarm: __NO__
Floors: __INCLUDED__ Carpets: __INC.__   Windows: __EXTRA__ Blinds: __NONE__
Lights: __NO__   Supplies: __ALL BUT PAPER*__ Density: __200 PEOPLE PER SQ.FT.__
Present Condition: __GOOD__   Initial: __NONE NEEDED__
Equipment: __WE FURNISH ALL__   Distance: __NO FACTOR__
Overall Dimensions: __200 x 250 – 2 FLOORS__ Gross Sq. Footage: __100,000__
Exterior Maintenance: _____

| Area | Dimensions | Floor Type | Number Units | @ Units | Estimated Time | Windows @ ___ | Blinds @ ___ | Other ___ |
|---|---|---|---|---|---|---|---|---|
| LOBBY | 40x50 | T | | | 30 MIN. | (NO WAX ON TERAZZO) | | |
| ELEVATORS | 4x6 @ | C | 2 | 3 MIN. | 6 MIN. | | | |
| CORR. | 10x50 | C | | | 5 MIN. | | | |
| EXEC. OFFC. | 12x12½ @ | C | 8 | 3 MIN. | 24 MIN. | | | |
| 1ST FLR. GEN. OFFC. | 45,460 | C | | | 15 HR. | | | |
| 2ND FLR. GEN. OFFC. | 47,260 | C | | | 14½ HR. | | | |
| RESTROOMS | 8x10 @ | CT | 8 | 10 MIN | 40 MIN. | | | |
| BREAK RM. | | R | | | 30 MIN. | | | |
| CONF. RM. | | C | . | | 10 MIN. | | | |
| STAIRS | | CC | 4 | 10MIN/WK. | 8 MIN. | | | |
| | | | | | | | | |
| — SWEEP STAIRS 1/WK. | | | | | | | | |
| — NO SERVICE IN MECHANICAL ROOMS OR CHASES | | | | | | | | |
| — NO LIGHT CHANGING | | | | | | | | |
| — CONF. RM. USED VERY LIGHTLY | | | | | | | | |
| — SEVERAL FAIRLY LARGE AREAS ON 2ND FLR. | | | | | | | | |
| UNOCCUPIED — ALL GEN. OFFC. LAID OUT | | | | | | | | |
| SIMPLY — WILL CLEAN FAST. | | | | | | | | |
| — NO SERVICE IN STORAGE AREAS | | | | | | | | |
| Totals | 32.05 | | | | | | | |

Key: C = Carpet; R = Resilient Flooring; CT = Ceramic Tile; T = Terazzo; CC = Concrete; W = Wood

\* OWNER FURNISHES R.R. DISPENSER ITEMS — PAPER SOAP, ETC.

can back them out using the Extra Work tables, and modify the Janitorial rates accordingly. As you get experience in bidding, you will come up with your own production rates which fit your operation, but the ones in the table will help you to get started. Use the published production rates only as a guideline until you can establish your own standards.

**Disclaimer:** The production rates, financial ratios and other figures, forms, and procedures I share with you in this book are the result of my years of experience in the Building Maintenance Industry. They represent my best knowledge of correct and workable systems. There is no way to guarantee that the figures and procedures will apply to your particular area of the country or your specific application, however, as too many variables enter in. The material is supplied to provide guidance to the user, but it is the user's sole responsibility to determine the applicability of the material to his use, and the author and publisher assume no responsibility for situations which may arise from the user's application of this material to his own operations.

### The Bid Work Sheet

Since janitorial work is so labor intensive, the cost of labor is **the big** expense item in a bid. Sixty-five to 75% of the cost of a typical job will be labor and payroll costs, so it is the one big item to be sure and get right. Once you get the correct hours figured for a job, computing the bid price is a simple matter. Again, I've included the form I like to use on pages 71 and 72, which gives you an organized format to not only figure your bid, but also to workload the job (plot the daily hours and work assignments for the different types of staff people). Look at the Bid Work Sheet, notice that under "Daily Work," it provides a place for you to list the various area types and their square footages from your survey sheet. You then plug in the appropriate production rates under the "Sq. Ft. per Hour" column, and divide the rate into the square footage to arrive at daily hours required for each area. The daily hours figure is then multiplied by a "Days per Month" factor to arrive at hours per month for each area. The factor used on the form is 21.1 days per month, which is the average number of work days in a month, assuming five work days per week and seven unpaid vacation

days. If your workers have paid vacations, or a different number of vacation days or work days per week, you can figure your own factor using this formula:

work days per week, times 52 weeks per year, less days unpaid vacation, divided by 12 months per year, equals average work days per month.

Even though months vary in actual number of work days, we usually figure an average monthly price for long-term contracts, and bill that price each month. Some contracts, however, are adjusted for the number of work days in the billing period. If you work on an average monthly billing, you will show more profit during those months with fewer actual work days, and less profit during long months. Just as we average the work days in a month, we also average weeks when figuring things like periodic work. The average month contains 4.33 weeks. (52 weeks per year divided by 12 months). If you have been figuring your costs based on four weeks per month, as many of the uninformed do, you have been cheating yourself!

After computing hours per month for each area type, you simply total that column to arrive at total daily hours per month. At this point, I like to do a little comparison to see if the daily work figure I've arrived at "fits" with the other things I know about how long a building should take to clean. I like to total the square footage column, to make sure it agrees with my overall gross footage from the survey. If it does not, I may have left an area off the Bid Work Sheet, or overlooked something. By totalling daily hours and dividing that total into total square feet, I can come up with an overall daily production rate. From experience, I know about what the average daily production rate should be for various types of buildings. I have shared a synopsis of that knowledge with you in the "Bidding Consideration" chart on page 62. By comparing your overall production rate to the models on the comparison chart, you can get a feel for whether or not your production rate (and, therefore, your daily hours), is "in the ballpark." If I come up with an overall production rate here that doesn't feel right, I go back to see what I did wrong, before proceeding with the bid computations. Incidentally, for smaller buildings and simple larger ones, you may decide you don't need to go through the detail of breaking the areas down by type and figuring each area at a

# Production Rates Table
# Daily Janitorial Work
(Daily production time in sq. ft. per man hours)*

| Area Type | Density/Traffic/Difficulty Carpeted Floors | | | Density/Traffic/Difficulty Waxed Floors | | |
|---|---|---|---|---|---|---|
| | Low | Med | High | Low | Med | High |
| General Offices | 3,600 | 3,300 | 3,000 | 3,200 | 3,000 | 2,800 |
| Executive Offices | 3,500 | 3,200 | ——— | 3,100 | 2,900 | ——— |
| Corridors | 6,500 | 6,000 | 5,500 | 6,000 | 5,500 | 5,000 |
| Lobbies | 5,500 | 5,000 | 4,500 | 4,600 | 4,200 | 3,800 |
| Elevators | 800 | 700 | 600 | 1,900 | 1,900 | 1,900 |
| Cafeteria | 2,800 | 2,500 | 2,000 | 2,500 | 2,200 | 1,800 |
| Restrooms | ——— | ——— | ——— | 600 | 500 | 400 |
| Mechanical Rms. | ——— | ——— | ——— | 10,000 | 8,000 | 6,000 |
| Auditorium | 6,000 | 5,000 | 4,500 | 5,000 | 4,500 | 4,000 |
| Conference Rms. | 3,600 | 3,200 | 2,800 | 3,400 | 3,000 | 2,600 |
| Data Processing | 4,500 | 4,250 | 4,000 | 4,500 | 4,250 | 4,000 |
| Stairs | 1,200 | 1,000 | 800 | 1,000 | 800 | 600 |
| Parking Garage | (Concrete) | | | 12,000 | 11,000 | 9,000 |
| Telephone Eqpt. | 8,000 | 7,000 | 6,000 | 7,000 | 6,000 | 5,000 |

*Daily Production rates include common periodic tasks such as high dusting, carpet cleaning, floor waxing, etc.

# "Extra Work" Production Rates

THESE PRICES ARE FOR **CLEANING ONLY** UNLESS SO NOTED

## "How to use the tables"

*RES: RESIDENTIAL        COM: COMMERCIAL*

THIS WILL IDENTIFY TASK

THIS WILL IDENTIFY TYPE & APPLICATION

THIS WILL GIVE YOU AN APPROXIMATE SUPPLY COST AMOUNT IS BASED ON TOTAL COST OF JOB W/ LABOR

THIS IS THE PER UNIT OR PER SQUARE FT. PRICE— IT HAS ALL COST INCLUDED— LABOR, OVERHEAD, SUPPLIES & PROFIT

| JOB | DESCRIPTION | SUPPLY FACTOR PER GROSS JOB COST | AVERAGE PRICE EACH OR PER SQ. FT. | DEGREE OF DIFFICULTY SQUARE FT. OR UNIT DONE PER HOUR | | |
|---|---|---|---|---|---|---|
| | | | | LIGHT | MEDIUM | HEAVY |
| LIGHT FIXTURE | EGG CRATE TYPE | 5% | 3.00 | 7 | 6 | 4 |
| | OPEN TUBE TYPE | 5% | 2.00 | 12 | 10 | 8 |
| | FLAT LENS TYPE | 4% | 1.80 | 15 | 12 | 10 |
| CARPET (SHAMPOO) | DRY FOAM METHOD | 6% | .06 | 1,200 | 1,000 | 800 |
| | BONNET PAD METHOD | 2% | .03 | 1,500 | 1,200 | 1,000 |
| | DRY POWDER METHOD | 10% | .12 | 600 | 400 | 200 |
| | ROTARY/EXTRACTION METHOD | 8% | .12 | 800 | 600 | 400 |
| | STEAM TRUCK EXTRACTION * | 6% | .08 | 1,200 | 900 | 600 |

*ASTERISK MEANS ALERT TO SPECIAL NOTE IN INDEX AREA

THIS IS THE PRODUCTION RATE, HOW MANY SQUARE FEET OR UNITS A PERSON CAN DO IN 1 HOUR - THE DEGREE OF DIFFICULTY. SIMPLY TAKE THE SAME TASK BUT PRESENT IT IN A SMALL, MEDIUM, OR LARGE CONTEXT. LIGHT MEANS IT ISN'T TOO DIRTY, THE AREA IS NOT CROWDED & SURFACE & CONDITION ARE EASIER.

MEDIUM - MEANS AVERAGE OFFICE OR CARPET OR FLOOR.
HEAVY - MEANS IT'S MUCH TOUGHER, MORE TIME CONSUMING THAN USUAL, DIFFICULT ACCESSIBILITY.

## CATASTROPHE—EMERGENCY CALLS

REMEMBER, THESE COLUMNS, UNLESS NOTED, ARE ONLY PRODUCTION TIME. YOU HAVE TO FIGURE COSTS.

| JOB | DESCRIPTION | SUPPLY FACTOR PER GROSS JOB COST | TOTAL PRICE PER EACH OR SQ. FT. | DEGREE OF DIFFICULTY, SQUARE FT. OR UNITS DONE PER HOUR | | |
|---|---|---|---|---|---|---|
| | | | | LIGHT | MEDIUM | HEAVY |
| HARD SURFACE FLOORS | SWEEP (BROOM) | 1% | | 20,000 | 10,000 | 5,000 |
| | SWEEP (DUST MOP) | 2% | | 30,000 | 20,000 | 10,000 |
| | DAMP MOP | 1% | | 8,000 | 6,000 | 4,000 |
| | WET MOP & RINSE | 1% | | 4,000 | 3,000 | 2,000 |
| | | | | | | |
| | MACHINE BURNISHING | 2% | .02 | 5,000 | 4,000 | 3,000 |
| | LAY WAX (PER COAT) | 25% | | 16,000 | 15,000 | 12,000 |
| | STRIP & WAX (2 COATS) | 15% | .10 | 400 | 300 | 200 |
| | SPRAY BUFFING | 5% | .04 | 1,500 | 1,000 | 800 |
| | AUTOMATIC SCRUBBER | | .06 | 20,000 | 15,000 | 10,000 |
| | | | | | | |
| FLOORS (WOOD-GYM) | CLEANING & 1 COAT SEAL | 15% | .25 | 800 | 700 | 600 |
| | CLEANING & 2 COAT SEAL | 20% | .30 | 600 | 500 | 400 |
| | STRIP & VARNISH-3COAT SEAL | 35% | .70 | 250 | 200 | 150 |
| | SANDING-3 COAT SEAL | 35% | .86 | 100 | 75 | 50 |
| POWER WASHING | WALLS-CEILING-FLOOR | | | | | |
| | TRAILER | | | | | |
| | TRUCKS-TRAILERS | | | | | |
| | BASEMENTS-GARAGE | | | | | |
| | STORE FRONTS/SIGNS/ AWNINGS | | | | | |

Too many variables to present controlled figures, call for a bid from a full time professional.

Power washer will give you closest cost-- see new price guide.

| JOB | DESCRIPTION | SUPPLY FACTOR | TOTAL PRICE | LIGHT | MEDIUM | HEAVY |
|---|---|---|---|---|---|---|
| COMPLETE JANITOR SERVICES | SMALL OFFICE BUILDING (5,000/20,000 SQ. FT. | 5% | 6.0 | 3,600 | 3,200 | 3,000 |
| | LARGE OFFICE BUILDING (50,000/100,000 SQ. FT.) | 4% | 5.0 | 4,200 | 3,500 | 3,000 |
| | BANKS | 5% | 7.0 | 4,200 | 3,500 | 3,000 |
| | MEDICAL OFFICE | 6% | 7.0 | 3,500 | 3,000 | 2,500 |
| | TELEPHONE EQUIPMENT BUILDING | 3% | 4.0 | 6,500 | 5,500 | 4,500 |
| DRAPERY | TAKE DOWN/SEND OUT/ RE-HANG | | | | | |
| | COMMERCIAL CLEANED IN PLACE | | | | | |
| | RESIDENTIAL CLEANED IN PLACE | | | | | |

I've never made a profit on drapes, either by doing them or sub-contracting them.

Have client call a professional drape person.

| JOB | DESCRIPTION | SUPPLY FACTOR PER GROSS JOB COST | TOTAL PRICE PER EACH OR SQ. FT. | DEGREE OF DIFFICULTY, SQUARE FT. OR UNITS DONE PER HOUR | | |
|---|---|---|---|---|---|---|
| | | | | LIGHT | MEDIUM | HEAVY |
| **CEILING CLEANING** | SMOOTH ENAMEL (WASH) | 3% | → COST PER SQUARE FT. | .05 | .06 | .07 |
| | TEXTURE ENAMEL (WASH) | 3% | | .06 | .07 | .08 |
| | LATEX FLAT (DRY SPONGE) | 3% | | .03 | .04 | .05 |
| | ACOUSTIC TILE (DRY SPONGE) | 10% | | .04 | .05 | .06 |
| | ACOUSTIC TILE (SPRAY BLEACH) | 20% | | .15 | .16 | .18 |
| | WOOD (FINISHED) | 3% | | .05 | .06 | .07 |
| | COTTAGE CHEESE / FLECK | - 0 - | | GET A NEW ARCHITECT NEXT TIME | | |
| **WALL CLEANING** | SMOOTH ENAMEL 10' OR LOWER | 3% | → COST PER SQUARE FT. | .04 | .06 | .07 |
| | TEXTURED ENAMEL 10' OR LOWER | 3% | | .05 | .07 | .08 |
| | ENAMEL WALL 10-15 FT. | 3% | | .05 | .07 | .08 |
| | WALL COVERING-SMOOTH | 3% | | .04 | .06 | .07 |
| | WALL COVERING-WEAVE OR FABRIC | 4% | | .10 | .11 | .12 |
| | TILE WALLS | 2% | | .04 | .06 | .07 |
| | PANELING | 2% | | .05 | .06 | .07 |
| | PAINTED MASONRY BLOCK | 3% | | .07 | .08 | .09 |
| **FURNITURE CLEAN & POLISH** | PIANO (CONSOLE) | 6% | → COST PER EACH | 5.00 | 8.00 | 10.00 |
| | PIANO (GRAND) | 6% | | 10.00 | 13.00 | 15.00 |
| | REFRIDGERATOR | 6% | | 3.00 | 4.00 | 5.00 |
| | AVERAGE T.V. | 6% | | 1.00 | 1.50 | 2.00 |
| | DRESSER | 6% | | 3.00 | 4.00 | 5.00 |
| | WOOD-METAL/WASHABLE CHAIRS | 6% | | 1.80 | 2.10 | 2.50 |
| | OFFICE CHAIRS | 6% | | 4.00 | 5.00 | 6.00 |
| | OFFICE DESK | 6% | | 6.00 | 7.00 | 8.00 |
| | MATTRESS | 6% | | 3.00 | 3.50 | 4.50 |
| **CARPET** (VACUUMING) | SMALL VAC UNOBSTRUCTED | 2% | | 12,000 | 10,000 | 8,000 |
| | SMALL VAC OBSTRUCTED | 2% | | 9,000 | 7,000 | 5,000 |
| | SPACE VAC OPEN AREA | 2% | | 15,000 | 12,000 | 8,000 |
| | EXTERIOR BILLY GOAT | | | 12,000 | 10,000 | 7,000 |
| **CARPET** (SHAMPOOING) | DRY FOAM METHOD | 12% | .08 | 1,200 | 1,000 | 800 |
| | BONNET/SPIN PAD | 10% | .03 | 1,500 | 1,200 | 1,000 |
| | DRY POWDER METHOD | 30% | .20 | 600 | 400 | 200 |
| | ROTARY/EXTRACTION | | .16 | 800 | 600 | 400 |
| | STEAM EXTRACTION METHOD | | .10 | 1,200 | 900 | 600 |
| | AUTOMATIC SHAMPOOER | | .08 | 3,000 | 2000 | 1,000 |
| **WALL PAPER REMOVAL** | GO TO HAWAII - YOU'LL SAVE MONEY! | | | | | |

| JOB | DESCRIPTION | | SUPPLY FACTOR PER GROSS JOB COST | TOTAL PRICE PER EACH OR SQ. FT. | DEGREE OF DIFFICULTY SQUARE FT. OR UNITS DONE PER HOUR | | |
|---|---|---|---|---|---|---|---|
| | | | | | LIGHT | MEDIUM | HEAVY |
| LIGHT FIXTURE | EGG CRATE GRILL | 4' | 8% | 3.00 | 7 | 6 | 4 |
| | | 8' | 8% | 6.00 | 6 | 4 | 3 |
| | OPEN TUBE TYPE | 4' | 5% | 2.00 | 12 | 10 | 8 |
| | | 8' | 5% | 2.50 | 10 | 8 | 6 |
| | SWING LENS | 4' | 5% | 1.80 | 15 | 12 | 10 |
| | | 8' | 5% | 2.50 | 12 | 10 | 8 |
| CONCRETE CLEANING & SEALING (WATERBASE OR OIL - 2 COATS) | *NEW CONCRETE (UNOBSTRUCTED) | | 25% | .35 | 600 | 400 | 300 |
| | *NEW CONCRETE (SHOP/DISPLAY AISLE) | | 25% | .38 | 400 | 350 | 250 |
| | *OLD CONCRETE (UNOBSTRUCTED) | | 20% | .38 | 450 | 350 | 250 |
| | *OLD CONCRETE (SHOP/DISPLAY AISLE) | | 20% | .40 | 380 | 300 | 200 |
| | RESEAL ANY SURFACE/ONE COAT | | 15% | .30 | 700 | 500 | 350 |
| WINDOWS PER SIDE | SMALL (HAND) | | 2% | access! | 300 | 200 | 100 |
| | SMALL - OPEN (SQUEEGEE) | | 2% | access! | 600 | 400 | 200 |
| | LARGE - OBSTRUCTED | | 2% | access is everything! | 3,600 | 2,000 | 1,500 |
| | LARGE - OPEN | | 2% | only | 6,000 | 9,000 | 2,500 |
| | TUCKER | | 8% | average | FREE FOR ALL--!! | | |
| UPHOLSTERY SHAMPOOING | COUCH REGULAR W/ CUSHIONS | | 10% | PER UNIT COST | 25.00 | 30.00 | 40.00 |
| | COUCH SUPER SIZE W/ CUSHIONS | | 10% | | 30.00 | 40.00 | 50.00 |
| | COUCH REG. W/O CUSHIONS | | 10% | | 20.00 | 25.00 | 30.00 |
| | COUCH SUPER W/O CUSHIONS | | 10% | | 25.00 | 30.00 | 40.00 |
| | CHAIR (OVERSTUFFED) | | 10% | | 15.00 | 16.00 | 18.00 |
| | LOVE SEAT & WOOD TRIM | | 10% | | 17.00 | 18.00 | 19.00 |
| | CHAIR (SEAT UPHOLSTERED) | | 10% | | 3.00 | 4.00 | 5.00 |
| | CUSHION - OTTOMANS | | 10% | | 8.00 | 6.00 | 4.00 |
| HARD SURFACE FLOORS | *TWO COAT | | | | | | |
| | SWEEP (BROOM) | | 1% | | 15,000 | 10,000 | 5,000 |
| | SWEEP (DUST MOP) | | 2% | | 30,000 | 20,000 | 10,000 |
| | DAMP MOP | | 1% | | 8,000 | 6,000 | 4,000 |
| | WET MOP & RINSE | | 1% | | 4,000 | 3,000 | 2,000 |
| | | | | | | | |
| | MACHINE BURNISHING | | 2% | .02 | 5,000 | 4,000 | 3,000 |
| | LAY WAX (PER COAT) | | 25% | | 16,000 | 15,000 | 12,000 |
| | STRIP & WAX (2 COATS) | | 15% | .10 | 400 | 300 | 200 |
| | SPRAY BUFFING | | 5% | .04 | 1,500 | 1,000 | 800 |
| | AUTOMATIC SCRUBBER | | | .06 | 20,000 | 15,000 | 10,000 |

# RELATED JOB PRICE REFERENCES

| JOB | DESCRIPTION | DEGREE OF DIFFICULTY SQUARE FT. OR UNITS DONE PER HOUR | | |
|---|---|---|---|---|
| | | LIGHT | MEDIUM | HEAVY |

**PAINTING**

Painting is a professional trade! Being able to paint Grandma's house once or doing a chair in high school shop does not make you a professional painter. However, experience, working with and around good painters can make you a fine and productive painting person. As a small contractor, you might need to do painting. I personally liked it, found that about one out of 10 good employees could learn to paint well. Painting is always available (even more than cleaning), so the logic of including it is good. Always use best grade paint, it costs a dollar more to go first class. Here are the basic pricing guidelines that I always use.

| | | LIGHT | MEDIUM | HEAVY |
|---|---|---|---|---|
| PREPARATION & 2 COATS LATEX (INTERIOR) | SQUARE FT. COST WITH SUPPLIES | .18 | .20 | .22 |
| PREPARATION & 2 COATS ENAMEL (INTERIOR) | | .20 | .22 | .24 |
| EXTERIOR AVERAGE | | .22 | .24 | .26 |
| ROOF (LINSEED OR PAINT) | | .18 | .28 | .24 |

**REMODELING**

Lots of you that are small operators know how, and will do handyman and minor remodeling work, or some dismantling and demolition.

After the measuring, figuring all replacement costs and the labor to do it, add 30 to 40%. Remember (which all forget) that everything has to be undone, taken down, hauled off and cleaned up and often the area needs to be repaired and brought up to code...

**ADMONITION:** Always do it by the hour, unless a simple job. How much rebar, how much glue, or nails, etc., was used in the old construction is always an unknown and can affect a job 500% either way. Convince them that you are a hard fast worker and can swing a sledge hammer. Convince them to give you a cost plus or a per hour job....

**AUTO**

There is a growing market here. A small dry (solvent) cleaner/extraction & good wet vac/spotting kit can get you into this business.

| | Carpet | Seats | Together |
|---|---|---|---|
| Passenger Car | $20.00 | $20.00 | $32.00 |
| Pickups (standard cab) | 12.50 | 12.50 | $25.00 |
| Vans & Wagons* | 29.00 | 25.00 | $49.00 |

\* Does not include carpet walls, door panels, or ceilings.

Auto Interior complete**..................................................(Firm Quote After Personal Survey)

\*\* Includes headliner, dash, seats, and carpets.

**SUPPLIES**

| | LIGHT | MEDIUM | HEAVY |
|---|---|---|---|
| PAPER PRODUCTS FURNISHED COST PER MONTH | 1.00 @ | 1.35 @ | 1.40 @ |

# Bid Work Sheet

Account Name: **ABC Co.**

Bid by: **JOHN JANITOR**          Date: **GREAT DAY**

## Daily Work

| Area/Type | Square Footage | ÷ | Sq. Ft. Per Hour | = | Daily Hours | x | Days Per Mo. (21.1) | = | Hours Per Mo. |
|---|---|---|---|---|---|---|---|---|---|
| General Offices | 92,720 | ÷ | 3600 | = | 25.75 | x | 21.1 | = | 543.33 |
| Executive Offices | 1200 | ÷ | 3200 | = | .38 | x | | = | 8.02 |
| Corridors | 500 | ÷ | 6000 | = | .08 | x | | = | 1.69 |
| Lobbies | 2000 | ÷ | 4500 | = | .44 | x | | = | 9.28 |
| Elevators | 48 | ÷ | 600 | = | .08 | x | | = | 1.69 |
| Cafeteria | 1050 | ÷ | 2500 | = | .42 | x | | = | 8.86 |
| Restrooms | 640 | ÷ | 500 | = | 1.28 | x | | = | 27.01 |
| Mechanical Rms. | — | ÷ | — | = | — | x | | = | — |
| Auditorium | — | ÷ | — | = | — | x | | = | — |
| Conference Rm. | 450 | ÷ | 3600 | = | .13 | x | | = | 2.74 |
| STAIRS | 480 | 3/4 | HR./WK | | .13 | | | | 2.74 |
| | | | | | | | | | |
| **Totals** | **99,088** * | | | | **28.69** ** | | | | **605.36** |

Total Daily Work Hours/Mo.

\* Does this agree with overall sq. footage estimate from survey?

\*\* Does this agree with estimated time on survey sheet?

GROSS SQ. FT. = 100,000
LESS DEAD SPACE
(MECHANICAL CHASES)   912
CLEANABLE SQ. FT. = 99,088

## Periodic Work

| Area/Type | Task | Frequency | Unit | Unit Rate | Task Time | Hours*** Per Mo. |
|---|---|---|---|---|---|---|
| Resilient Floors | Strip & W | | | | | |
| Resilient Floors | Scrub & W | | | | | |
| Carpeting | Surf. Cln. | | | | | |
| Carpeting | Shampoo | | | | | |
| Carpeting | Extract | ALL PERIODIC WORK | | | | |
| Windows | Interior | INCLUDED ABOVE. | | | | |
| Windows | Exterior | | | | | |
| Parking Area | Police | | | | | |
| Parking Area | Sweep | | | | | |
| Stairs | Sweep | | | | | |
| Blinds | Dust | | | | | |
| Lights | | | | | | |
| | | | | | | |

\*\*\*Weekly tasks x 4.33; Quarterly tasks ÷ 3; Annual tasks ÷ 12

Total Periodic Work Hours/Mo.

Total Hours/Mo.   **605.36**

## Bid Work Sheet cont.

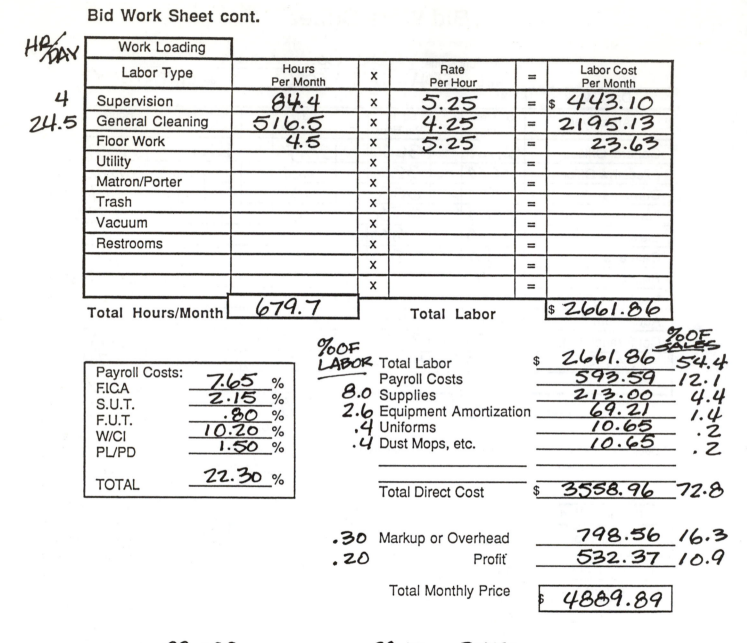

HR/DAY

4

24.5

| Work Loading | | | | | |
|---|---|---|---|---|---|
| Labor Type | Hours Per Month | x | Rate Per Hour | = | Labor Cost Per Month |
| Supervision | 84.4 | x | 5.25 | = | $ 443.10 |
| General Cleaning | 516.5 | x | 4.25 | = | 2195.13 |
| Floor Work | 4.5 | x | 5.25 | = | 23.63 |
| Utility | | x | | = | |
| Matron/Porter | | x | | = | |
| Trash | | x | | = | |
| Vacuum | | x | | = | |
| Restrooms | | x | | = | |
| | | x | | = | |
| | | x | | = | |

Total Hours/Month  679.7

Total Labor  $ 2661.86

Payroll Costs:
| | | |
|---|---|---|
| F.I.C.A. | 7.65 | % |
| S.U.T. | 2.15 | % |
| F.U.T. | .80 | % |
| W/CI | 10.20 | % |
| PL/PD | 1.50 | % |
| TOTAL | 22.30 | % |

% OF LABOR

|  | | % OF SALES |
|---|---|---|
| Total Labor | $ 2661.86 | 54.4 |
| Payroll Costs | 593.59 | 12.1 |
| 8.0 Supplies | 213.00 | 4.4 |
| 2.6 Equipment Amortization | 69.21 | 1.4 |
| .4 Uniforms | 10.65 | .2 |
| .4 Dust Mops, etc. | 10.65 | .2 |
| Total Direct Cost | $ 3558.96 | 72.8 |
| .30 Markup or Overhead | 798.56 | 16.3 |
| .20 Profit | 532.37 | 10.9 |
| Total Monthly Price | $ 4889.89 | |

Total sq. ft. 99,088 ÷ Total hours/day 28.7 = 3452 Overall Production Rate

Total Monthly Price $ 4890 ÷ Sq. ft. 99,088 = $ .050 Per sq. ft.

different production rate. You can just assign an overall production rate for the building, and divide it into the square footage to come up with overall daily hours. This is the "shortcut" method employed by the Boise Cascade estimator, and one which a lot of experienced bidders use.

Once you have a "Daily Work Hours Per Month" figure you feel comfortable with, you will have to decide if there are any periodic tasks that you need to add in. The "Periodic Work" section at the bottom of the Bid Work Sheet is provided to include any floor work or other tasks of a special nature which you have not included in the daily work section. I find the simplest thing to do is get in the habit of using production rates which include all the regular periodic items, so that the daily work hours reflect all the periodics also. On some jobs, though, it is helpful to be able to break out some tasks separately, so the space is provided to list these when needed. Any periodic work listed should be totalled and added to total daily hours to come up with the "Total Hours Per Month" figure on the bottom of page one of the form. Now it is time to workload the job.

## Workloading

Using the total hours per month from page one, go to page two of the Bid Work Sheet and break the hours down into the various types of labor listed under the "Workloading" section. It is difficult to give any hard and fast rules on this, because each building varies so much in its requirements, and it depends on how you set up your crews. Basically, I do it by a process of elimination. I assign hours for supervision, porter or matron, floor work, etc., and then plug whatever is left into general cleaning. I then check to see that the general cleaning figure "jibes" with my ballpark production rates, to make sure it looks right. This usually comes out pretty good. It is mainly a matter of experience, and you will just have to work with it awhile until you get comfortable with workloading. For starters, the above method will get you going until you get a feel for it. If your gang cleans the building, you can workload according to the production rates given for the various kinds of workers on pages 65 through 70. For this approach, you may have to add work categories such as "trasher," "restroom cleaner," and "vacuumer" in the blank spaces provided on the Bid Work Sheet. For a discussion of gang cleaning versus area cleaning, see page 74.

To figure supervision, plan on a full-time building supervisor for every ten to twelve production workers. In a smaller building with only three or four workers, the supervisor can be a working member of the team and actually clean an area personally, as well as supervise the rest of the crew. The super's full complement of hours should be entered in the supervision space, though, at the higher wage level usually accorded this position. It will depend on the building and its requirements whether or not you figure in any hours for a porter or matron, and any additional floor work must be figured individually for each facility. To determine hours required for floor work, use the production figures for floor operations in the "Extra Work" production tables.

## Direct Cost

Once you get your workloading done, total up the hours per month to make sure they agree with the total you arrived at on the bottom of page one. If they agree, go ahead and plug in the pay rates per hour for each category of worker, and multiply by monthly hours to get a labor cost per month for each work category. The sum of these, "Total Labor," is what we refer to as "Direct Labor" (labor related directly to the job, as opposed to administrative or clerical payroll). Now that you have a Direct Labor figure, carry it down to the bid computation section of the form, and we'll plug in the other direct costs.

To determine **Payroll Costs,** you will have to know what your particular rates are. This will take a little research the first time, but after you have determined it, you will be able to apply it to every bid. It's worth the hassle of gathering the information in order to accurately figure your bids. The current FICA rate is available from the Social Security Administration. It is the percent of payroll which is withheld from the employee's check (and which the employer matches), hence it is a payroll expense. State Unemployment Tax (SUT) may not apply in your locality, but most states have a percentage of payroll that the employer must contribute to the state fund. Federal Unemployment Tax (FUT) is the percentage of payroll that you contribute on your federal form 940. Your Workman's Compensation Insurance (W/CI) rate can be obtained from your

# Specialized Cleaning vs. Zone Cleaning

There are two basic systems in use for general cleaning of office space. There is specialized, or "gang" cleaning, where each member of the team performs a specialized task, and zone cleaning, where one person is responsible for an area and performs all of the necessary work in that zone. Each method has its strengths and weaknesses. Gang cleaning is unquestionably faster, especially in large buildings, and most high rises are cleaning using this method. Each member of the team has a specialty, at which they get very good, and the team as a whole can go through a building significantly faster than can one person doing all the jobs in one area.

To zone clean, a worker generally takes along the supplies and equipment necessary to "ash and trash" and do the general cleaning in office areas. They must then make a return trip to sweep or vacuum, and another to do the restrooms.  Also, while doing the general cleaning, the worker is constantly pulling along a trash cart, and switching off from one task and from one piece of equipment to another . By comparison, a general cleaner on a specialty team generally wears a "maid apron", containing all of the supplies needed, and has no trash cart to fight. A trasher has already whizzed through ahead and taken care of the ash trays and trash cans.  Not having to switch off from one job to another and to juggle equipment around, each member of a specialty team can cover a lot of ground.

You pay a price for all that speed, though. Usually,  both quality control and security are enhanced with zone cleaning. Because only one person works in the area, responsibility for any problems is easy to pin down. With the "gang" concept, each member of the team has been through the area, usually at a different time, and responsibility for such things as pilferage and breakage  is hard to ascertain. Also, when one person cleans the same area all the time,  they generally will start to think of the area as their own,  and to take pride in it.  Zone cleaning is  often used in smaller facilities, and where enhanced security and quality control are needed.

insurance carrier, and make sure that any experience mods or discounts are applied to the rate you are quoted. Your insurance agent can also help you figure your effective Public Liability and Property Damage (PL/PD) rates. You may have other payroll taxes or burdens which apply in your locality, which you should add to come up with a total Payroll Expense, which represents a percentage of your payroll. You then multiply this factor by the total labor to arrive at Payroll Costs. Depending upon locality, your payroll costs will probably run from 10–18% of direct labor. The rates shown on the sample work sheet are the average figures for a large regional janitorial contractor, operating in twelve western states.

**Supplies** and materials can be determined either on an actual basis, or as a percentage of payroll. I generally use 8% of total labor to figure basic small janitorial tools and chemicals. This doesn't include restroom dispenser items such as paper and hand soap, nor does it include large, depreciated items of equipment such as buffers and floor scrubbers. (I like to treat as current expense any equipment item under $100 and charge it to materials and supplies. Equipment over that amount I depreciate and expense under "Equipment Amortization." You can use the system that works for you.) If you use the percent of labor method, simply multiply total labor by 8%, or whatever factor you decide to use, and plug the figure onto the form. If the job calls for you to supply paper at your expense, you can use the cost and consumption figures supplied by the paper companies, or you can use a pat dollar amount per person occupying the building. I find that in 1991, $1.50 per person per month seems to be adequate. This is a figure that must be constantly updated, however, as paper prices fluctuate. You will note that I like to jot the percentage of labor figures I use in computing the bid right on the form, next to the item it applies to. Writing little notes to myself as I go along helps me immensely if I ever need to come back and reconstruct a bid or modify it. The dollar figures on the bid, along with my penciled-in notes on "% of sales" actually become a mini profit-and-loss statement for the job.

As I mentioned before, the expense for any large pieces of equipment which you depreciate on your financial statement should be shown under "Equipment Amortization." For instance, if you put a floor machine costing $3,600 on a job, and you want to amortize it over the three-year term of the contract, you expense $100 per month in the Equipment Amortization slot. On average, my big janitorial contracting firm spends 1.3% of total sales on depreciated equipment.

**Uniforms** are something I believe in. They give your crews a professional look and a sense of belonging to a team, and they really enhance security for the customer. I don't mind spending a few dollars a month to keep my people in good-looking uniforms on all my jobs. I usually figure .4% of total labor for my costs in this category, or $1.35 per employee per month. I don't use a linen service for uniforms, I just buy the garments and supply them to the employees, and they take care of them. I charge a uniform deposit when they are issued so I'm sure to get them back when an employee leaves.

**Dust Mops, Etc.,** and the blank lines can be used to estimate other direct (job-related) costs such as dust mops, towels and linen rental, on-the-job vehicle, etc. Before you total up the direct costs, here's the place to think about applying any extra costs generated by special factors. Remember the "Bidding Considerations" listed on page 62? If distance, occupancy, age or condition of the building, personality of the people involved, or any of the other modifying factors apply to this job, you may want to punch the additional costs in at this point. Some of these factors may affect the indirect costs, as well.

**Total Direct Cost** is your estimate of all job-related expenses. This should be the amount that it actually costs you to run the job, independent of any administrative costs, and is the figure we will use to mark up for overhead and profit.

## Overhead Markup

To come up with a total bid price, we need to add something in to cover overhead expenses and to provide for a reasonable profit. You will have to come up with your own overhead figures, because every operation is different in this regard. If you are operating a small company from an office in your home and doing all the clerical and sales work yourself, your overhead expense can range from next to nothing to 10% or 15% of total sales. For a larger, full-service company with offices, phones, clerical help, sales people, and all the expenses a full-blown operation generates, overhead can run anywhere from 12–25% of total sales. Average for all U.S. janitorial

# Crew "Gang" or Specialty Cleaning

Square foot per hour per worker rates for situations where individuals are assigned to specific duties as part of a team Cleaning System. This is in office buildings for regular janitorial duties and runs overall 6,000 sq. ft. high to 3500 low production per person. The below rates are potential levels in large, high-use complexes, and with a lean and mean Supervisor.

| JOB DUTIES | Easy, Light | Medium Density | Heavy Full |
|---|---|---|---|
| **TRASHER**<br>1. Empty all trash<br>2. Empty ash trays into metal containers<br>3. Wipe clean all ash trays<br>4. Replace all plastic liners as needed | 41,000 | 36,000 | 25,000 |
| **REST ROOMS**<br>1. Clean and sanitize all sinks and toilets<br>2. Clean all mirrors<br>3. Dust all edges and partitions<br>4. Spot clean all doors and kickplates<br>5. Refill all dispensers<br>6. Dry mop floor with treated dust mop<br>7. Wet mop floor with germicide | 800 | 700 | 500 |
| **VACUUMER**<br>1. Vacuum all carpets<br>2. Detail around and under all desks and do corners and edges periodically | 18,000 | 11,000 | 7,000 |
| **MAID OR GENERAL CLEANER**<br>1. Dust all desks, windows ledges, furniture<br>2. Spot clean desktops, and around doors, light switches, polish ash trays, etc. | 35,000 | 24,000 | 18,000 |
| **SWEEPER**<br>1. Dust mop all tile floors with treated dust mop<br>2. Spot clean floor for spillage | 40,000 | 30,000 | 25,000 |

**Remember:  this doesn't include floorwork (shampoo, strip, etc.)**

contractors is somewhere around 15%.

To estimate your own overhead markup for bidding purposes, you will need two figures from your existing operation: the percentage of overhead to sales you run, and the percentage of labor to sales. If you have a going concern with an income statement, getting this information is easy; just pull the figures from the statement. If your books are simple and you don't do income statements, get the figures by dividing average monthly overhead by average monthly sales, and average labor by average sales. If you are just starting out and don't have a track record, you will have to estimate what these figures will be. As a rule of thumb, overhead on a small start-up business should not run more that 10 or 15% of sales, and your labor factor should be in the neighborhood of 50-55%. (If you do some or all of the work yourself, be sure to include the cost for your labor when you figure your labor percentage.)

Once you come up with the overhead and labor percentages, compute your overhead markup factor for bidding purposes in this way: divide the overhead percentage by the labor percentage. For instance, if your figures looked like this:

|  | $ Sales/Mo. | % of Sales |
| --- | --- | --- |
| Total Sales | $10,000 | 100% |
| Direct Labor | 5,500 | 55% |
| Total Direct Costs | 7,000 | 70% |
| Overhead Costs | 2,000 | 20% |
| Net Profit | 1,000 | 10% |

Your overhead markup would be 36.4% of labor (.20 divided by .55 equals .364). So, to determine overhead expenses on our Bid Work Sheet, we would multiply Total Labor by .364 and plug the resulting figure into the overhead line. For most small contractors, starting out with limited office and administrative expenses, figuring overhead as 30% of Direct Labor will be sufficient.

## Profit

Marking up for profit is the individual bidder's prerogative and usually ends up being a compromise of several factors. We usually can't bid a job at too high a profit figure and stay competitive with other bidders, and yet we have to earn enough on the job to make it worthwhile and keep our business healthy. Don't be afraid to take a profit where you can. There will always be those jobs where for one reason or another you end up making little or nothing for a lot of hard work. Then, once in a while, you'll get a chance to make a good, healthy profit on a job and even things out. When you put your capital at risk, invest, work hard, and sacrifice to run a business, you deserve a profit!

The average profit margin for U.S. contract cleaners runs about 2-3% of sales, but that's an average of all sizes of companies and all sizes of jobs. You might mark up a small $300 insurance office bid 15% or more for profit, but you'd probably be willing to settle for 3 or 4% on a huge, easy-to-administer $50,000 per month industrial plant. You will have to make the final decision here. You may decide to shoot for 10% bottom line on your regular janitorial contracts, but you will probably want to go for a higher margin on your extra work jobs, 15-20%. For a lot of contractors, the regular contract work covers the overhead and pays the bills month in and month out, but the gravy is the extra work. Starting out, you might try figuring profit at 30% of labor on smaller jobs, 20% on larger ones.

## The Bottom Line

Now that you've agonized and sweated blood over all the figures, tried to guess what your competitors might bid, and hoped your paper supplier wouldn't pass on another price increase before you can lock in this job, you're ready to figure the final bid price. This is, of course, the simple process of adding up the Total Direct Cost, Overhead, and Profit figures to arrive at the Total Monthly Price. Here's the rub, though: now that you have it, do you trust it? By now, you've agonized over the numbers so much and pushed figures around to the point that you feel like you're swimming in a huge bowl of numerical soup. After all the decisions and value judgments you have made to arrive at the bid figure, have you arrived at a number that's right for this job? Doing some comparisons at this point can help you determine whether you've come up with a bid you can feel confident about.

## Comparisons

You have already computed the overall production time and plugged it in at the bottom of the Bid Work Sheet. Assuming you have an overall production rate that's right, your labor should be accurate. Now let's go to the next line down on the form, and figure the bid cost per square foot, to see how that stacks up. As the form indicates, simply divide Total Monthly Price by the Total Square Footage to determine cost per square foot. This is a yardstick that almost all cleaning contractors and building owners use to measure the costs of building maintenance. Once you get a little experience in bidding and comparing bids in your particular area, you will get a good feel for what the market price for a particular type of building is. Once you have bid enough, you'll find yourself walking through a building, making a few mental notes, and walking out saying to yourself: "This building will clean at about 3,500 feet per hour, and will go for about 4.5 cents per foot." With enough experience, you can come up with an extremely accurate bid in your head, without going through the mechanics of a bid work sheet, and most of it hinges on the production rate and the cost per square foot.

If you ever submitted a bid you weren't sure of, you know the awful pain and anguish that comes from waiting for the bid opening, sweating bullets over whether your bid will be either ridiculously high or low. There is nothing quite like the empty feeling in the pit of your stomach when they read the bids, and all the bidders are right together except for yours, which is 40% lower than all the rest. You know you've made a mistake in figuring the bid, and you are probably in for a rough go. If you've ever been in that situation, you will appreciate the sense of assurance that comes from comparing your bid to some known measuring sticks to see if it is reasonable. If you're new to bidding and pricing cleaning work, the "Buildings Comparison Chart" on pages 79 and 80 will give you some comparisons for various types of buildings.

## Computer Bids

Several companies market software packages to generate computer bids for cleaning services. Most of these programs use a computer to do essentially what we have just done with a pencil and a calculator. The computer is loaded with production rates, and you plug in the square footages for the various areas. The computer then makes all of the calculations and prints out a bid on a pre-programmed report form. Computer bids are no more accurate than what you can do by hand, and are often a bit inflexible because of the rigidity of the pre-programmed production rates. The computer-generated bid printout does help sell a job sometimes, because most people tend to lend more credence to a printout than they do to a handwritten or typed document. Except for the marketing edge that the printout bid may give you, I can see no advantage to computer bidding. It usually takes just as long for me to prepare and punch in the data and print a computer bid as it does to do one by hand.

## The Proposal

Now that you have come up with a bid figure you feel is right, be sure you present it to the customer in the most advantageous way. A well-designed proposal goes a long way in establishing your credentials as a professional. Even for a small operation just starting out, I would recommend spending a few dollars to have some nice proposal forms and contracts printed up. A full proposal should include:

1. A brief history of your company and background information on the principal people who will be dealing with the customer. Use this to establish your credibility and sell the strong points of your company.
2. References of companies you now work for who prospective customers can check with. If you are starting a new company from scratch, give personal references.
3. Specifications for the job, if the customer did not provide specs as part of a bid packet. You will find a copy of the spec form I use in the forms section of this book.
4. A contract agreement, which can be signed to formalize the contract. Again, you will find a sample agreement in the forms section.
5. Your certificate of insurance. Most customers will require a copy of your certificate as proof of insurance before you start the job, but it is a nice touch to include a photocopy in the proposal, just to show that you know how to stay ahead of the game.

For a small job, you may decide to just turn in specs and the contract agreement, and forego the full-blown proposal, but it is nice to have the capability to turn in a nice-looking package on a big, important job. I guarantee that if you

# Building Comparison Chart

"Ballpark" figures to help you assess the accuracy of your bids while you gain experience. Wide price and production fluctuations exist due to variations in building use and occupancy, and wage rates.

| Building Type | Factors To Consider | Production Rate (sq. ft./hour) | $ per mo. per sq. ft. |
|---|---|---|---|
| **Average Office Building** 40,000 sq. ft., 5 days/week | Bread and butter account for most small to medium-sized contractors. Production times vary widely with use and density of occupants. Carpeted building will be 15% faster to clean than one with resilient (waxed) floors. | 2,800 to 4,000 Avg. – 3,000 | .045 to .065 Avg. – .055 |
| **High Rise Office Tower** 300,000 sq. ft., 5 days/week | Be prepared to sharpen your pencil when you go after the high rises—you'll be bidding with the big boys here, and the margins are tight. The name of the game will be high production rates and low wage rates. It takes some experience to play in this ballpark. | 3,200 to 5,000 Avg. – 4,500 | .035 to .055 Avg. – .045 |
| **Small Office** 4,000 sq. ft., 3 days/week | This baby is going to cost you one and three-quarters to two hours per day no matter how you slice it. The actual work may only be one and one-half hours or so, but it takes just as long to get set up and put things away for this little gem as it would for a larger building. | 1,500 to 2,500 Avg. – 2,000 | .050 to .070 Avg. – .060 (3 days) |
| **Branch Bank** 6,000 sq. ft., 5 days/week | Usually demands a fairly high level of cleaning which, combined with size, means slower production rates. Better to have a number of branches and do them with route workers for better production times. | 2,000 to 3,500 Avg. – 2,500 | .045 to .080 Avg. – .065 |
| **Warehouse w/offices** 20,000 sq. ft., 3 days/week | Warehouse with small (1,000 sq. ft.) set of offices. Fast production time (10,000 sq. ft./hr. or better, sweeping warehouse) averages out to very fast time for overall facility. 3-day/wk. frequency keeps cost low. | 6,000 to 10,000 Avg. – 7,500 | .010 to .035 Avg. – .025 |

| Building Type | Factors To Consider | Production Rate (sq. ft./hour) | $ per mo. per sq. ft. |
|---|---|---|---|
| Supermarket 35,000 sq. ft., 7 days/week | Heavy on floor work—requires good knowledge of waxing and resilient floor maintenance. Requires automatic scrubber, propane or battery high-speed burnisher. Heavy equipment costs if not supplied by store. Many stores lock-in crews, reducing flexibility. 7-day-per-week service means personnel scheduling difficulties. | 3,500 to 5,500 Avg. 4,000 | .050 to .090 Avg. – .075 |
| Department Store 60,000 sq. ft., 6 days/week | Production time will vary widely based on use and traffic of store and amount of carpet versus waxed floor. Floor waxing schedules vary widely from daily to one time per week, depending on traffic and appearance level desired. Same cautions as supermarket on equipment and lock-ins. | 4,000 to 7,000 Avg. – 5,000 | .040 to .065 Avg. – .075 |
| Restaurant or Club 5,000 sq. ft., 7 days/week | Slow going, usually very late night or early morning work times—difficult to staff. Frequent changes in ownership/management. Worse than average in paying bills. | 2,000 to 2,800 Avg. – 2,500 | .07 to .10 Avg. – .08 |
| Telephone Switch Equipment Building 20,000 sq. ft., 5 days/week | Intimidating array of high-tech electronic switch gear. Requires specialized knowledge and cleaning techniques. Fast production times due to extremely limited occupancy and traffic. | 4,000 to 8,000 Avg. – 6,000 | .030 to .055 Avg. – .040 |
| Manufacturing Plant 6,000 sq. ft., 5 days/week | 20% offices, 80% large, open production areas with assembly lines and work stations. Electronic components assembly plant, etc. Fast production times in production areas. Workers usually clean around work stations. Add to price for day porter, clean rooms, etc. | 2,500 to 5,000 Avg. – 3,500 | .045 to .080 Avg. – .065 |

turn in something nicely-printed and professional-looking, it gives you a step up on the guy who scratches his out on the back of an envelope! On a lot of jobs, the customer will give you the specs, and will require you to sign the contract agreement he provides. In this case, be sure to look the contract document over carefully to make sure it doesn't contain anything you are not in agreement with. If unsure, it may pay to have an attorney read it and advise you.

Many contractors fall into the low bid trap. They talk themselves into believing that virtually **all** jobs are awarded on the basis of low bid, and they spend most of their time and energy trying to find ways to underbid their competitors. The problem with this is that soon all the contractors are in a price war, and everyone's profit margins erode to the point where it's hardly worth being in business. If you learn to **sell yourself,** you will find that you can often sell a contract to a customer based on service rather than on price, and you will beat out competitors even though they may quote lower prices. Part of selling yourself and your company is in convincing the customer that you are a true professional, and that you will take care of his problems. A well-presented, well-prepared proposal is absolutely essential to this effort, and will prove to be well worth the resources you devote to its development. I think this is such an important ingredient to success in this business, that I have devoted the whole next section of this book on how to present a bid.

## Price Adjustments

In your contract document, make sure you have a clause to provide for periodic price adjustments. You need to be able to adjust the contract price as occupancy of the facility goes up or down, or as additions are made, and as your costs increase over the term of the agreement. Some contracts are written with fixed prices, but it is much better if you can get an adjustment clause worked in. An escalation clause which allows you to negotiate a price increase when your costs for labor and supplies go up is a real help. It keeps things fair both for you and for the building owner.

As you negotiate prices with your customers, here is one trap to avoid: sometimes a customer will want to make a price cut, and will suggest a reduction in the frequency of cleaning to accomplish it. That's okay, but watch out how much you decrease your price! The customer might say something like this: "Well, Harry, you're cleaning now five days a week for $1,000 per month, why don't you reduce to three days per week and reduce the price to $600, or three-fifths of the current price?" Sound reasonable? Heck, no, it's not reasonable! When you come in on Wednesday, after not cleaning on Tuesday, all of Tuesday's trash will still be there to carry out, and there will be just as much detail vacuuming and high dusting and floor stripping to do, the costs will just be spread out over less total contract income. It will take longer to clean on the three days you now work than it used to take each day when you were there five days a week. You can't reduce it proportionately and come out. Also, it takes just as much equipment sitting in the janitor closet, depreciating away, to clean three days per week, but the fixed cost of the equipment is spread over a smaller contract base, and hence the percent of cost to sales goes up. Often times, you will need to negotiate a square foot price to apply to fluctuating footage in a building where the occupancy changes frequently, but keep the above example in mind when you negotiate such prices!

# HOW TO PRESENT A BID...

## 9

# ...AND CLOSE A SALE

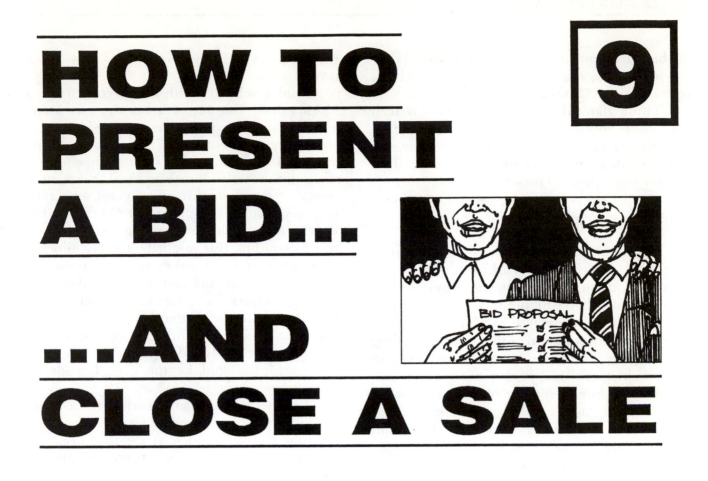

I saw a football game on TV once where the champions, with a one-point lead, held off a deadly charge of the opponent and got the ball back with 19 seconds left in the game. I shut off the TV and went to bed. The morning headline read "Champs Snatch Defeat Out Of The Jaws Of Victory" — **they lost in the last nineteen seconds!** In the cleaning business, we too can think we have cinched a contract because we have the best skills and the best prices, and still lose the job in the final moment. All because we don't know a few basics of presenting a bid and securing a sale. I'll condense and simplify the items that make the big bid-getting difference! Learn them well so you won't have to spend twenty years figuring them out. When I was doing most of my bid work personally I secured over 90% of the bids I submitted myself. Many contractors average only 20%.

I've snatched many a sale away from competent lower bid competitors, simply because of a skilled presentation and professional material.

## THE COST OF A BID

Only lawyers, doctors, and accountants can bill for the time they spend figuring their costs; the rest of us get paid only when we do the job.

We prepared, submitted, and presented a bunch of bids for several telephone companies once. We wanted them badly and for two weeks we prepared whole bid packages, met in bid conferences, checked local laws and licensing requirements. Our total cost for putting together the bid — in time, travel, phone, motel, secretarial expenses, etc. — was $26,000. **We were awarded none of them!**

To properly take a call, record and distribute all the communications involved, travel to and from the site, spend adequate time on the scene estimating and figuring the job, and return to the office to write and type the bid requires from five to fifteen hours for the average job. Considering time, office expense, vehicle expense, and basic overhead, it costs $50-$200 to make and submit the average bid. This quickly points to the importance of securing the work for most of the bids that you submit. If you were to bid only one job per day that you didn't get, it could cost your company $2,000 a month.

Think about that for a minute or two, then get serious about doing all you can to land all the bids you make. **Make them count!** I've covered how to calculate and figure bids earlier. This chapter shows how to present and secure them.

## THE CALL FOR A BID

A request for a bid can come through a telephone call, a sales call, through casual conversation, through a contractor's bid sheet, or a variety of other situations. When the initial request for a bid is received, **it's important to get all available information at that time, including:** names, phone numbers, addresses, the type of work desired, etc. The person receiving the call should show intense interest and desire to submit the bid, acting as if it's the greatest privilege he or she has had all day. Try to prepare and submit the bid as soon as possible. Delays allow people to "cool off," or other competitors to sniff out your job. Make sure you get all the details: where, when, and what. Avoid having to call back and ask questions. They'll instantly think you're a klutz and hold it against you later when considering the award.

## PERSONAL APPEARANCE

**Your presentation starts when you show up to bid.** Your appearance should be adjusted for the occasion. A suit, neatly cleaned and pressed will often allow you to gain more confidence of the customer and to be better accepted by and get more cooperation from the secretaries, especially on the initial contacts. However, experience has shown that there are times when it's just as effective to wear clean neat "whites" (work clothes) with your company emblem. This more informal "work" attire tends to give the bidder credibility as one who knows how to accomplish the work. I'd wear a suit when dealing with a similarly-attired executive, work clothes if dealing with an informally-clothed maintenance supervisor. It goes without saying that the bidder should be well-groomed in every way. Pay particular attention to hands and hair in addition to clothing. Your client won't know you're playing Grizzly Adams in the PTA play, and that rugged beard and those cowboy boots will only turn him off.

I did a bid walk with twelve contractors in Florida once. One brought his secretary along, and she had on an outfit that displayed her never-ending legs and enough of her bosom to cause several of the bidders and one of the clients to trip down the stairs. **Be professional.** Never, never smoke or drink anything, eat, chew, or scratch your ear around a client on a bid presentation. It weakens you. Clients are sizing you up in every way as you bid; this might be the last time the client sees you if you make a poor impression.

When I made bid calls myself I often wore whites, and carried a 12-foot tape measure. When I left the job site the customer was convinced that I was ready to go to work and no one in town could match me. My bid, regardless of the price, was practically sold by the time I made my presentation.

Unless the customer demands it, or unless the job is very small, **never** give a bid price at the time you go to look at the job. Leave the customer convinced that you are the best qualified company or person to do the job and that they will be missing out if they don't have you do the work. Then, return to your office, prepare the bid, and mail or deliver it to the customer. Always submit a bid in writing, never orally. Handing the customer the bid while you stand there and wait for a decision creates an unpleasant atmosphere. Especially when the expenditure involved is large, no customer likes to study a bid in haste, and undue pressure often develops into a bad attitude during the course of the job even if you get it, and in general it negatively affects the relationship you have with your customer.

If you can sense the customer hesitating or trying to delay a decision, the proper conversation may influence him. If you can see that money is a problem at the moment and if you know his credit is good, let him know that you'll work with him in arranging suitable terms. Then, of course, compensate for this by increasing the bid to cover the finance costs. Remember, some of the jobs you may consider small or common are a great and expensive decision for the customer. Take your time, discuss the whole job, and add your own personal touch to your relationship with the customer. An unconcerned square-footage estimator divorces himself from this personal touch, which is one of the biggest factors in whether or not you get the job.

Another secret to getting jobs and pleasing clients is to ask enough questions to get your customer talking about what they really want and why they're having the job done. You can get the information before doing the job when you're looking at it or bidding it. Knowing they want something cleaned and by what day isn't much to go on. Ask them why they're cleaning right now, what their previous experience has been, who has done work before, and how it came out. This will get you some answers about what they were pleased or displeased with before. They might say something like, "We are having visitors on the 15th from Palm Springs and they are real sticklers on housekeeping, especially windows." By knowing this you can concentrate efforts in your bid to solve these problems and anxieties. Consequently they gain a great deal of confidence in you and will probably award you the job — even if you bid higher.

What if your records show some minor problems on the previous job for them, on your side or theirs? Don't avoid mentioning any previous problems you or your company has had with the client, for they surely know about them and are thinking about them, and some doubts and wonderings of "Will it happen again?" are probably floating around in both your minds. Come out with something like "By the way, sir, these babies really shrink if overwet, as we found out last time. We know what caused it and how to avoid the extra time and effort of redoing them." Or, if it was their fault, ask directly: "Last time your people came in and tracked all over the floor during our wax job, surprising all of us, including you. How are we fixed on scheduling to avoid a repeat this time?" Remember, getting a job is more a matter of gaining confidence than of always having the lowest price. If customers can trust you for good timely work, it'll mean more to them than merely the cheapest price, so spend time figuring out how to do the job best and convince them you'll pull it off!

## PREPARATIONS

Other factors to consider when preparing and submitting bids include:

1. Obtaining a firm commitment as to when and where the work is to be performed.
2. If the job involves a "repeat customer," briefly review his previous record concerning type of work done, record of payment, etc.
3. During the on-site survey, check all the details that could complicate the bidding process: Are doors locked? Where are the keys? etc.
4. Be prepared for the specific type of bid it is. If it's going to be a bid for painting, have color books and chips available to display. Similar preparations should be made for other types of bids.
5. If the bid area is outside or in an unfinished building, wear appropriate clothes, bring a flashlight, etc. Your appearance and preparation will sell customers better than the price you are figuring.

If the bid is **really large or very significant** or the client requires it, you should make a formal bid presentation. Do it! Don't be afraid. Go back to the office and spend a day or two and even a dollar or two and make up a nice proposal. Maybe an eight- or nine-page bound booklet that:

- Introduces you, your company's history, and gives your credentials
- Shows some pictures of your operation and people
- Contains the price and proposal
- Outlines your quality control program
- Explains your training program
- Contains references from some of your accounts

This little volume, if done right, can convince clients that you are the deserving one, regardless of price. Make several copies, enough for each decision maker, and a few extra ones for the office.

The right goal: ever see a ballplayer score a point for the other side? Embarrassing! But worse, the point counts for the other side.

Likewise, if you are going to make a formal presentation, make sure you give it to the right person. The assistant manager and the secretary might love you, but if the head manager is the one who decides who to hire, your effort is all in vain.

## BID PRESENTATION FORMAT

I've seen bids submitted in many formats, from a sixty-page color-embossed booklet to scribbles on a folded piece of scrap paper. There are lots of ways you could present a bid, but

sticking to two basic formats can get the job done well.

Photos can lend credibility to a proposal. They make you real — not just talk. It's kind of like a fishing trip report, lots of talk and extended arms leaves the listeners scratching their chins and doubtful of your skill. One picture of the big fish says it all, and leaves the listener with a sagging jaw. Pictures are inexpensive to take, so include a few of the best, leaving behind the blurred or heads-chopped-off shots. A couple of the crew in action on the job or some before and after shots showing jobs you've completed are two possibilities. Photos add a testimony that you are what you say you are.

## FORM

A form is a standard pre-printed presentation, covering all the terms and specifications and basic understandings of the agreement between you and your customer. There are spaces for the account name, the building address, the date and the price, a section to briefly list the job description, and spaces for both of your signatures. A form assures that you won't forget any important legal aspects of the agreement. Designing one form tailored to your operation can give you speed and accuracy and save secretarial time. There are lots of standard forms that you can adapt to fit your needs.

I use a letter style for many bids because it lends a more personal touch. This can be a simple one-pager with:

- The client's name
- The date
- Job description

- Work and Material Description
- Cost
- Job completion commitment
- Signature

If the project is huge, your formal bid may be ten typed pages in all. Even these can be prepared quickly if you keep a sample layout to copy each time. For smaller jobs, where bids are often handed to the customer on the spot, a neatly handwritten bid is fine.

## HELPFUL TECHNIQUES

Unless specified by the client, a standard format to be used in submitting bids is nonexistent, so make your own! (Neatness and correct spelling are extremely important, however, no matter what format you use.)

Use color! Hire an artist — so you spend $50 trying to get a $4,000 a month contract, that's a good investment.

When preparing a bid, itemize and explain clearly and in descriptive terms the services that you are going to provide. Picture words are much more effective than just stating the minimum of information. For example, here are two ways a job could be described in the bid:

Example A:
   **Bid**
   Painting porch, one coat grey enamel
   $45.00

Example B:
   **Bid**
   Preparation of the complete back porch floor area, including light sanding, re-nailing of protruding nails, removing all dust and foreign material, and applying one coat of Benjamin Moore Floor and Deck enamel in Dover Grey color.
   Total Cost . . . $45.00

Almost anyone would accept the second bid instead of the first one, because it appears that they are getting much more for their money. The bidder on Example A is actually going to do as much as Example B. Preparation is simply getting the area ready and both will do that. But Example B tells the customer about it. "Light sanding" means removing the rough blisters or scaly areas and "removing all dust, etc." just means sweeping the floor. Example A didn't bother to tell the customer that the floor would be swept. Application is a professional-sounding word; "painting one coat of paint" is Tom Sawyer stuff. Paint is paint, but colors can become vivid if descriptive words are used, such as, Seaspray Green, Robin-Egg Blue, Fire-Engine Red, Eggshell Flat, Low Lustre Regal Gold, etc. Listing colors like this not only stimulates the customer's imagination but also provides more information concerning the exact material to be used.

Another very important technique in preparing a bid is the manner in which the price is quoted. Consider the following bid:

Example A:

**Bid**

Removing grill plates and lamps from light fixtures; cleaning of base units, grills and lamps and replacing units, leaving entire fixture clean.

Total cost for cleaning all light fixtures in the building — $2,100.00

This is a real bid! Light fixtures are very difficult to clean, especially the grills. To thoroughly clean one takes more than ten minutes a fixture. Most people are not aware of just what is involved. It's much better to submit this kind of bid on a per item basis. For example:

Example B:

**Bid**

Removing grill plates and lamps from 1,200 light fixtures; cleaning of base units, grills and lamps, and replacing the entire unit, leaving completely clean fixtures.

Total cost for each fixture to be cleaned: $1.75.

Remember hearing announcers selling color televisions for only 60¢ a day? That seemed much better than "our color televisions are selling for only $657.00" which is 60¢ a day for 36 months. The same principle applies to bidding a job.

## RECORDS OF BIDS

All bids should be prepared at least in triplicate, with the original going to the customer, and one carbon copy to your main office, if you have one, and one for your files. It is essential that your home office receive a copy of all bids submitted with a notation as to the status of the proposal, whether (1) accepted; (2) rejected; or (3) pending.

## FINAL TACTICS

Preach benefits, not hot air, in the final presentation. They really don't want to know how good you are or all about your magnificent accomplishments, they want to know what you will do for them. Do you just talk big or can you work big?

I asked one of our most successful bid-getting managers how he did it. He said, "I just tell them how good it's going to look when I'm through."

Everyone will spend money if they are convinced they will get their money's worth, but after they spend it, what do they get? Use statements like:

- We can't make it new again, but we will make it look new.
- Your rooms will also be lighter and safer after we finish. Close your eyes and imagine the finished job, and then describe it to the customer!

A MAJOR KEY FACTOR OF YOUR SUCCESS will be remembering that you are the **PROFESSIONAL**. If the customers knew what and how to do the job, and had the time, they would probably do it themselves. They called you to bid and do it, so assume the position. Grab hold of the situation and tell them what needs to be done and what to expect; if you determine that carpets will shrink, are worn, ruined, or that the color will bleed — tell them ahead of time. Just like a doctor tells you before surgery, "You have a 10% chance of not making it," or "Your age is against you on this," etc. I was asked by an older woman to remove eight coats of wallpaper and then paint the walls in the bedroom of an old, old home. Because the plaster was cracked, it would have cost me $400 to do the job. I explained to the lady that the age of her home would make the job expensive, and I knew she could save $200 and be happy with the new pecan paneling that was on sale at Anderson's. She was thrilled. We did the job one morning, made good money, and she was a lifelong customer. If you can't do the job, or can't do it at a reasonable price, then help the customer by suggesting other alternatives, other companies (even your competitors). They'll love you and trust you forever and from that day on, look for an excuse to call you back!

## REFERENCES

Because you are brand new in the cleaning business, this business of references may seem frustrating to you. It's like the guy trying to get a job as a bartender from a bar which precludes hiring anyone without experience; the only way he can get experience is to be hired. References carry weight because they back up all the big talk and promises. Have you been as good in the past as you say you are: dependable, on time, honest, etc.? References give a real answer to those questions to a would-be customer. List all of the buildings that you now service, or the ones most like the buildings you're trying to get. As sure as you hold out your dissatisfied customers, the client (who has ways of knowing what accounts you have) will call you on the one you didn't put down on the list. Be honest on your references.

Good references help tremendously. When we put down Bell System, American Express, IBM, or others we have serviced for thirty years, it goes a long way toward letting our would-be clients know we are a bit better than others might be. If you don't have any buildings yet, put down past job or personal references. Personally, I'd give you a lot of mileage for that. Reinforce with the would-be client that you are competitive, dependable, and an honest person. Most folks will give you the benefit of the doubt. When you give a reference, give the name of a specific individual, an address, and a phone number. Make it easy for the client to contact them.

## THANK-YOU LETTERS

When ten of us bid on a job, there are going to be nine people disappointed, and often you will be one of the nine. This doesn't mean you're a failure, or a bad guy, and not necessarily that you bid too high or too low. In some way, maybe money, maybe personality, maybe experience, someone has outsold you. This has happened to me thousands and thousands of times and I've survived it beautifully. One reason I've survived is that even after losing a job or bid, I write to the clients and thank them for the opportunity to bid. I reassure them that we'd like another chance if and when it comes up for bid again, or if things don't work out well with the successful bidder. Very few professionals do this! Instead they stomp away and call the winning bidder a cutthroat, etc. The minute your thank-you and acknowledgement letter reaches the client, you remind the customer of your estimate, and it puts pressure on the present contractor. The client knows he has you waiting in the wings if they don't perform. You'll pick up lots of work after losing the first bid. Keep calling on the account and, some day, you will get it, even from big guys like me. The personal touch just can't be beat.

# YOUR STAFF EMPLOYEES

## 10

APPLICATONS

## THE BOSS

For the majority of people who are striving to become "the boss," their prime motivation is a desire for power, not merely to succeed. We've been blaming our bosses for all our problems, for years. The word "boss" represents power and even fear: someone Dagwood is constantly cringing before and begging for a raise. Much of your desire to start your own company is from wanting to be the boss. You want the power to make money, decisions, to decide when you have free time to do anything you want. Well, you're in for a big surprise: bosses are just employees too. When you're the owner and boss of your own company, you'll discover you have forty bosses over you, where you only had one before. Boss is just a better position from which to grow, to love, to learn, and for sure, not an instant crowning of a little king. Things don't go your way nor can you get your own way just because you become boss — and people won't automatically respect you because of your position. You still have to earn respect. You'll find out that getting fired was an easier and more pleasant experience than firing someone. You'll find that the boss gets the last paycheck (if there's any

money left). You'll find that the boss's position carries with it a great deal of incentive, but it is demanding. You learn quickly that your livelihood depends on the employees and not vice versa as you'd previously thought. I think becoming a boss will end up being the best experience you ever have in your life — go for it — but go for it compassionately and with commitment. The multitude of employment laws are complicated entanglements involving unions, discrimination, absenteeism, overtime, leaves of absence, vacations, etc. Obeying them as an employee was easy because you kind of let them herd you around like sheep. Well now, as the boss, you have to learn, apply, and enforce the rules. Don't be scared by them — all the officials and the different departments of government will see to it that you are educated. Read the literature carefully, structure your business within the letter of the law, and follow the rules. The generally understood rules are outlined in this manual; you'll find others that pertain specifically to your state, county, and city. It's worth the little extra attention, so don't let the fine print keep you from becoming the boss.

This chapter is not intended to be a comprehensive treatment of employment practices.

That would be a book in itself, and there are a number of them written on the subject, plus scores of government pamphlets and publications you can get for free. I'm just trying to give you some of the nuggets of wisdom I've picked up over the years about how to find, hire, and keep good people. I also try to point out some of the pitfalls in hiring — most of them traps I fell into and had to fight my way out of!

First, don't hire anyone until the workload gets so heavy that you're exhausted and stumbling over your own eyelids. Then work with the person yourself for a long time before you send them out on their own. It's the only way to start a staff.

There seems to be an anxious sense of anticipation of the power to hire someone to work for us. It seems that all our lives someone else has told us when to jump and how far, but at last we are the owner, the king, the BOSS, the one who does the whip-cracking. The first hour or two may be enjoyable, but actually now, as an independent contractor, you have three hundred bosses (owners) telling you not only how high to jump, but exactly when, why, and where to jump. Being an owner and boss doesn't free you from having to answer to someone.

Hiring people to work for you can be very dangerous because, remember: they have to be paid at the rate you agree upon, whether they produce or make you money or not, and not many people are naturally good, fast, and productive workers. The people readily available to go to work for you will be the chronically unemployed, the discouraged, someone looking for a second income, or a young person who's never had a job in their life and needs to be taught. That sounds fair enough — you've heard of training programs for the underprivileged, but the training isn't free. Where you were once out on the job producing $10 to $30 per hour, you suddenly have to spend two hours a day helping, teaching, training, and looking after some new employees. That means they're costing your company $50 of income not coming in any more. Of the four groups of people above, those looking for a second income are your best bet (more on finding good employees later).

Too many cleaning company owners get a $3,000 contract and run out and hire "people to do all the work" for them — they're just planning to sit back and run things. At the end of the month

the employee payroll is $4,000. What are you going to do then? You've spent all your time training them, not working yourself, and they were slow and fumbled and didn't do it as fast as you bid it. Now you're a thousand dollars in the hole and you have six eager new employees ready to go out and lose a thousand dollars again next month. Employees don't make you money if they are non-productive. Good, productive workers don't come beating your door down to go to work cleaning toilets for you — you have to go out and find them. In our business, some refer to many of the people who go to work for us as "marginal employees." That means they're at the end of the line, they couldn't get a job in the big money, or for that matter anywhere else, and have to resort to cleaning to survive. They generally have a poor attitude and almost always are taking the job as a stopgap survival move until something better comes along. Lines of unemployed and chronic underachievers will answer your employment ads, and seldom will the superman employee drop out of the sky. There is no magic difference in selecting male or female, age or race. But getting good employees is the key to building your business, and if you succeed it will be through your selection of, treatment of, and the production of your employees. It's really pretty sobering when you add it all up, and I'm not stacking the deck or exaggerating. Good employees can be found, and it will even be a great source of personal satisfaction to be involved with their lives and their families. I've built and retained some employees for thirty years and some are now running entire states for my company, but it wasn't storybook or TV fiction activities that did it; it takes planning and effort. Last year our general manager got our trade association's "President's Citation for Excellence" and one of my custodians in Phoenix was "Custodian of the Year." Thousands of books and directions and philosophies have been written on the skills of finding, training, keeping, and motivating employees. I will give you the cream of what I've learned, not only from my own experience but from speaking with highly credible employers all over the U.S. We are a close-knit, personally committed, employee-oriented company. Maybe we're even too much so for your personality; you'll have to level out with your employees where you feel right and comfortable.

## EMPLOYEE SEARCH

Even when unemployment figures are as high as 10% many people would rather draw unemployment then do janitor work. That's their attitude before they get involved with it, at least. Remember, most all your competitors will be paying minimum wage for their production workers, so you'll have to be somewhere in there too, to be competitive. We would all like to be able to pay our people top dollar, but the competitive bid process most often limits us to "market" wage rates, and that's usually around minimum wage. This limits somewhat the people we can draw on to fill our cleaning jobs.

First, be careful with the people that are forever unemployed and can't seem to find or hold a job. Most of the good workers are already working. When a factory lays off 20% of their work force because of a slowdown, guess who they let go? The fast, productive, responsible workers, or those who are a little slower, who don't always show up on time, and who don't get along well with others? We all know the answer. Although there are always a certain number of good producers who are justifiably unemployed for one reason or another, they don't stay unemployed long. They want to work, they are good producers, and they can give good references. A savvy boss snaps these types up quick. If you limit your recruiting largely to the ranks of the unemployed (which is what you do with "help wanted" ads and job service placements), you'll learn an important lesson: there's usually a good reason why the person was unemployed! Your best source of employees will be moonlighters. Look for established, responsible people who already have a solid daytime job, who want to earn extra money working part-time after hours. Always get lots of applications and screen them carefully and use your own judgment of character to make your selections.

I re-emphasize: screen and hire carefully, because once someone is working for you they assume an unbelievable amount of **rights,** and they can sure run you in directions you may not want to go and stick you for the bill. One of the biggies, that looms bigger all the time, is the dishonesty problem. Your people are in a prime position to steal, and are always the ones to be blamed first by the tenants, so you'll be getting it from two fronts. Even if you know for sure that an employee did, or is, stealing, laws and the lawyers and the do-gooders are making it more and more difficult to dismiss people, even when you have good cause. You dismiss any employee for stealing, even if you catch them red-handed, and if the court happens to acquit him for any reason (pity, insanity, or anything), he can come back and sue you for improper dismissal. He can put you right out of business. Several government and private volunteer organizations work intensively with low-income workers and have really been educating them to their rights. They can get free legal help and beat you to death with trumped-up charges of discrimination and improper hiring practices. So screen, screen, screen, and do everything possible to not pick shysters and crooks, and remember that just because someone goes to the same church as you, it's no guarantee that they'll never rip you off. I tend to upfront trust everyone and probably always will, but I have learned, sadly, that everyone isn't always worthy of trust.

Hands down, my best source of people has been referrals from other employees. Good employees are your kind of people, they know what you're looking for, and will most times send you the kind of people you're looking for. Plus, the existing employee will often take a proprietary interest in the newly-hired referral, and will help to make sure they do well. Classified ads work fairly well, but we've had poor results from employment agencies, professional job placement groups, etc.

Have people report to your office and fill out an application. Make your application form as complete as possible, without breaking the minority and equal opportunity laws. Ask all the questions you can, then be sure to ask for at least three past references from previous jobs and three past references for character. **Be sure to check the references. Do it!** A three-minute phone check on a person can save you three months of agony or three years of claims and lawsuits. The world is full of people who get jobs, work a week, have an injury crop up (they actually got it twenty years ago), and they stay home and collect insurance and unemployment off you indefinitely. It is total misery and it pushes your insurance rate way up. Remember this, and never forget it: up front, before you hire people, you have lots of liberty; you can consider their work habits, employment record, language, grooming, attitudes, etc. You can say **yes** or **no** to them before hiring. After you get them on the job and find them on drugs or sleeping on the job, you try to ditch them and it's often "arbitration" or civil liberties material.

Before you get into hiring very many employees, you need to become conversant with the many employment practices governing discrimination, proper dismissal, record-keeping, etc. A session with a good labor relations attorney could be a wise investment for you, and there are government publications and agencies to help you out. I've included the "Reference Check List" I use in the forms section in the back of the book to help you in screening.

Interview each person as if you were keeping them around for the rest of your life, as if they were going to be around your kids and home, drive your vehicles, and represent your investment. Find out, when you call the reference, why they left, what kind of people they were, their speed, their character, get all the information you can. Now is the time to do it. This is critical to your success in the future, because if you're going to pour hours of your time into training and trusting them, then you better make sure they're worthy of it. There are lots of good people around; be patient and go after them. Most of your competitors won't; they'll be in a hurry and take the first live body through the door that can mumble "Ajax" and read a "Wet Floor" sign. When you aren't around on a job, those employees are the total representation of you and your image, it's as clear and simple as that, and poor employees will destroy you.

Always have a backup. Don't wait until someone leaves to find a replacement. Average turnover in the cleaning business is 300% annually, and that simply means that if the bank or doctor's office your company cleans requires

one person to clean it, over the course of the year you'll need to hire three, because two will have quit before the year is out. Your objective is not to have any turnover.

## HIRING

When you hire a person for any position, give him or her an on-the-spot written description of the job, tell the person what is expected, and what the salary will be. My company now has an employee manual. It has all of our policies on sick leave, absenteeism, vacations, etc., but you can just type your own descriptions up on a little form, run it off at the instant press and make two copies, one for employees and one for the personnel file. This is a quick, inexpensive little move that will save your bacon. When they start, there is no doubt about exactly what they're supposed to be doing, and when and exactly how much they will be paid. All rules and regulations also need to be carefully spelled out in a set of employee policies, so the employee knows exactly what's expected. If you're interested in having a copy of the employee manual we use in my big cleaning company, it's included in my *Clean Up For A Living* kit.

My experience is that most cleaning employees will have a dispute at the end of the first month as to the amount paid them or the hours or days worked. The fact that they have and you have a copy of the agreement is a real deterrent for any crowding from either your side or theirs. Ninety percent of employees think bosses and companies are "out to get them" and it takes time to convince the worker that you love and need them, and will treat them right.

## RAISES

As your employee's goals will be the same as yours, to work, grow, and make better money, they need to know how they can advance and get raises. In cleaning this is difficult because "clean" is hard to measure. Working hard and doing a good job are abstract terms, unless you define how hard is hard and how clean is clean.

You'll have to set a quality level based on inspection and record, and set a production level based on how much has to be done in how much time. If your employees can accomplish both of these, they deserve a raise, and future raises as they increase quality and production.

# Employment Application

**EQUAL EMPLOYMENT OPPORTUNITY POLICY**
Applicants are considered for all positions without regard to race, color, religion, sex, national origin, age, marital or veteran status, or the presence of a non-job related medical condition or handicap.

Date of Application ————————————

Position Applied For ————————————————————————

Name In Full (last, middle, first) ————————————————————

S.S.N. ———————————————————— Phone ——————————

Home Address ———————————— City ———————— State ———— Zip ————

Are you over eighteen years of age?  ❑ yes    ❑ no

Highest Education Level Completed ————————————————————

Do you have any physical condition that may limit your ability to perform the job for which you have applied?    ❑ yes    ❑ no

If yes, please explain ————————————————————————

————————————————————————————————————

Does heat, standing on your feet, or lifting cause you any difficulties? ————————————

————————————————————————————————————

## WORK HISTORY
*(Start with present or last job)*

| Date Employed | Employer | Position | Supervisor | Reason For Leaving |
|---|---|---|---|---|
| FROM | NAME | | | |
| TO | ADDRESS | | | |
| FOR OFFICE USE ONLY | | | | |
| | | | | |
| | | | | |
| FOR OFFICE USE ONLY | | | | |
| | | | | |
| FOR OFFICE USE ONLY | | | | |
| | | | | |
| | | | | |

Indicate languages you speak: _____ read: _____ write: _____

### REFERENCES:
(Name 3 persons other than relatives, former employers, or persons whose identity might reveal or suggest religious or ethnic affiliation. Include address and phone numbers.)

NAME                          ADDRESS                          PHONE

_____

_____

_____

What kind of work can you do? _____

_____

_____

Do you have reliable transportation? _____

HAVE YOU EVER BEEN CONVICTED OF A CRIME OTHER THAN MINOR TRAFFIC VIOLATIONS?   ☐ yes  ☐ no

If yes, explain fully. A criminal conviction will not necessarily be a bar          _____
to employment. Any relevent factors such as age at time of the offense,
seriousness and nature of the violation, and rehabilitation will be taken          _____
into account.
                                                                                   _____

_____

I AUTHORIZE INVESTIGATION OF ALL STATEMENTS CONTAINED IN THE ATTACHED APPLICATION. I UNDER-
STAND THAT MISREPRESENTATION OR OMISSION OF FACTS CALLED FOR IS CAUSE FOR DISMISSAL.

Signature _____

Date _____

# Employee Reference Checklist

NAME _____ SSN_____

CHECKED BY _____ DATE _____

PERSON TALKED TO _____ PHONE _____

COMPANY_____ DEPT. _____

EMPLOYMENT VERIFICATION:

Employed from _____ to _____ Dept. _____

Position _____ Supervisor _____

**Could you please rate the employee on a scale of 1 to 10 for the following traits, 10 being best:**

Reliable (dependable) _____

Punctual (showed up for work on time, etc.) _____

Trustworthy (honest) _____

Job Skills (accomplishment of assigned job) _____

What did you like about this employee?_____

_____

Did you notice any problems or weaknesses which might cause

difficulties in the new job?_____

Would you re-hire this employee?_____

Any other comments? _____

_____

_____

The perfect example of this is the Larry/Keith competition. Keith was a quick, personable kid from the LA area, a super worker, ambitious, handsome, and competitive. He worked in a fury, almost running. Larry was slow moving and quiet, but was paid double what Keith made per hour (much to Keith's dismay.) Larry would go into a home and clean two rooms for every one of Keith's, consistently — and Larry did the best work. The two guys were the same size, age, weight, and had the same family status, but Larry just out-produced Keith in quantity and quality two to one.

All of us are over-optimistic about our ability and application. When I used to interview and hire a person, I would say: "We will start you at the regular $5.00 per hour," (they'd only expected to get $4.50) "and if you're a real outstanding producer, in time you can work up to $8.50 per hour." At the end of the first month when I'd call them in to terminate them for total non-production, they'd honestly think they were being called in for that $8.50 raise, and really expected it on their final check. **Make sure your agreements are clear.** If you promise a raise or a bonus, then write out exactly when and make it 100% clear; don't say "if you do well, you'll get a raise" because everyone thinks they "do well." Say instead: "If you can get your production up to 3,200 feet per hour, and can hold a quality index of 85 or better, you will get a raise of fifty cents per hour." Then you've eliminated all arbitration, pressure and wild thoughts, and you also won't be stuck making a value judgment in a squirmy situation. They'll know at the end of the time whether they have it coming or not. They'll also realize that they, not you, will eventually determine what they get.

## PERSONAL HABITS AND GROOMING

As you've observed for many years, "the janitors" too often look like the dregs of wino row. This is an image our profession has picked up and it's hard to shake. Don't add to it; set some standards up front in the interview, and spell them out in your employment agreement (see page 103). This is key. Would you want some shaggy, unshaven, unwashed, dirty-clothed worker cleaning your nice living room or plush office downtown? Or would you rather have a sharp, clean-cut, and well groomed person? Once you allow bad language, drinking, drugs, sloppy clothes, smoking, and bad language in your operation, you'll never get it out. The bad employees will poison the good ones. This also goes for allowing blasting radios or tape decks on the job; never do it. It's offensive to the customer, and we are in a service business and are a guest in the place. Just because we have a pocketful of keys doesn't give us the authority to make ourselves at home in other people's places.

**Remember: you can't clean a building good enough if people don't like you.**

## APPRECIATION AND RESPECT

Treat your employees with importance and as your friends. We all want to be loved, recognized and appreciated, and if you treat your employees with appreciation and respect, they will show love, loyalty, and trust in return. Work with and around and for them, and show them that you're willing to do the dirtiest and toughest jobs while you are with them. They are human and have homes and families just like you do, and they live for that check. Just because you can wait for your money if accounts are slow, they can't. Whatever you do, be on time and exact with their money. Keep them busy and work them hard. Employees love to work hard and feel part of the business. Again, whenever possible, work with your employees on the job. There are several good reasons for this:

1. It builds respect, loyalty, and trust and you can get to know them better.
2. You can train them while you yourself are in a productive, money-making situation.
3. You can evaluate their performance firsthand and know who will be the best for promotion and future upward moves; no one else can tell you this.

The whole secret here, which will be one of the keys in making your company better than your competitor's, is practicing the art of having your employees work with you, not for you. The art of asking them more than telling them what to do. I'm not talking manipulation and textbook psychology, but genuine caring for them as human beings. Here are a couple of principles that will work magic for you.

When you have a challenging job or problems on the job, ask for help to solve them. Instead of appraising the situation yourself and telling workers what to do, ask, "What do you think?" It's the magic question of all time in cleaning and you'll be surprised that, in most cases, they will have a better solution than you, and will make it work ten times better because it was their idea!

Instead of solely making the decisions for purchasing supplies and equipment for your crew all the time, get them involved: hand them brochures or let them sit in on the salesman's visit and get their opinions. You'll be surprised at what you can learn in minutes.

Aggressively question your employees every chance you get: how do you do that; why do you do that; what has happened here last week; any funny stories; how long have you been with us; how are you feeling, etc.

You'll begin to love your employees when you learn about them. You'll be overwhelmed with what they know about the job, and can teach you.

## HOUR CARDS

Dollar signs should come up in your eyes the minute your employees show up to work, because they are getting paid the minute they get there, but they only make you a profit when on the job. If you are paying for break time, breakdown time, travel time, job wasting time, look at it this way: if eight employees show up to work at 8 A.M. and you don't get around to starting the job until 8:30, you've paid for four total hours of nothing which has to be subtracted from the job. That means if you show a $21 profit on the job, the $24 in wages paid for waiting around and getting ready will erase the profit and put you $2 in the hole. Wouldn't you have been ahead if you hadn't taken the job? There is no magic government or "they" that pay your people — it's you. No one else absorbs the expenses; it comes out of the money taken in for the job. I've seen some of my $20-an-hour managers spend thirty minutes to sell a $4 profit item, thinking they really accomplished something. In fact they lost $6 dollars on the deal because it cost $10 of their time to sell it. To be successful in your own business, you have to start thinking this way!

## SUPERVISION AND SNOOPERVISION

Too many new business people think supervision is detective work: to find out what's happening, or what went on, and then keep the record in a little book to take to a meeting. Supervision is just the opposite. It is making sure nothing wrong happens in the first place. Supervision is preventative, restorative, not listings of what happened and how to correct it, but anticipating and giving lists before there is trouble. Supervision isn't finding out who done it and why and what. It's active not passive. It's catching them in the act or before and steering behavior to a positive result.

The simple laws of supervision are:

1. Keeping people informed as to where they are and what is expected. Don't complicate it; keep your evaluations and job assignments simple and to the point. Ninety-nine percent of the people can take it from there and get the job done if they know where they stand and what they must do.
2. Doing it regularly, even if there are no complaints and everyone is happy.
3. Requiring the supervisor (even if it's you) to be the best example of all workers, in looks, attitude, production, and enthusiasm.

We use a simple hour card and our employees keep their own time (example on page 98). They fill it out, sign it, and submit it at the end of the pay period, or a supervisor can do it every night with them.

There are instructions on the card, and it acts as a legal record of the location, time and amount of the work. As a rule, if you check them from time to time, and they know you do, they will be honest. In some big plants where we have as many as thirty or more employees, we use a standard time clock.

## PAYDAY

Don't forget, payday is the big reason most of these people are working, so be prompt and accurate. Paydays cost money, so pay once a month if it's legal in your state. You might have to go to twice a month. Avoid weekly payrolls; payroll days are hectic, cost lots of office time, and it puts a real pressure on cash flow. You get

# YOU MUST READ FIRST

Please fill out time card completely. They must be signed by employee and supervisor before processing. Time cards must be in the office by the 15th and 30th of each month. Employees are responsible for their own time cards. All overtime prior to working must be approved by manager. Late time cards will be held and processed in the next pay period.

NAME OF BUILDING _____

MONTH _____

NAME _____

ADDRESS _____

CITY _____ STATE _____

ZIP _____ PHONE _____

SOCIAL SECURITY NUMBER _____

"I CERTIFY THAT THIS RECORD WHICH HAS BEEN MAINTAINED BY ME IS COMPLETE AND ACCURATE. I FURTHER ACKNOWLEDGE THAT I WAS GIVEN AN OPPORTUNITY TO MAKE CORRECTIONS."

_____
EMPLOYEE SIGNATURE          DATE

**Do Not Write in This Space**

EMPLOYEE NO. _____

| BLDG | HOURS | O.T. | RATE | TOTAL |
|------|-------|------|------|-------|
|      |       |      |      |       |
|      |       |      |      |       |
|      |       |      |      |       |
|      |       |      |      |       |
|      |       |      |      |       |
|      |       |      |      |       |

MILEAGE _____ OTHER _____

_____
SUPERVISOR

| DAY | DATE | NAME OF BUILDING BLDG. # | NAME OF BUILDING BLDG. # | NAME OF BUILDING BLDG. # | NAME OF BUILDING BLDG. # | NAME OF BUILDING BLDG. # | TOTAL |
|-----|------|------|------|------|------|------|------|
| M |  |  |  |  |  |  |  |
| T |  |  |  |  |  |  |  |
| W |  |  |  |  |  |  |  |
| TH |  |  |  |  |  |  |  |
| FRI |  |  |  |  |  |  |  |
| SAT |  |  |  |  |  |  |  |
| SUN |  |  |  |  |  |  |  |
| TOTAL |  |  |  |  |  |  |  |
| M |  |  |  |  |  |  |  |
| T |  |  |  |  |  |  |  |
| W |  |  |  |  |  |  |  |
| TH |  |  |  |  |  |  |  |
| FRI |  |  |  |  |  |  |  |
| SAT |  |  |  |  |  |  |  |
| SUN |  |  |  |  |  |  |  |
| TOTAL |  |  |  |  |  |  |  |
| M |  |  |  |  |  |  |  |
| T |  |  |  |  |  |  |  |
| W |  |  |  |  |  |  |  |
| TH |  |  |  |  |  |  |  |
| FRI |  |  |  |  |  |  |  |
| SAT |  |  |  |  |  |  |  |
| SUN |  |  |  |  |  |  |  |
| TOTAL |  |  |  |  |  |  |  |
| M |  |  |  |  |  |  |  |
| T |  |  |  |  |  |  |  |
| W |  |  |  |  |  |  |  |
| TH |  |  |  |  |  |  |  |
| FRI |  |  |  |  |  |  |  |
| SAT |  |  |  |  |  |  |  |
| SUN |  |  |  |  |  |  |  |
| TOTAL |  |  |  |  |  |  |  |
| M |  |  |  |  |  |  |  |
| T |  |  |  |  |  |  |  |
| W |  |  |  |  |  |  |  |
| TH |  |  |  |  |  |  |  |
| FRI |  |  |  |  |  |  |  |
| SAT |  |  |  |  |  |  |  |
| SUN |  |  |  |  |  |  |  |
| TOTAL |  |  |  |  |  |  |  |
| M |  |  |  |  |  |  |  |
| T |  |  |  |  |  |  |  |
| W |  |  |  |  |  |  |  |
| REG. HOURS |  |  |  |  |  |  |  |
| O.T. HOURS |  |  |  |  |  |  |  |
| TOTAL HOURS WORKED |  |  |  |  |  |  |  |

paid at the end of the month from most accounts, so when you pay mid-month, it's with your own money.

## ADVANCES

Don't give employees advances. They'll get addicted to your pre-payroll cash injection and it will cause all sorts of problems: irregular bookkeeping entries, employees showing up at odd emergency hours, etc., and they'll eventually hate you for it when you turn them down, which someday you will have to do. And the problem will escalate until they're asking for advances bigger than the earnings they have coming.

Most of the forms and outlines I've used as examples and illustrations are the ones we use. I've seen lots of companies' forms and think they are overly complicated — they tend to bury you in the office and paperwork. You can come up with an adaptation of mine or others' forms to fit you, but please keep it simple. Have the necessities; leave out all the cute, puffy stuff.

## PART TIME OR FULL TIME?

Eight full hours of cleaning is not very stimulating for an active, hustling individual. Cleaning is somewhat boring after you've been doing it for for five or six hours, especially late at night. A person working four hours with hustle can generally do almost as much work as they would do in eight. After the first few hours of working, cleaning people really lose their zip, and it saps their attitude, too. Schools and governments are full of cleaners stretching two hours of work into an eight-hour day. Part-time people can be of high quality, have their own insurance and benefits somewhere else, and often don't even want to take breaks. Many of our moonlighters do office work all day, and they use their part-time cleaning jobs as a welcome opportunity for physical activity. They come to us physically fresh and eager, hustle through their work, and go home happy. Part-time workers are generally wage-earners who are using the job for supplementary income. They want to buy a boat or pay for a family vacation. Also, having full-time workers usually means benefit programs, such as Health Insurance and Retirement, which cost you extra money, programs that moonlighters have at their regular jobs. Trying to support a family, make house payments, car payments, etc., on a full-time janitor's wage is rough. You will almost always get higher quality people and achieve better production levels with part-time moonlighters.

## NON-COMPETITION CLAUSE

It will be a bleak day for you when you open up the paper and see a competitor's ad for cleaning, and the new operator is one of your best, and most trusted, loyal employees. It happens to all of us and it will to you. The one you were going to ordain a manager someday comes in this morning to tell you he's resigning his position with you. This is not at all uncommon; where do you think all the cleaning companies come from? At least a third of you reading this book are thinking about leaving your present cleaning job and going into your own business. Can we expect our own workers not to want what we want someday? Nope! People have the right to go into their own business, open their own store, buy their own backhoes or buffers, and be our competitors, and they will! I've lost numerous good people who have gone on their own, but all of them are still my friends, too. The catch here is that indeed people do have the right to leave you and develop their own thing, but they don't have the right to take your customers or your trade secrets.

They've been grooming themselves while working for you. After all, they have all the information on your prices, they know all your accounts, etc., and they in fact are in a good position to step in and steal it all. You could almost say they have a key to your safe, because your basic business is out there in the accounts, in your reputation and good will. Believe it or not, I've even had my own supervisor use my stationery to bid against me and submit the bid on the day I gave him a bonus check for loyalty. If you are going to go, be upfront about it, and don't steal accounts. If you do, you are a thief and a person who can't be trusted, and word will get around. Customers and clients are also business people and they will hate your guts for your dumping on another business person. We business people are pretty loyal to each other.

To prevent or deter this from happening, have each employee sign a non-competition clause when you hire him or her. This is a simple agreement that protects your interests and territory. Basically, it's an agreement between you and the employee that he or she won't go into business against you for a period of one year and within fifty miles of your operation. Have this form OK'd by your attorney, because states have different regulations about this sort of thing. People will always sign them the day they come to work for you, because they usually have no interest in leaving you then, but it may be hard to get later on. If they decide to leave, you have no right to keep them from making a living in the work they know best, but can keep them from competing with you unfairly. Get your noncompete form legally checked out and go down to the instant press and run off $5.00 worth of them and get them signed and in the file. Even as Chairman of the Board and major stockholder of my company, I've signed one. It would be unfair if, in my position, I got a real deal with you to start a business personally in one of my company's areas. It would hurt the other stockholders, so I have a non-comp agreement that I won't do it.

## EMPLOYEES' PERSONAL PROBLEMS

In the cleaning business, you're going to get your share of employees with personal problems. None of us like to see people down and out, unhappy or depressed from home or life problems, and we often think we're helping by giving them advances in pay, or listening to their woes for hours. Sometimes we even end up getting involved in their personal lives. Helping people is our responsibility in this life, but there is a lot of difference between helping and doing, and you can get in too deep. When you refuse them an advance, (they already owe you for four previous advances), they'll stomp off and call you an SOB, and all the time you were sacrificing, going without personally, to help them. People have to solve their own problems, and too often when we try to be guide, God, protector, and preserver of them, we don't allow them or force them to face their own problems, and thus we actually weaken them. There is a fine line between help and hurt. Be careful, or you'll be used as a full-time counselor, and welfare source. You especially want to stay out of people's marriage problems. Your job is to clean floors! Too often your compassion for a fragile employee will

evolve to passion and then everyone's in trouble and the business is down the drain. It happens thousands of times a day in this business, so don't fool yourself. Set standards and keep the rules yourself and make your employees do the same. Even close friends and relatives, husbands, wives and children should keep the rules.

## STEALING: A RED FLAG FOR FAILURE

Most of the people you hire will be honest, maybe only one in a thousand a thief, but to your customers finding that one in a thousand in their building will mean throwing that contract away. Every contractor eventually ends up with at least one bad apple who thinks being a cleaner is being a gleaner (supplemental income, you understand). Client trust is more important than quality, price, and all the P.R. in the world. This is something you'll have to face and control in your cleaning business. Stealing is a costly problem. A missing $2 item may cost you $200 or even $2000 to replace in terms of time and lost trust. Society thinks poor, uneducated, low-end employees — like us janitors — always do the stealing. A ready-made scapegoat and it's really no big deal if it costs them their job. The truth is, the white collar boys we work with are often caught with their hands in the cookie jar, too, but are seldom prosecuted. Like it or not, being a janitor means coming under suspicion when things turn up missing. We have access to all of the keys, we work in the building when no one else is around, and the opportunity is certainly there. It's no big mystery why building owners and tenants tend to suspect us first. About all you can do is carefully screen prospective employees to weed out the bad apples, make sure you have crews you can trust, and then support your people and stick up for them when someone points an accusing finger. In my experience, people almost always suspect and accuse the janitor first, but a careful investigation will clear the janitors of blame in most cases. Be sure you demand a full investigation before you jump to conclusions. The client will always be hot to have you fire the poor janitor, but I refuse to let someone go unless I have a criminal conviction or reasonable proof of guilt. If the client is adamant, you can always move the cleaner to another job location.

## SUPERVISORS

For some reason, office jockeys always want to execute around and make a long precise list of perfect assignment schedules. Personally, I expect a supervisor to work his tail off. I think it's useless to walk around with a clipboard, humming and looking under the lips of sinks for fingerprints. **This business can't afford dead weight!** If you're a supervisor, it means you're capable of more responsibility and get a little more pay, but you should do as much or more work than the crew. Everyone has this idealistic picture of supervisors as being off the firing line, people who just drift and snoop and coach. Bull! A supervisor should have hot shoes, a wrinkled brow, be a good P.R. person, and be able to get his work done faster than the rest. The same is true of most managers in this business; they don't ride around in a pickup in a white shirt, clearing their throats and dropping off paychecks and supplies. Just like you when you start your business, a manager should be on the job whenever possible. You don't make money and get accounts and beat your competitors sitting in an office shuffling papers and making analysis charts. You win by doing a job neater, faster, and more efficiently.

## SUB-CONTRACTING

Somewhere in the beginning, after we pay a bunch of payroll taxes, we hear of the wisdom of sub-contracting some of our work out to other contractors, or better still, to our employees. Say one of them is faster than the others and wants to make a little more money, so we say, "Hey Morgan, see that $600-a-month branch over there? I'll contract that to you for $400 instead of by the hourly rate." Morgan eats that up, because he and his wife are fast, and they can clean it in two hours and average $10 per hour instead of $5.00, their usual pay. Plus there's no payroll tax, unemployment insurance, or other deductions. Lots of contractors figure that out fast and do it, thinking they are fooling the world. When you get caught, and you will in time, maybe a month, maybe a year, or maybe five years, **you'll regret it!** They **will** get you ("they" in this case is your insurance company and the government).

And what if Morgan's butane buffer blows up one night and burns the bank down? Three million dollars lost and the employee goes with it. When you try to put in a claim to your insurance or to Workman's Comp, they will look through their records of premiums you were paying on Morgan and there is none. Does Morgan have business insurance or an IRS number? Nope! Was he a legitimate contractor? Nope! So you'd better hit your petty cash for the three million bucks! Then, there's the federal government to deal with, who thinks you should have been paying FICA and Withholding on Morgan for all those years.

Just in case that didn't convince you, let me give you another, better one. In another bank across town, you have Herkem and Betty Slowgoer cleaning for $5.00 an hour, and they get wind that Morgan is averaging $10. If they scream to the labor board, the board will make you give the Slowgoers equal pay ($10, as Morgan was averaging). You'll explain the deal, that Morgan is faster and does get paid more because he does more work in an hour. But equal pay is the law. You'll have to go back five years and reimburse the Slowgoers, which will undoubtedly put you out of business or in debtor's prison.

Any legitimate work you sub-contract, like outside windows you can't reach, you'd better sub to a licensed and insured bonafide contractor, and do it right. Sub-contracting is smart in some cases.

See the Sample Employment Contract that follows and the forms section in the back of the book for samples of the employment forms I use, including employee application, employment contract, evaluation, etc.

# Managerial Evaluation

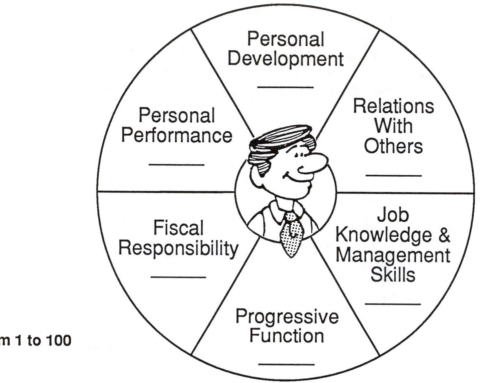

**Rate from 1 to 100**

**Personal Development** means individual growth and progress, the effort you make to improve yourself through educational opportunities, personal study, and other resources.

**Relationships with Others** indicates how you get along with other people, including co-workers, customers, and business associates.

**Job Knowledge and Management Skills** assesses your understanding of maintenance technology, company practices and procedures, managerial skills, and other information necessary to the successful operation of your assigned area.

**Progressive Function** rates your ability to build and expand upon a given assignment, your ability to make creative or innovative contributions and maintain an overall progressive attitude.

**Fiscal Responsibility** indicates you overall understanding and performance in financial planning, cost control, accounting systems, profit and loss, and related financial matters.

**Personal Performance** is an assessment of your personal performance as a manager in keeping your own life and your business operation in order and harmony, and also rates your use of time, ability to plan, responsiveness, etc.

# Employment Contract

THIS AGREEMENT made and entered into the date and place hereinbelow identified, by and between VARSITY CONTRACTORS, INC. (hereinafter the "Company"), an Idaho corporation, and _____John Janitor_____ _____ (hereinafter "Employee").

## Introduction

The Company is engaged in the business of providing janitorial maintenance and related services, especially to large enterprises. Company desires to employ Employee for the period specified herein in accordance with the terms and conditions hereof and Employee desires to be so employed.

NOW, THEREFORE, IN CONSIDERATION OF THE MUTUAL PROMISES CONTAINED HEREIN, COMPANY AND EMPLOYEE AGREE AS FOLLOWS:

1.    **Retention of Employee.** Company hereby employs Employee to perform the duties hereinafter set forth and Employee hereby accepts said employment and agrees to perform said duties during the term of this agreement.

2.    **Duties.** Employee agrees to perform whatever duties may be required of him by the Company, including, but not necessarily limited to, the following:

Area Manager of Centerville Area #3

Job Description per Policy & Procedure Manual Pg. 4.05

and to otherwise assist in the successful operation of the Company's business as it is now or may hereafter be constituted. Employee shall discharge such specific responsibilities as the Company shall from time to time assign to him.

3.    **Term.** The term of employment under this contract shall commence _Feb. 1_, 19_86_, and shall continue thereafter until December 31 of the same year, and shall be renewed automatically each calendar year until terminated under the provisions of this contract.

4.    **Compensation.** Company agrees to pay Employee for all services rendered pursuant to the provisions of this Contract, and the Employee agrees to accept as full compensation, a salary of $_2,000_, per _month_, to be paid [(1) during the first week of each month] or [(2) in semimonthly installments] for the previous month's service. Said salary shall be reviewed at regular intervals by the Company and may be increased as the Company may direct.

Payment of salary is contingent upon Employee filing with the Company such report forms as the Company may direct, documenting Employee's activities for the week.

5.    **Exclusive Service.** Employee promises to work [(1) exclusively] or [(2) part time] for the Company during the term of this contract and to devote his entire time, attention and energies during his working hours to the business of the Company, and shall not be connected with or have any interest in any business similar to or competitive with that of the Company.

6.    **Incentive Compensation.** As additional compensation provided as an incentive for Employee to excel in his assigned duties, Company promises to pay Employee a portion of the Company's profits according to the following plan:

Management Profit-Sharing Plan per Policy & Procedure Manual pg. 5.19

7.    **Fringe Benefits.** The Employee shall be entitled to participate in the following fringe benefit programs of the Company:

Profit-Sharing Retirement Fund

Group Health & Life Plan

8. **Vacation and Sick Leave.** After one year's continuous Employment, the Employee shall be entitled each year to a vacation of __1__ weeks, during which time his compensation shall be paid in full. After several years employment with the Company, this agreement may be renegotiated to increase the amount of vacation time. In no case does vacation time accumulate beyond one (1) year.

9. Restrictive Covenants.

9.1 **Confidential Information.** The Employee acknowledges that Company possesses certain proprietary information including but not limited to customer lists, service or personnel requirements, pricing of services or contracts, Company procedures, methods and processes; Company financial position or activities; and other privileged information. Employee promises that he will not at any time or in any direct or indirect manner divulge or communicate to any person, firm, or corporation any proprietary matters relating to the business of Company, Employee and Company stipulating that as between them, such information is important and gravely affects the successful conduct of Company's business and goodwill, and that any breach of the terms of this section shall be a material breach of this Agreement.

9.2 **Noncompetition.** The parties recognize that Employee will perform services of a unique, unusual and extraordinary character by reason of his training and abilities. Employee therefore agrees that he will not, either during the term of this agreement or for a period of one (1) year thereafter, engage directly or indirectly for himself or as a representative or employee of others, in the janitorial maintenance business or other business activity which is in competition with that of the Company, within an area of fifty (50) miles of Employee's principal place of business under this contract. Employee further agrees that he will not, during such period, directly or indirectly, for himself or for any other employer, solicit or divert or attempt to solicit or attempt to divert the patronage of any Company customers.

9.3 **Remedies.** In the event of a breach or threatened breach by the Employee of the provisions of this section, Company shall be entitled to an injunction restraining Employee from any breach by whole or in part, of the provisions of this section. Nothing herein shall be construed as prohibiting Company from pursuing any other remedies available to it for such breach or threatened breach, including the recovery of damages from the employee.

10. **Termination.** The term of Employee's employment as set forth herein at Section 3 shall be subject to the Following:

(a) Without cause, either party may terminate this agreement at any time upon giving thirty (30) days' written notice to the other party, and in that event, Company shall be under no obligation to Employee except to pay such compensation as Employee may be entitled to receive up to the date of termination.

(b) Company reserves the right to terminate this agreement without advance notice for gross insubordination, repeated drunkeness, addiction, theft or embezzlement, fraud, disclosing of confidential or private Company information, aiding a competitor of the Company, violation by Employee of any of the provisions of this agreement, or failure or refusal to perform the services referred to herein.

(c) Company shall be entitled to terminate this agreement in the event Employee dies or is permanently disabled from substantially performing his duty as assigned, in which event Employee shall be entitled to receive his salary computed to __30__ days after termination and such other Employee benefits under the plans of the Company to which Employee is properly entitled only to the date of termination.

(d) Company shall be entitled to terminate this agreement in the event Employee is temporarily disabled (whether by one or a series of events) so that he is unable to perform his duties during sixty (60) business days (whether or not consecutive) during any period of six calendar months.

11. **Assignment.**

(a) By the Company. This agreement shall be binding upon and shall insure to the benefit of the transferees, successors and assigns of the Company.

(b) By Employee. Because this agreement is based upon the unique abilities and personal confidence in Employee, he shall have no right to assign this agreement or any of his right hereunder without the prior written consent of the Company.

12. **Waiver.** A waiver of any term hereof shall not be construed as a general waiver by the Company, and the Company shall be free to reinstate any such term or condition without notice to Employee.

13.    **Company Policies.** Employee hereby acknowledges receipt of a company EMPLOYEE'S HANDBOOK which contains policies and guidelines for all levels of employees. Employee agrees to abide by said policies personally and to direct their compliance by employees under his supervision. Special note should be taken of the sections titled "Code of Conduct,' "Safety," and "Security," in this regard. Employee further agrees to abide by and enforce company policies contained in the company Policies and Procedures Manual, which may be added to or deleted from time to time. Employee agrees to take a lie detector test when and if requested to do so by the Company to verify the compliance of Employee with the terms of the above named policies. Employee further understands and agrees that his failure to pass said lie detector test or refusal to take said lie detector test may result in his immediate termination under this Employment Contract.

14.    **Severability.** The provisions of this contract are subject to compliance with state and federal laws and regulations governing such employment where applicable. The finding of any court of law that any portion of this contract is void or inoperable as a matter of law or equity shall have no effect as to the remaining parts and provisions of this contract.

15.    **Attorney's Fees.** In the event of any breach of this contract, the defaulting party shall pay any and all costs incurred by the other party for a reasonable attorney's fee or for arbitration in settling the claim or a controversy.

16.    **Integration.** This instrument contains the entire understanding of the parties with respect to the subject matter hereof. It may be amended or cancelled only by a written instrument signed by the party against whom enforcement of such amendment or cancellation is sought.

17.    **Prior Contracts.** This agreement voids any prior contracts between Employee and Company.

IN WITNESS WHEREOF, Employee has executed this agreement and Company has caused this agreement to be executed by a duly authorized employment officer, this __1st__ day of __Feb.__, 19_86_, in the city of _____Centerville_____, state of _____Bliss_____.


_____
                    Employee

VARSITY CONTRACTORS, INC.


By _____
      Duly Authorized Employment Officer

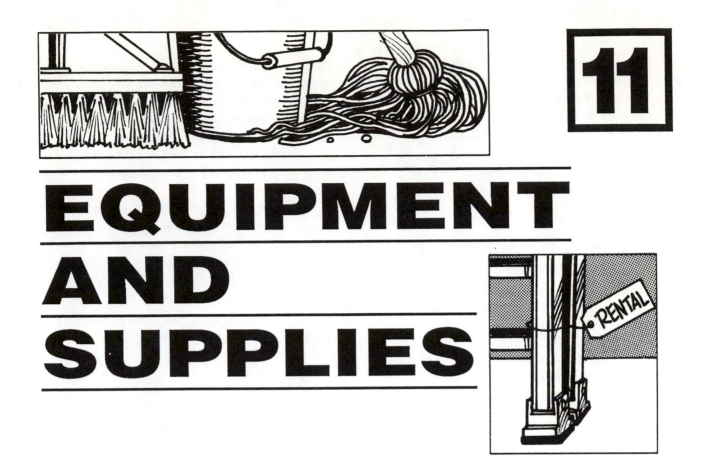

# EQUIPMENT AND SUPPLIES

## 11

This is the "Christmas morning" for most people going into the cleaning business. We just can't wait to get our hands on all that new shining commercial and industrial equipment that does everything faster and better. The machines, the tools and the cleaners — **wow!** Remember what Christmas always does to us? We overspend! It's so easy to let your imagination go wild and buy all sorts of stuff, and those suppliers are good guys and know their stuff, but believe me, they'll let you purchase all the supplies and equipment you want and even string out the payments so you can be sure to be able to get it **now.** Slow down, back off, and be reasonable. First, don't buy anything until you need it. Why get a big parking lot sweeper when you have no parking lots? Why get a 40-foot ladder until you get some 40-foot windows to clean? If you happen to not get many 40-foot windows in the first couple of years, then a $300 fiberglass 40-foot ladder isn't very smart to own. Go rent one each time you do need it for $10 and you'll be ahead of the game. I suggested earlier that you watch the newspaper for used equipment and supplies. People in trouble or moving or going out of business are

selling, and you should do this a few months before you actually go into business.

## OVERBUYING

In fact, if you're real crafty, you'll do your best to get the customer to furnish all the supplies. Many of them are happy to, and it makes your total bill for the service look cheaper and more competitive. I was doing a contract for $1,200 a month once and the company was happy. They were furnishing the supplies. A new manager came in and didn't want to ding around with supplies and equipment, and so asked us on the next bid to include them. This meant providing things like lights, paper, cleaning compounds, snow melting chemicals, and fertilizer for the lawn, which came to over $500 a month. So our next year's bid was $1,700 (the $1,200 plus the new $500, and we weren't making anything on the supplies, either). About halfway through the year the head of the company noticed our bill for cleaning was higher and hit the ceiling. He ranted and raved and ordered us fired for raising the price, even though we explained it was the supplies inflating the cost, that he was paying the same as before, only in a different set of checks. It didn't dent his thick head, the only thing that came across to him was the fact that the price was higher. Not everyone in a high place has a matching I.Q.

## USE OF SUPPLIES

Wasted, unnecessary, or lost supplies are an expense to watch. Your time shopping and looking around and listening to salesmen is also a time to watch. There are millions of salesmen zipping across our country. Their goal is to sell you stuff, and they will oversell if you let them. They'll drop off a case of expensive baseboard cleaner that will take you a year to use up. I'm not criticizing the salesmen and their suppliers, they can and will be your best friends, they know the business and they'll help you learn it — it's **your greed** for too much, too soon that I'm cautioning you about.

You especially want to be sure you train your people to dilute chemicals properly and to conserve supplies. Lock up all supplies and keep good inventory records to discourage pilferage. An unlocked janitor closet is an open invitation for you to supply toilet paper and garbage can liners to every tenant in the building.

## LOCAL BUSINESSES

Do business with local people as much as you can. The out-of-towners might be as good and even a little cheaper, but there's more than comradeship to keeping the dollar in your own city. Someday when you need help or supplies in the middle of the night, and those long-distance boys can't deliver, you may lose an account. My wife always questioned my buying gas at the station right next door to the office instead of going down the street and getting it at a self-serve place. The place next door always checked my oil, etc. One day the motor of her brand new car burned out because it was out of oil — she'd forgotten to check it. **Good service is cheap in the long run.**

## QUALITY

Good service is more important than saving 5% on a gross of something. Ninety percent of your operating expenses are labor and overhead.

Most cleaning companies' supplies and equipment run only 5–6%! I've done business with lots of suppliers who are 10% or even 20% higher in cost than others, but their products are superior and their contributions to my business are a plus.

Payroll is almost 60–70% of your operating expense. You're a lot further ahead to pay $10 for a gallon of wax than $4 for a cheap brand, if the good one lasts longer and performs better to cut your labor costs. In janitorial equipment and supplies as well as in most things, you generally get what you pay for. Go the few bucks extra to get the good stuff. Don't be caught wasting $50 in labor while your crews thrash around trying to get good results from an inferior wax you saved $6 on.

## SERVICE

Remember your smart friends of yesteryear who bought cute little foreign cars that got forty miles to the gallon? It grated on your old Chevy and Ford nerves for a while, until they broke down. The parts had to come from Bangladesh, and when they did get there at an arm-and-leg price, no one knew how to install them.

Likewise, I see some real cute little vacuums and miracle floor machines from all kinds of exotic locales and all kinds of experimental models of stuff that come in, and it scares me to death, yet dozens of people buy a gross of them immediately. There isn't a lot of difference between most cleaners, waxers or other machines, but nothing is as important as being able to get the repair done when you're in down time. Losing your Sukahama sake-powered buffer one night when you have two big supermarkets to clean could be a real disaster. If you are solid with a good supplier and a piece of standard equipment goes down, they'll generally have another one for you, often at no charge. You can't beat good service and it's worth paying extra bucks for.

For breakage or non-performance you should have 24-hour service, for either repair or replacement. Warranties and five-year guarantees are useless if it takes six months to get service and satisfaction Speaking of breaking down, be sure to follow the manufacturer's recommendations for preventive maintenance on all of your machinery, to avoid costly down time. Preventive maintenance pays!

## SOURCES FOR BUYING EQUIPMENT

In most cases, I buy. Leasing has some short-term cash flow and deduction benefits, but in the long run it washes out, and owning and caring for your own is the best way to go. When I need something big fast and haven't the cash for it, we lease, but when I do this the object is to keep the reserve cash. Remember, they make money on the leasing of cars, for example, and you'd just as well make it yourself.

Before you get into business, and depending on how many areas of service you offer, go to some suppliers and pick up brochures, or mail off inquiries to the sources I've listed in Chapter 15 and read up on the equipment that fits you. If you happen to be going into window cleaning only, $80 worth of stuff can get you going. If carpets are your goal, then you might need to go big money and buy or lease an $8,000 truck-mounted unit. It isn't real difficult to figure it out. This may be hard for you to believe, because of all the mystery and hype for the big equipment and all the different brands of chemical supplies, but, no matter what it is, directions and instructions for the use of everything should come right along with it. Salesmen will do your first on-the-job demo if you ask. There are books, manuals, and lots of experienced people to show you. For that matter, many of you reading this have already used the equipment and know exactly what you want.

Bear in mind that things can change fast. Ten expensive machines once bought from one of the biggest suppliers in the world were obsolete and useless in one year, and I ended up junking them. Again, ask around, call your competitors (if you keep calling your competitor he might start liking you and might even pass some extra work your way), visit the janitorial supply houses and trade shows to keep current.

## DOWN TIME COSTS

When it come to supplies and equipment, remember that the well-established "big" company generally puts out good products, but they aren't infallible, and it's that fact that contains the real cost factor of supplies and equipment. I've bought and used many hundreds of machines from the best and the biggest companies. During one year we replaced gears in 80% of the floor machines we bought from one of the leading manufacturers. In one phone office in the South, three of six new 22″ deluxe floor polisher machines had faulty micro switches and grease leaks. When a machine or chemical doesn't work or isn't there when you need it, this is where you really pay, because you're paying for:

1. Six janitors (drawing pay) wandering around hunting for parts.
2. Two janitors standing by while one tries to fix a broken machine.
3. The grease leakage that ruins the rug because there were no plastic bags handy.
4. The cheap cord plug that gets yanked off, so the janitor seeks one for an hour, then goes to a helpful maintenance man; he hunts for one, then has to replace it for the janitor.
5. Re-doing the floors with a four-man stripping crew after the wax powdered because it was frozen in shipment.
6. This list could go on and on and on with many dozen more examples.

## INVENTORY CONTROL

Having supplies when and where you need them without lengthy delays is critical. Order enough supplies so your crews always have what they need, and don't have to "juggle" supplies or do without. Don't go overboard, though, and lay in a year's supply. You don't want to have all of your working capital tied up in supplies inventory. This is one of those little balancing acts that separate the good managers from the crowd. And by the way, mark everything you own, even if it's just with a stencil of your company name and a can of spray paint. When others "borrow" your ladder, your name on it helps them remember where to return it. Keep a list of all your equipment with serial numbers and locations assigned to, and do a physical inventory of it once a year.

## STANDARDIZATION

Standardization is using the same supplies and equipment throughout the servicing area. All-purpose cleaners, for example, come in green, red, blue, pink, and neutral, as do strippers, disinfectants, window cleaners, and some deli-mers. Smelling, tasting, dipping fingers, and trial and error is an inefficient (as well as dangerous) way for determining what is what. Machines with parts, tanks, brushes, etc., that can interchange and provide replacement parts for each other are great, and so is having all your all-purpose cleaner blue, your stripper red, your window cleaners green, and your shampoo neutral.

**Remember: You already have 80% of the knowledge and sense you need to run a business, just use your head.**

# OFFICE AND OVERHEAD

## 12

It's kind of a prestigious pastime. After all, who has the nerve to question you when you have to "go to the office" or "work late in the office." In our society, the **office** has held a fine aura of authority (and unaccountability). Everyone has always wanted his own **office**. A big desk, an impressive row of books, maybe a tiger skin or two on the floor or wall, and a ship in a bottle right beside the desk blotter. An office will become necessary as a communications center, and a softer workbench of your business operation, as you grow. But opening an office too soon is like letting the fox inside the chicken coop; you better watch out. An office is generally your first introduction to the magic word **overhead.** Once the office is established as your base, you have to serve it just as you serve your customers. The basic and ultimate caution of overhead is simple — namely, you may gradually need to support and serve it even more than you do your customers. It happens to almost all businesses, but some do manage to survive the bureaucracy, all that government and political overhead. I promise you that not long after coming down with "office-itis," you'll have your bout of overhead.

Look at the drawing on the next page for one hour, then hang it up in front of you for several days — or forever — it'll teach you a business overhead principle that four years of business college won't teach you.

Overhead starts with office rent (which you have to pay whether you're there or not), lights, heat, phones, office machines, water coolers, alarm service, chamber of commerce dues, garbage pickup, satellite TV, parking permits, taxes, solicited donations, and thirty more items. Then there's staff: first a secretary, and next a bookkeeper lurketh in the corner. Soon, with two people in the office, you need an office manager to administer their quarrels, and then a clerk to do everyone's menial work. It's gradual, but suddenly you realize your **overhead** is $5,000 per month, which means it takes days of working to just pay for the machine that supports your operation. Then the real killer comes, the day you begin to work less on the job and more in the office. Now you're really into **big-time overhead!** There's a lot of appearance and facade in an office, kind of an ego trip, a pre-casket for those dying in the business, or at least getting

# THE EVOLUTION OF BUSINESS

**ONCE IN THE BEGINNING . . .**

YOU HAD ONE PERSON TO HELP IN THE OFFICE TO TAKE CARE OF THE END OF THE YEAR TRANSACTIONS.

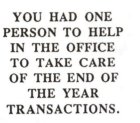

## GROWING . . .

## TODAY . . .

rigor mortis. **Don't get office-itis!** Make it a goal to spend as little time as possible in "the office" and keep your costs down.

## AN OFFICE AT HOME

There admittedly isn't much prestige when someone says, "Henry, where's the office for your new cleaning business?" Your eyes fall and you say, "I work out of my home." They say "Oh well," and kick dirt with their feet. Live with it! An office costs lots of money and it isn't worth days of slaving with your head in a toilet bowl away from your family to maintain a plush office. No account ever comes to the office anyway. You go to the place of business. Employees might need to come to your home for job interviews, or if you wish, you can arrange a meeting place at the building they will work in. When you need and can really use one, then get a small office. When you get one, don't go wild with decor and furnishings and decorations. Keep it in the cleaning field. Hang some pictures of accounts and employees, and some of the better complimentary letters you've received. Buy used equipment when you can, and keep it simple.

For my first five years (and my operation was a good size) I worked out of my home, and it was a superb experience! Later while I was still a student, I had an enormous garage/shop complex connected to the house. One monthly mortgage payment covered my house, office, supply storage, and repair shop. It sure was nice, in fact it was the best deal I ever had. Everything was there. I could get lots more done because I could work and still play with the kids, have fun and be involved with my family. If your family can handle the books and calls for a while, do that too.

When things start to get heavy, the first employee in the office should be a competent secretary. She or he shouldn't be just a typist, either. Nothing is worse than getting a dingy, primping secretary on the phone preoccupied with personal calls and problems. A good secretary is almost as important as you are. They can take calls and handle problems, set things up and free you from administrative details. Remember, that's your goal: to get free of twinky administrative work and get out and keep out in the field, **hustling work,** and **bidding,** and **doing jobs.** You should never be the errand boy running to the bank, getting things signed, picking up parts and mail. One secretary worth his or her salt can handle a business grossing up to $25,000 a month easily, and keep the books and do all the other miscellaneous stuff.

Don't ever allow your secretary to read books or do personal things on the job. During the slow times, have her call accounts to get work, organize and update records, even do your personal stuff, but don't let her do her personal stuff, ever. Notice that I'm saying "her": whether you're a man or woman running your own business, I'll tell you that in thirty years of running numerous offices, my experience is that women are faster, neater, more loyal, less cry-babyish; they inject cheerfulness and they're just plain better!

## OFFICE HOURS

Yes, I know you have a personal life, but keep yourself available. Come early and work late. Because your business is yours you will actually enjoy it. Be around on Saturday, too — that's the best cleaning day of the week. Be in at 7:00 A.M. and still cheerful when the phone rings at your bedside at 11:00 o'clock at night. Never be out to lunch. If your office is open for the day, be open. When I call someplace to give them a job, my business, my money — and I get "I'm sorry Mr. Aslett, everyone is out to lunch," I'm thinking "Man, I want them now." Remember, the good, sharp big wheels who handle the good jobs and the big accounts will often call off hours because **they** work off hours.

## ANSWERING SERVICE

There are few things I actually hate in this world, but an answering service is one of them. I even like the machines better than the answering services and I hate the machines. You call to get Mr. Hansen, and some operator answers the phone trying to fake you out that it's actually Mr. Hansen's office. You start asking questions and giving messages and they rudely interrupt you: "We are just the answering service. We'll give him your number and have him call." When people call, most of them would rather get no one than someone who, while talking to you, has to jump to another line and put you on hold.

## THE BOOKS

I can't give you a course here on bookkeeping and accounting, but let me try to steer you in a few helpful directions. When you first start out, you won't need a lot of fancy bookkeeping. Just get a local CPA or bookkeeping service who is reasonable in price to help you get set up. The "write-once" pegboard systems work pretty good, or use some other system. The important thing is to simply have an organized way to keep track of the data you'll need to keep control of your business. Basically, these are: Receivables (money owed to you) and Payables (money you owe others). You will need a form on which to invoice customers, and a filing system to keep track of invoices billed out, and when they're paid. It's best to be on a cash accounting basis when you first start out (as opposed to an accrual system). This means you just write out a check to pay your bills at the end of the month, and the amount you wrote the check for becomes an Expense. By knowing your Income and Expenses, you can work up a little Profit-and-Loss Statement, so you know whether you're making money or not. A simple Profit-and-Loss (or Income Statement) would look something like the table on this page.

When your books are simple, you can keep track of everything yourself, and crank out your own income statement monthly, or whenever you want. Your CPA should help you figure year-end totals, depreciation, and your taxes. Get his input for tax planning, too, as your business grows. There are things you can do through your business that benefit you personally and help you save personal income tax. As your business grows, you may want to have the CPA or bookkeeping service do your financial statements for you. This is easy. They will help you develop a chart of accounts, which assigns each income and expense item a number code. For instance, Vehicle Expense might be 625. Then, if you write a check for gas, you just write "625" on the check. At the end of the month, you give the bookkeeper your income figures and a copy of all your checks, and he or she whips out the reports on their computer. Don't let anyone talk you into overly-detailed reports and charts of accounts, though — you don't need it. Keep your system simple, and you will find it a lot easier to use.

|  | Amount | (%) |
|---|---|---|
| **Income** |  |  |
| Contract Income | $ 8,000 | 80.0 |
| Extra Work Income | 2,000 | 20.0 |
| Total Income | $10,000 | 100.0 |
| **Direct Expenses** |  |  |
| Labor on the Job | 5,500 | 55.0 |
| Payroll Expenses | 800 | 8.0 |
| Equipment Expense | 200 | 2.0 |
| Vehicle on the Job | 300 | 3.0 |
| Materials & Supplies | 600 | 6.0 |
| Uniforms, Dust Mops | 200 | 2.0 |
| Total Direct Expense | $ 7,600 | 76.0 |
| **Indirect Expenses** |  |  |
| Administrative Wages | 500 | 5.0 |
| Administrative Payroll Expense | 100 | 1.0 |
| Administrative Vehicle | 200 | 2.0 |
| Travel & Entertainment | 100 | 1.0 |
| Interest Expense | - 0 - | 0.0 |
| Accounting & Legal | 100 | 1.0 |
| Advertising | - 0 - | 0.0 |
| Office | 100 | 1.0 |
| Telepone | 100 | 1.0 |
| Total Indirect Expense | $ 1,200 | 12.0 |
| **Total Expenses** | $ 8,800 | 88.0 |
| **Net Profit** (Loss) | $ 1,200 | 12.0 |

## RECORD-KEEPING

As you get set up, you will get instructions from a lot of government agencies on the records they require you to keep and reports you have to file. Some payroll records and hour cards have to be kept for three years, others for five, etc. You just need to set up a filing system that will organize these records and allow you to store them and retrieve them when you need to. One very important record you will want to keep, though, is not required by any agency — it's called a job sheet. Just as mechanics fill out a work order on every car they fix, you will want to keep a job sheet on all of your extra work jobs. This handy form shows the customer information, what you did, who worked on the job and all the costs involved, and how much profit you made on it (see sample on page 115). Next time a repeat customer calls, instead of running clear across town and spending $20 worth of time and gas to look at the job, you can just flip to the previous year's job sheet and say, "Oh, yes, Mrs. Winters, we can do your job for the same price as last

# Extra Work Job Sheet

ORDERED
BY: _____   BILL TO:_____

_____ DATE _____   _____

_____ PHONE _____   _____

| DESCRIPTION OF WORK COMPLETED | UNIT COST | COST |
|---|---|---|
| LOCATION | | |
| | | |
| | | |
| | | |
| | | |
| JOB SHEET No. _____ | | |

TOTAL BILLING

| DATE WORK COMPLETED | SIGNED: |
|---|---|

## EXTRA WORK JOB SHEET

| FOR OFFICE USE ONLY | | | | FOR FIELD USE | | NUMBER_____ |
|---|---|---|---|---|---|---|

| CHECKED BY | DATE | POSTED & BILLED BY | DATE | PAY COMMISSION TO | AMOUNT | TOTALS |
|---|---|---|---|---|---|---|
| | | | | | | |

TOTAL BILLING

| LABOR EXPENSE | RATE | •••••• DATE •••••• | | | | TOTAL HOURS | TOTAL COSTS |
|---|---|---|---|---|---|---|---|
| BOSS | | | | | | | |
| | | | | | | | |
| | | | | | | | |
| | | | | | | | |
| | | | | | | | |
| | | | | | | | |
| | | | | | | | |
| | | | | | | | |
| | | | | | | | |

OVERHEAD
(20% OF JOB COST)

TOTAL LABOR

| TOTAL LABOR EXPENSE | |
| PAYROLL EXPENSE 15% | |

PAYROLL EXPENSE 15%

GENERAL EXPENSES

| GENERAL EXPENSES | RATE | | | | | | |
|---|---|---|---|---|---|---|---|
| VEHICLE | .18/mi | | | | | | |
| PHONE | | | | | | | |
| EQUIP. RENTAL | | | | | | | |
| | | | | | | | |
| | | | | | | | |
| SOAP & CLEANERS | | | | | | | |
| WAXES & FINISHES | | | | | | | |
| TOWELS | .10 ea | | | | | | |
| | | | | | | | |
| PAINT | | | | | | | |
| THINNER | | | | | | | |
| OTHER PAINT EXP. | | | | | | | |

GENERAL EXPENSES

TOTAL COSTS

PROFIT OR LOSS

| BID BY: | | |
| WRITE RECOMMENDATION ON BACK | TOTAL GENERAL EXPENSE | PROFIT OR LOSS |

year. Will you want the Scotchgard treatment on the carpet this time, too?" Boy, is that impressive to a customer, to be remembered and to be handled in such a professional way.

Of course, there all kinds of records you will need to keep track of as you go along, such as copies of all your contracts and change orders, work schedules, personnel files, etc. These will depend a lot on the nature of your business, and developing your own forms and systems is half the fun. Just be sure you have some way to keep hold of everything you need to meet government requirements, and to keep track of where you are in your operation.

## OFFICE AIDS

The **computer:** Computers have done their best to put me out of business for the last twenty years. They are wonderful machines and can save time and money if you have a genuine, direct use for them; if not, they're an albatross around the neck. Computers don't run a business, they're only a tool to do the work faster and better. Remember that — skip the ego trip and the temptation to play big business with them. Right now we have computers in all our offices to do our bookkeeping. Last year, one mistake in programming judgment cost $75,000 — money totally wasted. We have our payroll checks done by a computer center for about 58 cents a check — computer agencies are fast and cheap! They keep all the payroll records, punch the W-2 forms and all of that. Someday we might do it right in the office, but not yet. When you're small, you can keep your books easily by hand, or have one of the bookkeeping services do it (see **Record-keeping** section).

When the time comes to get a computer you should call a local cleaning company that's doing well and ask them what computer and program they use to run their books, receivables, payables and other things. There are simple, inexpensive, off-the-shelf programs that can handle your operation in a breeze and not cost you much. Talk to other contractors, get a recommendation from your CPA, and talk to the computer salesmen to see what is available.

In the computer area, things can change overnight — the computers we bought last year for $2,800 each are $800 this year, and a better version of the $25,000-custom program we had developed for us is available off the shelf now

for $500. Computer salesmen (who failed at their own business) will lay all sorts of gizmos on you that you "can't get along without" — you can.

## CLUBS AND ASSOCIATIONS

We have a great tendency, when starting our own business, to seek as much help as possible in the areas where we lack skill and confidence.

This is all well and good if you don't overdo it. There are four hundred associations and organizations that "businesspeople" can join. Cities are full of clubs and groups and institutions that offer brotherhood and promise the security of a group. In the cleaning business, very few of them fit. You won't have oodles of time for lunches and dinners and parades and parties and barbecues and ticket-selling and trophy-awarding. I'd say limit your activities to one trade group and one civic service organization, unless you get a big kick out of club membership. I'm not knocking the idea of giving to others, but remember, success in the cleaning business is being on the job and getting the cleaning done. Your clients don't care about your trophied walls or the support you give to the Grazer's Gazette or the county fair circular. Limit yourself and be careful with this, or you'll end up being a full-time supporter. It isn't the money, but the time you have to spend at meetings, committee groups, breakfasts, and all that. The cleaning business is keeping on the job. It's not like some sales-oriented businesses that depend a lot upon social interaction. We are a service business and only get praised and paid when service occurs.

## OFFICE-RELATED COSTS — A WORD TO THE WISE . . .

The more money and time you dedicate to the office, the more expensive your overhead will be. When your office and administrative costs and time get out of balance with your service operation (on the job), you are quite simply out of business. Remember, in the cleaning business you don't earn money in an office, even if you're the owner and big chief. Office work is administrative, and you can get someone to do it. You need to have your brain and muscle and enthusiasm out in the field and on and around the job, doing work, cutting costs, dealing with customers, eliminating troubles. As soon as you make your quarters the office, the dollars will disappear.

# CONTROLLING QUALITY ON THE JOB

Every building needs an effective Quality Assurance Program! Most buildings have a program, but only a few have one that really works. The Quality Control in most buildings is what I call "reactionary." They wait for a problem (complaint) to appear, then they deal with it (react). This is what the business consultants call fire fighting. Instead of running around putting out brush fires all the time, you need to learn the skill of fire prevention. This is what a good quality control program does for you — it keeps complaints from happening, and keeps you out of trouble. It's not uncommon to find a fine structure, caring and capable management, a well-qualified cleaning crew with the most modern equipment and methods, and yet a rapidly depreciating building with an unacceptable appearance and a throng of unhappy, complaining people. This is what happens when there is no Quality Control.

The solution to this problem is simple and inexpensive! The purpose of this chapter is to explain how you can attain a smooth, clean, happy, economical quality control program.

## A SAD, SAD, STORY

About thirty years ago I enrolled as a student at Idaho State University, totally committed to my college education. But leaving a hard-working farm home, I had only enough money to enroll, and needed to make more to stay in school. My independent agricultural background led me to organize my own business — a **cleaning service.** I pushed my way through school and upon graduation **my cleaning service was a full-fledged company,** operating over a three-state area! Since I ended up knowing more about cleaning toilets than about dissecting frogs, I decided to stay with my regional building maintenance company and build it into a large national business.

Our growth and success, when told in a single sentence, is a glorious, spirit-tingling story; but in real life, between the lines, it was a gut wrencher. After years of grinding and serving, we had a gradual increase — mighty gradual — then suddenly we jumped and jumped. During this jump, little changed in our business, it cost us nothing to take this tremendous rise. And your operation can do the same, so let me share the secret.

## THE BEGINNING

Pocatello, Idaho, my home base, isn't exactly the ideal metropolis from which to build a national company. We have a few five-story buildings and a couple of commuter airlines in and out, but it certainly isn't a hub of commerce. We soon realized that expansion to other cities was a priority. We branched out to Boise, Salt Lake City, and nearby towns, setting up operations, and then worked to keep them afloat, which meant pressure and problem-chasing. We survived and grew a little through sheer commitment and endurance. Then one day, a real opportunity came our way. Near the border of Southern Utah (450 miles away) a Bell Telephone manager called me and asked if we were interested in contracting his main building and twenty other remote CDO's (Community Dial Offices). I'd previously pioneered the Bell contracting concept in our area, so I speedily drove down to bid the job. The buildings came up, my bid was right on. They were ecstatic, and so were we. We were awarded the contract, a nice package of buildings in a beautiful setting of Zion National Park and Grand Canyon land, and the manager of the buildings, Mr. Harris, was a prince of a man.

We were the same age, had the same size family, both of us had small farms, we even belonged to the same church. It was ideal! I opened the area personally and stayed there two weeks stripping floors. Then I hired another gentleman to supervise it for us. It was an easy area to reach, and the buildings were easy to clean. I mean it was almost impossible to foul up! I scheduled a visit once a month to check up and oversee the operation and they liked that.

The first month I was right on schedule. I drove down and solved a couple of minor start-up problems and all was well. They patted me on the back and I went home. Next month I showed up right on schedule and checked everything. They raved over me and my company.

I got busy the next month with another expansion and so it was two months before I showed up again. All was well, they praised our progress and our local supervisor. Although he was new and inexperienced, we'd checked him out carefully before we hired him and he was doing fine.

It was spring now and we were busy, and it was four months before I made it down there to check, inspect, and evaluate. Things were good,

they were happy, we were profitable and productive. They said they missed me, but understood I was busy.

The next visit was — guess how long? You all know the pattern — it was a year later and guess what prompted it — a threat of cancellation!

This is the common conduct of almost all cleaning people: we start off big and impressive and then only show up when there are complaints or problems. I made this exact mistake! On this visit there was seat kicking, not back patting. Our friendly, fun relationship was now an "I'm out to get you" negative standoff.

Interestingly enough, when I got down there I discovered that it wasn't that the service was so bad, but my absence had allowed the little things to build up. Minor problems, left uncorrected, end up being major issues. Little things like our cleaning folks occasionally eating an operator's leftover donuts, and one of our cleaners parking his motorcycle on the front lawn. One important, highly verbal secretary didn't like the smell of the ammoniated cleaner being used. And things did get pretty exciting when one of the janitors hung his dead deer in the janitor closet. But had I been making regular checkups or inspections, all of these little things would have simply been handled and laughed over. Added together, the incidents built a strong case that seemed to say that we, the contractor, didn't care.

The straw that broke the camel's back and prompted the threatening call was the hardest blunder to smooth over. Our people who stripped the business office floor poured the dirty stripping water into a deep pothole outside the front of the building. That night it froze and a quarter-inch of snow fell, so that the hole looked just like a soiled piece of the driveway. Well, as you might expect, a Bell System vice-president for the State of Utah — the very head man — stepped on it and went in half way up to his shin. As he emptied his alligator shoes of mop string threads and gunky stripping water, he had a pretty good idea of its origin.

What an agonizing, miserable time I had trying to patch up and repair things — and our relationship was never quite the same!

This "hit and miss" inspection system is the way about 95% of all cleaning operations operate. We do a great job of selling our service, but then sit back and wait for the threats and complaints to roll in. Then we rush in a restorations crew to try to appease and amend. This explains why most cleaner/owner relationships are so negative, because the only communication occurs in volatile situations. With no feedback, the cleaners don't know where they stand until the customer is enraged. Most cleaners are capable of doing the job, but they need constant input from supervisors to keep things running smoothly. The key to good cleaning service is **supervision!**

Reputation, skill, financial strength, honesty, and effort mean nothing and will go to waste without supervision and inspection!

I knew the why, when, what, and how to supervise my Southern Utah operation. It was profitable and I loved the area and people; what went wrong? I simply wasn't there regularly. A good **quality control** program is nothing if you're not out there implementing it regularly.

## A HARD LESSON

Until now, I still hadn't caught on to why success in the cleaning business was so elusive. Even after the Southern Utah fiasco, it didn't all sink in until about a year later. A call came from Denver requesting our services for a million-square foot building. In a few weeks we signed the contract (our biggest up to that point). As we sat in the office of the "big boss," he explained that the building was currently at a rather low 74% quality rating and said he knew that we could bring it up to an astonishing 80%, maybe 84%. We enthusiastically reinforced his faith in us with confident smiles and head nodding.

He then showed us how his salary advanced as he obtained his objectives, and how if we did in fact reach our goals, he would be financially blessed. Our heads nodded and we again pledged that we could do it.

He said, "I know you can, and to make sure you do, you will formally inspect the buildings **every month without fail.**" Again, like all cleaners, we had heard this four hundred times before and nodded assuringly. But for the first time in our lives, this guy meant it, and we did it. He made it clear that if he didn't get his attainment bonus, we wouldn't be around long. He held our feet to the fire, and made certain we did inspect every month, and we did get the quality rating up to 85%!

We still have that building today. A building with thousands of potential problems, but one that's had very few complaints for many, many years. The quality of the relationship and feelings we've shared with this client have always been positive and productive.

We applied the lesson we learned in Denver to our entire operation, and this has been the key to our successful growth!

## THE ANSWER

We instituted a simple practice, it took hardly any time, cost us little, we followed through, and made sure it was done — regular inspection.

## THE SECRET

Keep it simple. This is the place too many of us get carried away and ruin the whole inspection process. We try to design a complicated, all-encompassing form. **Remember, the fact that you actually do the inspection is 95% of its value.** The leftover marked-up paper is just a byproduct. It's also a nice, convenient way to reach a mark and keep a record. But ideally, after each inspection, you could wad up the paper and toss it in the waste can and still retain 95% of the importance of the inspection. Why then, is the form important at all? Because **the form,** that little bit of paper, can easily encourage or discourage us in performing the inspection! Really! It's just like an entry form for a contest. If it's too long or hard to fill in to register, people won't participate, even for a wonderful prize. "Win A New Buick," a contest where you only have to spend fifteen minutes filling out information on an entry form. Few people will enter, because the form is long, detailed and requires a few ounces of mental concentration. If it's a simple card, with boxes to check and a place to sign, everyone goes for it. It's the same for the paperwork of a workable, effective **quality control program.**

We've evolved into a convenience society. We want things **quick! Easy! Disposable!** People simply won't use things that are complicated. They won't read things that are complicated. No matter how good or good for you a product is, it'll be ignored if it can't be used quickly and disposed of easily.

The inspection we ran on that big, million-square foot building took only a couple of hours a month. It was complete on one sheet of paper — a form we put together after we had tried a number of different forms. This form has a success

# Let's take a very SIMPLE LOOK at the job we have—it consists of only 3 basic objectives...

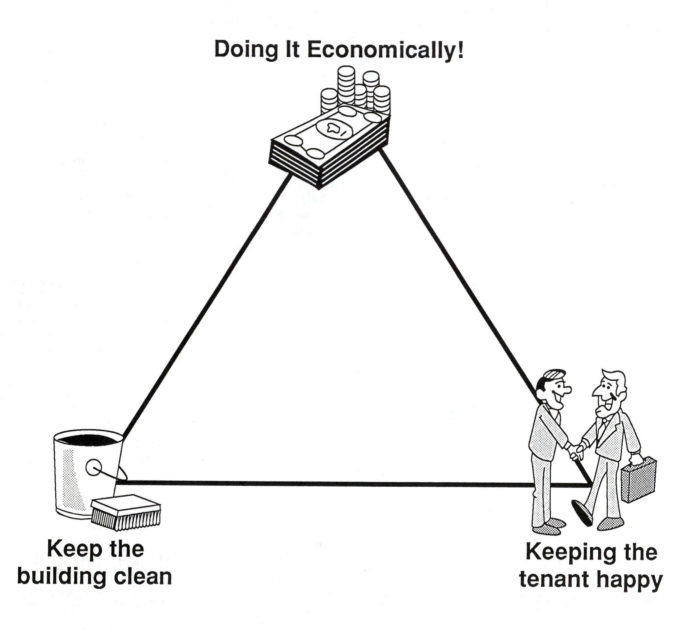

**Doing It Economically!**

**Keep the building clean**

**Keeping the tenant happy**

# No single one of these objectives or other combination will work...You have to do all 3

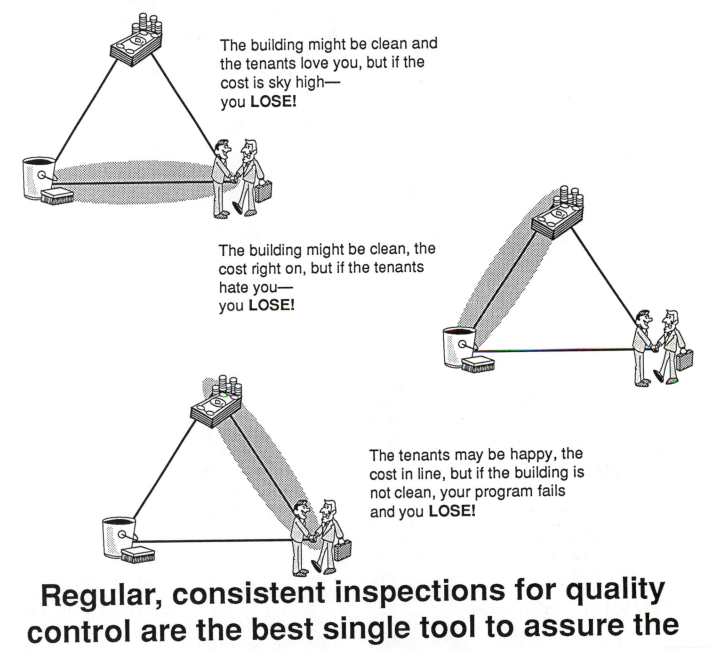

The building might be clean and the tenants love you, but if the cost is sky high—
you **LOSE!**

The building might be clean, the cost right on, but if the tenants hate you—
you **LOSE!**

The tenants may be happy, the cost in line, but if the building is not clean, your program fails and you **LOSE!**

# Regular, consistent inspections for quality control are the best single tool to assure the accomplishment of all three

story all its own. It went on to be adapted by the nation's largest corporation to develop and teach a Building Service Management Course. It was highly successful and resulted in a series of seminars that trained over 1,400 Executive Managers.

## BASIC GUIDELINES

1. **Only one page:** This keeps it simple and it's all that's needed. It's convenient and, most importantly, it implies a quick, efficient inspection.

2. **Make it a distinctive color:** White paper is lost in the shuffle. Avoid a neutral or newsprint look. Design your form to assert itself and to be instantly recognizable in hand or book. Our form is printed on three-part carbonless paper, one each for the customer, the office files, and the cleaning crew.

3. **Make it a checklist:** The less writing you have to do, the better — especially while moving. Design your form so that the inspector can easily check off items and ratings rather than have to write an an essay of an appraisal sentence. A concise form is attractive and easy to use, whereas long drawn-out epistles scribbled down on the page are generally ignored. Make sure the form is constructed so it says **yes** or **no,** and shows what and where the needs are. Remember, you're appraising a training course that should have been perfected long ago. The form serves to jog the memory, a checklist to see if it's all working.

## THE RATING

Although the act of inspecting is 95% of its value, as with any test, there has to be a bottom line — a standard of how good or bad things are. We call this an Index Rating. Your inspection form should be designed to produce a bottom line rating, not a vague judgment.

Satisfactory or Unsatisfactory ratings aren't enough. They don't communicate the specific discrepancies or target the areas that need improvement.

The inspection form should be designed to produce a score or number that represents the sum total of all services. The best numbering system to use is 1 to 100. One hundred percent is readily recognized as perfection. Don't use 1 to 10 or 1,000 to 10,000, these scales cannot be

interpreted at a glance. The index number 8.5 or 850, for example, is confusing. Most of us know the 1 to 100 value system from school, and it works best because it is pre-learned. We all went to school and got grades, so we know that anything under 80% isn't too good. A "C" grade might be good enough to get by, but it won't win you any honors. Anything over 90% is high merit, indeed. The index rating has to be so basic and simple that a third-grader could instantly comprehend it.

The index rating must be easy to compute and understand, but must also be designed to reflect the relative importance of the different tasks accurately. **For example,** more weight should be on critical areas like restrooms and floors, less weight on light dusting, plant watering, and ashtray wiping. When we first used our form every box equaled 10 points. The restroom and floor could have been filthy, but if the other areas were OK, the index rating could have been 80%. By shifting more weight to critical items and less to minor areas, you'll have a much fairer measurement of the building's overall appearance. Again, a number rating works best because it pinpoints the areas that need improvement and enables you to accurately weigh different tasks.

## THE IDEAL INSPECTION

**Keep it positive and uncomplicated!** In my opinion, having people who do nothing but inspect is a waste of money. The cleaners end up worrying more about pleasing the "Inspector" than they do about cleaning the building. I've never seen a specially created "Inspector's" job work well. They become power gods, whose job is to walk around with a clipboard and find problems — not affect a positive change. Political and emotional conflicts are sure to arise, too. The designated inspector doesn't have enough to do, so he stirs up trouble to keep busy and look impressive. It works much better to do the inspections yourself; then you know exactly what is going on, and it gets you in the building, seeing the customer, where you need to be.

**Remember:** inspections only take a little time if they're consistent, because they force supervision, and with supervision the cleaning people will eliminate most of their own oversights and problems.

Most "inspections" are considered to be the

wrath of the building management raining down on the fumbling cleaners. Don't let it become a witch hunt — too many do! The ideal inspection should be like an awards banquet — an opportunity to recognize your people for a job well done. If you have to put a critical comment on it for a sub-standard item, make sure you offset it with praise for something well done. If you can't find anything praiseworthy to note, you need to reassess the cleaner you have on the job!

## ATTITUDE CHECK

Cleaning people get enough abuse from the public and all the people who litter, spill things, spit, sneer, and otherwise abuse the building and the staff. They don't need, and won't respond to, dictatorship. You might think you've "shaped them up," but a resentful cleaning employee can turn two hours of work into eight hours of being busy. And you can't do anything about it, even if you're **aware** of it.

There are positive, constructive ways to do a good inspection.

For a poor performance, after the first and second inspection, and a correction attempt, try a personal plea. If it doesn't change the service, change the employee, but don't strip dignity from another human being by browbeating them.

Our Miami manager, frustrated because his crew consistently missed a dead cockroach in a corner, constructed a clever little cardboard funeral tent over the deceased insect. His action delighted everyone, the crew even laughed over it, but never allowed other bodies to follow!

Regular inspections should catch and fix the problems, before they fester and spread. There's a common hangup that we (the public and tenants) all have with the maintenance staff: if anything goes wrong, is stolen, if it's too hot, too cold, too noisy, or there's any kind of nuisance in the building, it's unquestionably the maintenance staff's fault. It's up to us to follow through with inspections and quality controls which will effectively diffuse this kind of attitude.

Avoid cancellations or job termination threats as a measure to get your building clean. Regular inspections are easier and more effective. You may know of bosses that draw contracts or employment agreements — like a gun — on non-performing companies or individuals. Again, the negative feelings generated will backfire on you tenfold.

## A TRAP TO AVOID

Inspections will also eliminate the need for "trap-setting." Setting traps is an underhanded approach to detecting cleaning neglect. For example, management (or even tenants) will mark an object (like a paper clip, a bottle cap, toothpick, rubber band, or match) and place it around, in back of, under or on something to measure the cleaner's thoroughness. No one with any class at all "sets traps." It has no dignity, and is less productive than any other approach. What will you say to the cleaner the next morning when you call him in and display your handful of planted junk? "Look what you are missing — this stuff I laid around to trap you." How much improvement is that going to generate? **None!** Instead they will hate you and spend time looking for traps rather than cleaning the building. If you have to resort to traps to know and prove the building isn't clean, you aren't qualified for your job. Never set traps, they will ultimately trap you.

A perfect "entrapment" example is the cleaner who found a "planted" clip on a shelf a little above eye level. Each night he'd lift the clip, dust under it and replace it. The trapper would find the clip and call the cleaner down to say he didn't dust the shelf. Then the cleaner would ask if there was any dust on it. Nope! He almost drove that trapper to drink. In another case, a medical office, one of the staff sutured (sewed) a leaf to the carpet. When it failed to come up with the vacuum, the cleaner discovered it was attached to the rug. It made him so angry he took out his knife and cut the piece of rug out, threw it away and left it in the waste can; no one said anything about it or set any traps again.

## INSPECTION SCHEDULE

Varying of the exact day you do the inspection on is OK, even beneficial to keep crews from "salting the mine," or from "gearing up for inspection day." Of course, even if they do white-glove it a little to prepare for a coming inspection that's part of the value of inspection, to get the building clean, employees motivated, and tenants happy. Never skip a scheduled inspection, though — it's the consistency that keeps you out of trouble. I like to do an informal "walk-through" — just a quick look to make sure nothing is slipping — weekly. Once a month is about right for the formal, written inspection with a customer representative along if the customer wants to be a part of it.

## A SILK PURSE FROM A SOW'S EAR

What kind of a building are you giving your cleaning crew to work with? We cleaned a storeroom office in the Los Angeles area and did a good job, but never could raise our quality index rating above 78%. One day, the owner came in and repaired the deteriorating baseboards, replaced the carpets, and painted the place. Our index rating instantly went up to a superb 84%, even though the cleaning didn't change. The physical construction or condition of a building has a big influence on its appearance, and the cleaning staff has no power or responsibility to change this. If the sinks are stripped of finish, the faucets and fountains oxidized right back to pre-chrome days, the light grills stained from twenty years of tar and nicotine, the waste receptacles bent and scratched, then you have to figure those items into the inspection results. The age and condition of a property can influence the apparent production and quality of work by a cleaning staff more than 50%.

Another factor you, as a manager, must consider when setting your expectations, is the quantity, quality, and age of your cleaning equipment and supplies. Are you expecting your crews to achieve super results with substandard supplies and broken-down equipment? This book isn't about cleaning methods, you already know how to clean. If you don't, get my *Cleaning Up For A Living* kit, which contains my books on how to clean. The point I'm trying to make is that you, in your leadership position, must adjust your rating system to be fair and flexible when you're evaluating maintenance work. Too often, physical damage of the building is directly blamed on the cleaning operation. Even you, as a cleaning manager, will often be criticized for poor structural conditions in a building that have nothing to do with how well you do your job. I would go to some pains to correct this if I were you. At least call it to the attention of the owners, so it won't hold your performance rating forever at a 78% when you're actually giving them a superb 84%.

## THE USE OF SPACE

Consider how heavily the building is used; too often we judge production by how big a building is, forgetting that how many people occupy it and how concentrated they are is the biggest factor in cleaning cost and quality. You spend more time and supplies to clean a one-room hair styling school than the three-story telephone building across the street, because of the heavy use and number of occupants. Remember, space itself means very little — it's how many people are using the space and what they're using it for that counts.

I recall a classic example of this in a large leased office building: when it was first contracted, there was one occupant to every 240 square feet of space. Cleaning crews, supplies, cost, and quality ratings were all based on these figures. As the company grew and put more personnel in the building, the cleaning people couldn't keep up! Quality slipped and all sorts of complaints resulted. The icing on the cake was when the building manager said "Humph, we are covering up more square footage with desks and furniture all the time, so there is **less** area to clean! The janitors should have plenty of extra time to pick up the items they're missing." Nice logic, right? Wrong! By now, there was one person to every 120 square feet — or twice the concentration of use. This meant double the trash, double the desks to clean, double the toilet paper, double use of fountains, double the number of feet to carry dirt in and double the number of hands to put prints on everything, double the amount of cleaning supplies and double the complaint factor! Empty space square footage is easy to clean; concentration is the key factor in cleaning. We had to put additional cleaners in the facility to cover the additional work and get the quality up. Here's an interesting guideline:

| Square Feet per Person | Density |
|---|---|
| 100 | Awful |
| 125 | Heavy |
| 150 | |
| 175 | Average |
| 200 | |
| 225 | |
| 250 | Delightful |

NOTE: When you conduct inspections, be sure to point out or adjust for this factor.

Remember, too, that just as a saturation of people can adversely affect speed and quality of cleaning, a concentration of **objects** will have the same effect. Offices cluttered with excess furniture, boxes on the floor, and plants and other personal objects, will be harder to keep at an acceptable quality level.

## FAIRNESS

Interestingly enough, in the first few inspections you'll find a gap between the two inspectors. They obviously view dirty and clean differently when the supervisor comes up with a rating of 68% and the building manager, 82%. This is the great thing about a written record of an inspection. Instantly it's clear that one is too picky, or one is too casual, or a little of each. You iron it out and agree on "how good" is good, what you expect and what to look for together. I'll bet you a new toilet brush that the next inspection ratings will be right together and will stay that way.

If you don't reach an index rating agreement point, you will fight each other with accusations of "He's never satisfied" or "He doesn't know what clean is!" Time after time I see situations where people with opposite views will arrive at the same index figure when they use this handy form. What a great positive piece of work that is. No questions, no arguments, no suspicion, just an agreement on how to measure the appearance of the building.

Don't get your maintenance people to reach a high rating, then use their own accomplishment to beat them with. Be fair — a building may be at 72%, and the crews slave and work and finally get it up to 85%, (much higher than you expect). Then, once in a while, they slip to 81% (which is still commendable and much better than the 72%). A supervisor may be tempted to hammer on the crews, using the 85% rating. That is a low-class way to try to motivate workers and will only bring negative results.

## SHORT AND SWEET

So you're set. You, as manager, have scheduled the monthly inspection with a representative of the owner, and you each appear with form in hand. A basic inspection survival principle is "make it short and sweet!" If an inspection is a long, draining, tiring ordeal, it will gradually disappear and not be done. Fifteen to twenty minutes in a small building or a couple of hours in a huge building should be the limit.

Crews working a given area won't vary much in their strengths and weaknesses. If the same people clean the restrooms on five floors, you can bank on them being about the same in quality. Check a couple — the others will be the same. If the dusting is bad on the eighth and twelfth floors, and the same person is dusting on the seventh and fourteenth, you can usually assume those floors will be of a like quality.

Entrances, elevators, lobbies, (items there are only one of), should be checked every time, but you needn't look in 4,000 wastebaskets to evaluate wastebaskets. A few in each separate crew's area will tell you the story.

Don't wander aimlessly from room to room, hoping something will jump out at you. Follow a schedule. Develop ways to evaluate the entire building without looking at every single square inch. The secret is to learn to visit and appraise representative areas of your building. If the building is too big to cover on one inspection form, use a separate form for each floor or area.

Inspecting in pairs is most inconspicuous and effective. (Take along more and you'll look like a touring United Nations task force.)

Remember you aren't performing or preparing a remodeling bid, only doing a "flight check" of the building.

Observe the area, and concentrate on the appearance and quality of the job as a whole. If you fragment yourself and get caught up in too much detail, you'll lose the whole value of the inspection as a tool.

You know what to look for. What I'm trying to tell you here is how to use and present this information in a positive, relevant manner. As you inspect, be brief, fair and positive.

## THE INSPECTION FORM

Using the inspection form really makes it easy. As you walk through the building, refer to the corresponding section along the left margin of the form. For instance, as you first enter the building, go to the section titled "Entrance." Take a close look at each item listed, and simply mark

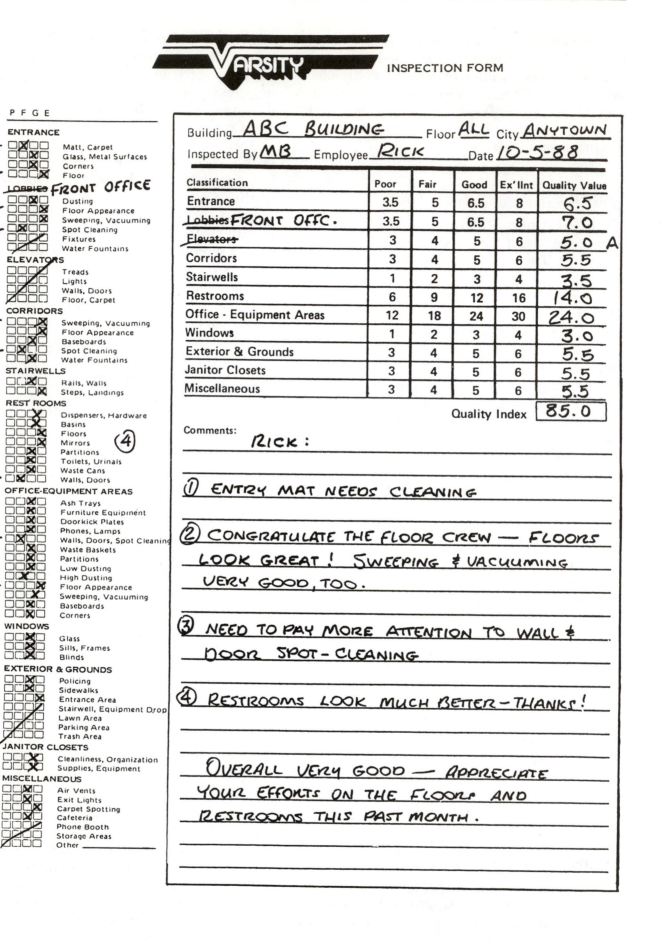

## VARSITY    INSPECTION FORM

Building ABC BUILDING    Floor ALL  City ANYTOWN
Inspected By MB  Employee RICK    Date 10-5-88

| Classification | Poor | Fair | Good | Ex'llnt | Quality Value |
|---|---|---|---|---|---|
| Entrance | 3.5 | 5 | 6.5 | 8 | 6.5 |
| ~~Lobbies~~ FRONT OFFC. | 3.5 | 5 | 6.5 | 8 | 7.0 |
| ~~Elevators~~ | 3 | 4 | 5 | 6 | 5.0 A |
| Corridors | 3 | 4 | 5 | 6 | 5.5 |
| Stairwells | 1 | 2 | 3 | 4 | 3.5 |
| Restrooms | 6 | 9 | 12 | 16 | 14.0 |
| Office - Equipment Areas | 12 | 18 | 24 | 30 | 24.0 |
| Windows | 1 | 2 | 3 | 4 | 3.0 |
| Exterior & Grounds | 3 | 4 | 5 | 6 | 5.5 |
| Janitor Closets | 3 | 4 | 5 | 6 | 5.5 |
| Miscellaneous | 3 | 4 | 5 | 6 | 5.5 |

Quality Index  85.0

Comments:

RICK:

① ENTRY MAT NEEDS CLEANING

② CONGRATULATE THE FLOOR CREW — FLOORS
LOOK GREAT! SWEEPING & VACUUMING
VERY GOOD, TOO.

③ NEED TO PAY MORE ATTENTION TO WALL &
DOOR SPOT-CLEANING

④ RESTROOMS LOOK MUCH BETTER — THANKS!

OVERALL VERY GOOD — APPRECIATE
YOUR EFFORTS ON THE FLOORS AND
RESTROOMS THIS PAST MONTH.

---

P F G E

**ENTRANCE**
① — Matt, Carpet
Glass, Metal Surfaces
② — Corners
Floor

**LOBBIES** FRONT OFFICE
② — Dusting
Floor Appearance
Sweeping, Vacuuming
③ — Spot Cleaning
Fixtures
Water Fountains

**ELEVATORS**
Treads
Lights
Walls, Doors
Floor, Carpet

**CORRIDORS**
② — Sweeping, Vacuuming
Floor Appearance
Baseboards
③ — Spot Cleaning
Water Fountains

**STAIRWELLS**
Rails, Walls
Steps, Landings

**REST ROOMS**
Dispensers, Hardware
Basins
Floors
Mirrors ④
Partitions
Toilets, Urinals
Waste Cans
③ — Walls, Doors

**OFFICE-EQUIPMENT AREAS**
Ash Trays
Furniture Equipment
Doorkick Plates
Phones, Lamps
③ — Walls, Doors, Spot Cleaning
Waste Baskets
Partitions
Low Dusting
High Dusting
② — Floor Appearance
Sweeping, Vacuuming
Baseboards
Corners

**WINDOWS**
Glass
Sills, Frames
Blinds

**EXTERIOR & GROUNDS**
Policing
Sidewalks
Entrance Area
Stairwell, Equipment Drop
Lawn Area
Parking Area
Trash Area

**JANITOR CLOSETS**
Cleanliness, Organization
Supplies, Equipment

**MISCELLANEOUS**
Air Vents
Exit Lights
Carpet Spotting
Cafeteria
Phone Booth
Storage Areas
Other _____

one of the boxes to indicate whether you think the cleaning deserves poor, fair, good, or excellent. If you think it falls in between, mark in between the boxes! After you have rated the mat, glass, corners, and floor in the entrance, go on to the lobby, and so on through the building. If you need to rate an area type that doesn't have a place on the form, improvise. Re-title one of the sections to meet your needs. If you find no elevators or stairs or whatever, don't worry about it — just leave it blank.

After you have checked the boxes for all areas in the building, it is time to figure the quality index. Go to the top center of the form, and you'll see that each area is again listed, and that a numerical value is assigned for "good," "fair," "poor," etc. To come up with a number, you will have to **average** your ratings from the boxes at the left. Suppose I had marked the entrance good for glass and corners, had found the mat to be only fair, but had judged the floor excellent. I would average the overall entrance out at a solid "good," and so would assign a numerical rating of 6.5. If you feel it rates a little better than good, give it a 7, or only a 6 if it falls a little short. Do this for all of the areas you rated. Now, it's time to go in and do something with those blank spaces, so that the zero values in them won't affect the rest of the figures. Simply go to each blank section and **average** it in. If you didn't find any elevators, but it appears that the overall building is averaging "good," I'd give elevators a 5. Doing this just loads the unrated areas into the figures at whatever level the building is averaging, so that the unrated areas don't affect the figures for the rated areas one way or the other. I like to put an "A" in the margin by any figures I average in, so I can quickly see how I arrived at the numbers. After you have a number on the line for every area type, simply add them up to come up with the overall building rating. You will have to set your own standard, but generally speaking, you'll keep yourself out of trouble by holding your commercial buildings at 85 or so. If you want to receive praise and admiration, they'll have to be in the nineties.

The mechanics of a good inspection: quick, simple, and discreet! Simplicity and consistency must be part of quality control. If it takes too long or is complicated — you'll quit doing it!

## THE VALUE OF DISCRETION

Not long ago I presented a cleaning management seminar to some southeastern telephone companies. Midway through my presentation — when I get to the part on quality control — I always have the group run a fifteen-minute inspection on the telephone building itself. Usually the seminar is held very close to the building, but in this case it was a large, isolated Holiday Inn.

Without considering the possible consequences, I pumped up, enthused, and excited my inspectors — and offered a prize to the most accurate inspector. Then I turned the whole meeting room full of competitive cleaning managers loose on that hotel.

They attacked the lobby, the restrooms, the entrances, the vents, the carpets, the windows and forty other places, with the aggressiveness of germ wardens! There were guys and gals on their knees and tiptoes everywhere, looking over and under every possible lint hiding corner.

Now the hotel employees (especially the manager) were instantly alarmed. They didn't know what they'd done to deserve twenty-five instant radical inspectors. From the way these inspectors were writing on their forms and shaking their heads, the hotel people figured they were about to be part of a grand sanitization closeup! It caused some very tense moments and some hurt feelings.

I mention this to remind you that inspection — no matter of what or by whom — is always a sensitive business. You want to do it quietly and quickly. QUIETLY AND QUICKLY.

## CRUMB CATCHERS

Be careful about letting others help you evaluate things. During an inspection, you never want to stop and ask someone (a secretary, clerk, boss, etc.) "How are things?" or "How is the cleaning?" WHAT A MISTAKE! You'll find everyone's an expert about the cleaning! They assume that the purpose of an inspection is to find fault and air discontent, and they'll do just that. Your short and sweet inspection will get hung up but good, and you'll have every crumb catcher in the place bending your ear (and it puts the burden on you of following up on each and every piddly complaint). You have to sound out your official customer contact to make sure they're happy with your job, but leave it up to them to receive any complaints from people with the building. Don't query every person you pass about their satisfaction with the cleaning.

A true professional doesn't have to ask, "How are things?" If both you and your crew are doing your job, you'll know how things are. When you ask a tenant if he or she has any complaints, they feel obligated to come up with some problem. They'll start rounding up and saving every little smudge and dust particle to present to you. That totally throttles your inspection. You'll never get past the first floor, and you'll be riddled, chewed out, torn and strained. You'll begin to dread making an inspection, and bang, your program is dead.

If you show that you are aware, interested and conscious of the cleaning level, then whistle through on your regular inspections. People will love it and leave you alone. If someone has a legitimate complaint, it will usually get to you. Asking for problems from every person you pass on your inspection tour is a real killer.

## A FINAL INSPECTION: THE STAFF

Because the cleaning people are moving around and are seen throughout the building, their condition and appearance is often more apparent than that of the facility. It's hard for a scroungy scrubber to do spotless work. The appearance of your people leaves an impression with building owners and tenants that is often more lasting than the quality of cleaning. Set some dress and grooming standards. Uniforms and grooming should be part of the quality control picture. Set your requirements! Your staff will enjoy being part of a sharp, professional team. Inspect them at least twice a month, too.

## SUMMARY

### Why Inspection Programs Fail:

1. Not simple enough! (in form, function or time).
2. Not administered fairly and objectively (handled like a witch hunt).

3. Not communicated positively to the staff. (If the janitors resent it, it will not work. They are the only ones who can effect change.)
4. Not kept up! One good inspection deserves another and another and another! Never skip or miss an inspection. Ninety-five percent of the inspection's value is the fact that it was done.

A regular inspection, done as I have outlined, will keep a check on all three of the basic parts of our job: (1) keep the building clean, (2) keep the tenant happy, and (3) do it economically.

### What a Proper Inspection Does:

1. It forces supervision. Silently and easily, regular inspection requires supervisors to do their jobs. Almost everything in maintenance success relies on supervision. If it is done, 90% of cleaning problems will disappear.
2. It generates a positive relationship. Most relationships between cleaners and management are negative, making it awkward and uncomfortable to work together — if communication doesn't occur until there's a problem. Inspections force more regular meetings where things can be noticed and conveyed positively, before they get to the point that a complaint is necessary — and inspections produce positive feelings.
3. It maintains and enforces standards. Standards will only be effective if they are never allowed to slip or be reduced. Nothing cements and enforces standards like consistent inspections.
4. It establishes a record. Short memory and short patience are common to cleaning operations. Making and having a tangible, written record quells many emotional, and even legal problems, and diffuses accusations.
5. It reduces management time and stress. Inspections are the "ounce of prevention" that eliminates the pound of problems.
6. It gives a vote of confidence. Inspections tell the cleaning staff and crews that their work is worthy of evaluation. A simple inspection is one of the most important motivational and public relations moves you can make.

# BENEFITTING FROM YOUR COMPETITION

## THE PARADE

I started my cleaning business with such gusto and enthusiasm, I didn't think anyone else around could even keep in my dust. Nor was I aware of a thing called a competitor lurking outside every janitor closet in town. My company grew fast. I was the largest in our little city of Pocatello, Idaho — and I was confident I was the best. I'd heard of a couple of mom-and-pop outfits who wielded a few brooms out of the back of their station wagons, but nothing threatened my fleet of four-and-a-half vehicles (I sneaked my wife's station wagon in on some occasions). But then a truly upsetting experience happened to me during a Fourth of July celebration. A banker friend had invited me and my six kids to sit in his plush, air-conditioned second-story office on Main and Center, with a big picture window — right on the parade's finest vantage point. Prominent city people and customers viewed me (one of the city's real whiz kids) there in the executive suite, drinking lemonade and watching the parade. Suddenly, at the end of the parade, the last entry brought me to attention. There, following the parade (and the two hundred pooping horses that had passed in review) was one of my newest competitors — Jon Bell.

I'd heard he was in town, but ignored him as another small operator soon to be washed away in his own mop water. But his appearance at that Fourth of July parade made me suddenly wonder who indeed was going to be washed away. What a clever devil he was. There, in bright clean uniforms, with emblems sparkling in the sun (and everyone taking pictures of them, too) came his crew. One pushed a gleaming wheelbarrow with a sign that said "Bannock Window Cleaning Co./ We Clean Everything!", as his crew, armed with manure forks, brooms, and shovels, cleaned up all of the horse droppings, candy wrappers, and other parade residue. Two of them even had little deodorant aerosols and were spraying the freshly cleaned spots. The crowd was cheering and clapping, they loved him, and he was passing out business cards like mad. Boy, did that ruin my day!

I was so upset at being outsmarted, I couldn't contain my disgust. There I was sitting on my fanny, lounging in my success, thinking I had the world by the tail, and some young hustler comes into my territory and steals my business. For the first time, I realized that there were others out there who would be competing for those same accounts I was feeding my family with, and those people would keep coming and coming. My despair over the matter however, had its lighter side. A week later I received a fine letter from the mayor of the city saying:

Dear Don,

How can we thank you and your crew enough for the clever and thoughtful job you did cleaning up behind the horses and cows. Our streets never looked so good. Many people have told me how impressed they were with you and your fine crew. We will be giving you some work and contracts shortly to show our appreciation.

Sincerely, THE MAYOR

My reputation was so strong, many people just assumed it was my crew and hadn't even read the sign!

So I did get some work from the parade, but so did he. You can be sure he went on to be one of my toughest competitors. He was a hustler and he worked long and hard and kept his crew sharp. Today, twenty-five years later, one of his former supervisors is now in his own business and is one of my tough competitors in another city. Jon's Bannock Window Cleaners made my company better, because I didn't like windows and so I rarely did windows, and Jon would get all the ones I let go. Once he got their windows, he often got the floors and the walls and the carpets, and then their office buildings. So, you guessed it, I learned to do windows, and I learned to push and keep my crews sharper and faster and better than his. He wasn't my enemy, he was my competitor, and competition can end up being your best asset, providing you have moxie and commitment. Jon and I even became good friends; we competed for work, but we didn't have to fight for a living, because there was work enough to go around and our work and our efforts rewarded us both.

## A NEW PERSPECTIVE

About the time I got used to Jon's competition, I noticed some others in town. Remember my story in the bidding chapter about bidding the Boise Cascade building? That building was the biggest thing I'd ever seen, and the contract on it would have doubled my gross sales overnight. I was hot to get it, and was sure I had the inside track, because they were so happy with my work on the construction cleanup. The big, easygoing fellow who showed up to bid against us was from Seattle, representing a company called ABM (American Building Maintenance), who happened to be the most successful national company in the industry. This tall John Wayne-type stranger spent about three hours in the building, then left and submitted his bid. Three of my best men and me had spent three days bidding it. ABM was awarded the bid — ("Those rats snatched our building right out from under our nose!") As it turned out, his bid was accurate, within fifteen minutes a day, and ours was off 40%.

This was my second real chance to meet my competition and in this case it was in a form we all come to know: "the big boys." I had to learn to play in the big leagues because of them. Life went on, and competition became common and plentiful. On one building in Denver, Colorado, we had eighty-one competitors all bidding for the same building. (I learned later that this was a selected, pre-screened group.) Have you ever wondered how many janitor companies there are in a city like Denver? 500? 1000? A lot of competition.

A bunch of California contractors in the Los Angeles area really put me in perspective about competition. We'd traveled to L.A. to bid work, especially the Bell System business, for which we were one of the most efficient in the world at that time. The other contractors, instead of pooh-poohing us or muttering obscene phrases about these invaders from Idaho, came over, shook hands, and asked if there was anything they could do for us. They pointed out some of the things in California to watch out for, offered their cars to us to take us around to bid, and in general treated us like professional colleagues. Their attitude was, "Hey, there's tons of work around, enough for us all. If you are the best and can do it better and faster than us, then you deserve it and vice versa."

Ever since then I've carried that attitude about my competition, and I suggest you do the same. There's no way you're going to get rid of competition, ever. If you do the work cheaper and starve them out, fresh ones dutifully arrive to make you keep your price down. After two or three of these, you will be the one who is starved out, if you continually fight it.

## COURTESY

Here is a logical and very practical reason you should treat and respect and support your competitors and be fair with them: to the average customer and account, contractors all look about the same; they don't care about your name and claim, you are simply a janitorial contractor and fit the same mold. So when you bad-mouth, cut, and squeeze your competition, you're hurting yourself and cutting your own throat because you are one of them.

We may hear from one dissatisfied customer that our competitor really fouled up a job, stole something, and was always late, so we blab it all over to other accounts and customers and all our crews. This just fouls the nest for the rest of the industry. Think how many times you have lost an account — it will happen, and may be unjustified — usually because you deserved it. Meanwhile, comments like these just contribute to a bad public attitude about the whole cleaning industry. It happens to the best of us.

Some of your best competitors will be former employees. Once you have nurtured, trained, weaned, and helped them, they leave you and take your accounts with them. This happens to all of us, and even here you'd better turn the other cheek and be friends. (Don't forget that I've given you some good ways of preventing your people from competing unfairly with you earlier in this manual.)

Some of your competitors will be bidding very low all the time, and that will keep you awake at night. If they do a poor job, sooner or later it will keep them awake at night, too, and probably end up taking them out of competition. You don't have to share the family secrets or anything else with them, of course, but be courteous to your competitors and treat them decently. Good ones are your best friends and will stimulate and force **you** to be better.

## ASSOCIATIONS

There are a number of cleaning associations, and they all have some value in getting all of us cleaners together to share our experience, etc. But don't figure them as lifesavers with all the answers, for they are NOT. They cost money, and they often take you away from work. Treat them as a place to gather a certain amount of information and to meet the competition, and let it go at that.

You're definitely not going to get from the organization itself an endless flow of great mastermind truths that will make you more successful than any other member. Some associations are an expensive way to get a magazine subscription. Consider the actual makeup of the organization, check their track record, what they actually do. Too many, in my opinion, are just social gatherings where you spend 90% of the time and money electing officers and organizing committees over and over. If the leadership is the best around, the association may well prove to be valuable.

## SUMMARY

Your competitors aren't out to ruin you, they're just trying to build their own business like you are, so don't treat them as enemies. Treat them well, and in years to come, they'll probably end up working for you or with you. As someone once said, just when you think you're winning the rat race, the other rats will show up. Competitors will always be a fact of life, and they usually fall into the following categories:

1. Well-established local companies: These are the stable and long-term citizens and families who have been around a long time, have a lot of friends, and know how to run a cleaning business. They've bought Fords from Johnson Ford for forty years, and they've had the cleaning account for twenty years. They're hard to beat on their own established turf. Sooner or later, someone will leave, divorce, or die, or they'll sell out, or management will change, or you'll begin to buy more Fords than they do.

2. Your former true-blue people: You will sire, breed, and inspire a lot of your own competitors by running a good company yourself. Any employee worth his salt has the right to want what you have, so lots of them go out and try to take it. I like to help those who go on their own, if they do it ethically. If they don't, I don't go out of my way to pass new accounts or people along, or make referrals to them when I'm too busy to handle something.

3. The national giants: There are ten or so of these biggies, like ABM, Prudential, or Service-Master, which are made up of exactly the same kinds of people as you and your little company. They just have more employees, they've been in the business longer, and they have more leverage and clout. They earned their position and deserve it, and you have the right to do the same. If you stay at it long enough you can be big and powerful, too.

4. Mom-and-pop outfits or the mop-buckets-out-of-the-station-wagon society: How can we criticize or dislike them, when that's the way we all began, and that's what some of us still are? Lots of mom-and-pop operations are good competitors; they do custom work and are careful with their accounts. A lot of them do excellent work, better than some of the biggies.

No competitor is much richer or faster, nor do they have hundreds of hidden secrets on how to clean. They just do several things better if they are beating you: and that is servicing the customers, keeping their buildings clean, keeping the people happy, and doing it for a fair dollar.

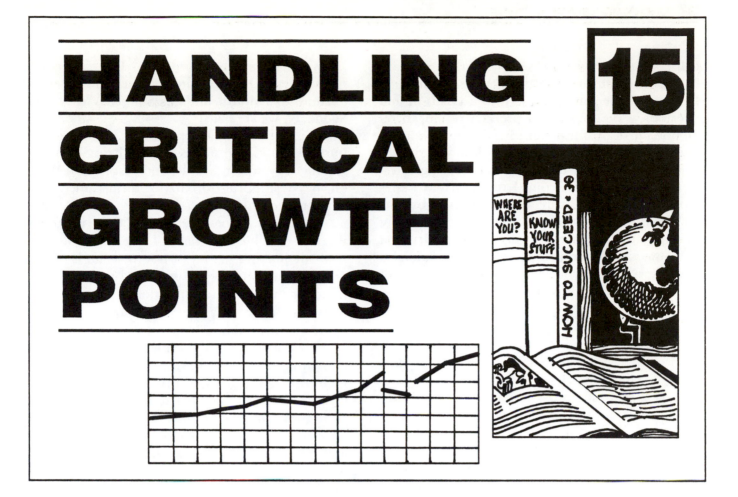

# HANDLING CRITICAL GROWTH POINTS

# 15

As I've repeated over and over in this book, this is a tough, close-margin business with an over 95% failure rate!

Before we get into the critical growth points, let me warn you of the three major reasons cleaning businesses get into trouble. It's not lack of work, lack of capital, or lack of opportunity as most people claim. The three conditions that kill us before we even get to a critical growth point are **nepotism, not knowing where you are, and not knowing your business.**

How many of these negative conditions do you already have built into your business? These conditions must be eliminated before your cleaning business can grow.

## REASON #1: NEPOTISM

Nepotism is the practice of hiring family and relatives (and I stretch this to include close friends). When you get going in your business and have things flowing your way, **all** the desperate "down and out" people **who know you** will naturally come to you for a job. This is a compliment; basically we all have heartfelt urges to give and to help others, and we all love to be needed. It makes us feel powerful and

accomplished. We envision ourselves as the great godfather of the cleaning world. A struggling brother in the family could be a supervisor. The old college friend, down on his luck after two bankruptcies, might be a good branch manager. The unemployed fellow you know from church, your best friend, and the banker's wife and father-in-law all need a part-time job. You hire them all and extend your best efforts to help them, forgetting that the purpose for which you hire any employee is to help your business succeed. You soon find out that most of them are in their respective down-and-out situations because they don't perform, or they lack experience. So you spend lots of time helping them and patching up complaints about their work and filling in for their missed days of work. Anyone else would fire them and get on with it, but nepotism works against you here and you carry the burden. After all, they're family or friends and even a totally justified dismissal would create a rift. The whole family would come down on you; and what about their children who love you and call you Uncle Johnny?

It's great to have close family and friends work with you, **if you can handle it, but few can!** Trying to fit people into positions where they can't perform will cause a business to fail. Millions of businesses transfer or promote a family member or associate into a position and overlook a deserving and productive employee. Nepotism in business can cause a loss of respect and loyalty to the point where you, the owner, can't recover and restructure. Some of my greatest moments in life have come from family working close with me, but some of my lowest moments in business have also resulted from giving "family" a preference over others. Hiring a customer's children to give them a break is also risky business. If you fire them, your chance of keeping the account is about zero.

Nepotism usually means that:

- Relatives won't respect and obey you as their boss — they'll still treat you like "Uncle Charley."
- You'll kid yourself about their qualifications for the job, and won't appraise their results objectively.
- If you're able to overcome the above two items, it'll probably ruin your *personal* relationship with them.
- The other employees will resent the situation, will lose respect for you, and the ambitious ones will probably go elsewhere.

In business each step must be **up**, and nepotism is the first step **down**! To avoid unnecessary struggle and possible failure — avoid nepotism!

## REASON #2: NOT KNOWING WHERE YOU ARE

It's amazing how many of us fail in business right at the time when we are reaching a peak. We have all the work we need, spirits are high, and we're giving good quality service. One day, we come into the office and find that we've overdrawn at the bank; one of our most trusted employees has been embezzling money from us. One $15,000 job we were waiting to get paid for has gone into bankruptcy. Our shop and building taxes have doubled since a year ago (we haven't had time to read the notice since it came in a month ago). Our spouse hasn't been able to stand us for the past five months, and has left a divorce note. We hadn't anticipated car problems, but notice the engine has 130,000 miles on it and is

likely to go at any minute — and we've no replacement. Our top manager is starting his own business in a month, and has just given us notice. Suddenly, we are had!

How many of us see plenty of money going into the bank, and plenty of jobs being done — assume they are profitable, and just keep rolling on, never stopping to balance things once in a while to see where we really are?

The disaster doesn't end there. Once we know we're in trouble and haven't the slightest idea if we are making money or not (or what is going on, for that matter), we run scared to a $100-an-hour accountant who plays doctor for a month or two treating only the symptoms and telling us we are in trouble — which we already knew.

You never win ball games or bids without knowing where you are in price, in service, and in public relations. Sadly, many cleaning businesses don't know where they are. They just slave away and never look up or ahead. If we know what is coming in and what our labor costs and other expenses are, we should know where we are. Few of us do. We get so absorbed in the pressing, short-term details that we never take the time to sit back and assess where we're at. Some of you reading this right now are bankrupt and don't even know it. Many are headed in that direction.

Have the guts to face the truth. Add up and balance your payables, receivables, assets, liabilities, workload, and work needs. Project your cash flow and write out a financial plan. Know what your actual status is, not what you're hoping or wishing for!

## REASON #3: NOT KNOWING YOUR BUSINESS

If you think that just anyone can run a janitor company you're fooling yourself. I own and run six operations: real estate, mail order, consulting, publishing, marketing, and janitorial. The first five are simple and easy compared to our cleaning operation. It takes a real effort to own and run a cleaning business, more skill than any other business I know! We professional cleaners have to be bankers, accountants, marketers, and laborers, and have to have an acquaintance with at least ten trades. We're salesmen, engineers, purchasing agents, and forty other things. You don't inherit cleaning or management skills, you have to learn them. You have to know your stuff, in all phases of every operation. Knowing how to do a floor perfectly and efficiently is of zero value if you can't sell your clients and get the floors to do. Too many of us don't know how to care for our own machines, or we don't know heads or tails about our own accounting systems. In short, we don't have all the skills we need. Lots of skillful, competent athletes get cut from ball teams simply because they don't know the plays. They don't have the knowledge they need to operate their business. Many times I was so busy working that I fouled up huge jobs. (I had no time to read the directions on the paint can, etc.) **I didn't know my business.**

I am now fifty years old, and still put in sixteen-hour cleaning-related work days and have for the past thirty years (this book is an anniversary edition.) I study one to two hours a day on cleaning and management skills. I get together daily with people who know a lot to ask and listen and learn.

You should be studying much more than you did in your school days. That was just play and practice, now we are in the real game.

We all have to start at the bottom rung of the ladder as far as knowledge goes, but climb the ladder as you can. Study, learn, read, ask others, and get to know as much about the business as you can, as fast as you can.

Be sure to read the business section of your local newspaper. If you don't live in an urban area, subscribe to a newspaper from a large city to keep abreast of business news.

## CRITICAL GROWTH POINTS

For years, we had a massive and successful contract to clean facilities at Sun Valley, the Idaho ski resort. Eventually, Mr. Earl Holding, one of America's truly successful businessmen, purchased the resort. Mr. Holding surprisingly chose a young, relatively inexperienced department head named Wally Huffman to run the whole resort. They utilized their own maintenance people and things went very well. Months later, I visited Wally and expressed my amazement at his rapid rise up the corporate ladder. Wally said his success was due to a five-minute training course he'd received from Earl Holding at the

**THE 3 PRIME REASONS THAT CLEANING BUSINESSES FAIL ARE NOT LACK OF WORK, LACK OF CAPITAL, OR LACK OF OPPORTUNITY AS MOST PEOPLE CLAIM . . .**

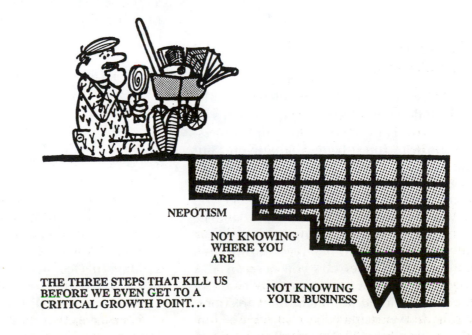

NEPOTISM

NOT KNOWING
WHERE YOU
ARE

THE THREE STEPS THAT KILL US
BEFORE WE EVEN GET TO A
CRITICAL GROWTH POINT . . .

NOT KNOWING
YOUR BUSINESS

time of his appointment as the general manager. This "short course," he said, had taught him more than five years of study in a university school of business.

Wally said Mr. Holding had looked him in the eye and said, "Wally, there are only four things you need to do to make a profit and succeed: (1) **Know** what's coming in, (2) Know what your payroll is, (3) Know what your expenses are, and (4) **Sign** EVERY check yourself! UNDER-STAND?"

Wally said, "Yes sir!" and Holding said, "See that table over there, Wally?" "Yes, Sir!"

"That table is never going to move if **you** don't move it." Mr. Holding left the room, his multimillion dollar resort in the hands of the newly-trained General Manager.

Business really is that simple. If we followed the instincts we have of business, we wouldn't have any critical growth points. We would have the usual strains, surprises, and adjustments to keep things going, but no **critical growth points**. We want growth, but we want the transition from one stage to another to be smooth and controlled. As our business revs up, we reach a point at which we must shift gears. We call these critical growth points because it is critical that we handle the transition well, but they shouldn't be critical to the point of giving you a heart attack. If you follow Mr. Holding's advice, you can avoid a lot of the heartburn when these critical points are reached in your own business.

## The First Critical Growth Point: Doubts

This is simply reaching a time when you want to or start to rely on others to run your business. You begin to let meddling accountants, bankers, lawyers, brilliant friends, would-be managers, and family start taking the reins of your business away from you. It is your business! You know how to run it better than anyone, but then you run up against a problem you're not sure how to handle (or more likely, you know what to do but just don't want to do it). So, you bawl to your accountant, for example, and he sells you on the solution of changing your whole company to being completely computerized overnight. Or the banker says you need an SBA loan; or your lawyer says you need a board of wise directors nodding and grunting directions. So you turn it over to their hands and press on. **There goes the business!** If they were so good,

they would have had their own janitorial company.

Trust your instincts and have the courage to do what you feel is right at critical points. Don't relinquish control to well-meaning "consultants" just because you're a little unsure. Keep the reins in your hands and follow your gut feelings — 90% of the time you'll do the right thing.

## The Second Critical Growth Point: Employees

When you start to hire others, you've reached the second peak. You'll see the time when you *have* to move from self-management, because you simply can't do all the work and still watch everything; you will need to hire another person or get a bigger machine. Go the machine route until you've exhausted your efficiency level, then pull in some help. But get it out of your mind at the outset that there exists an abundance of people who are knowledgeable and are as committed as you are to the cause of building the biggest and best janitorial company in the world. Finding someone like you takes a long time, and is extremely rare. Those you hire are working for the money mostly, and that's their only interest in the company. Adding to management is a critical but necessary step in growth. The process of getting others to operate productively is never easy but my simple guidelines are:

1. Hire ambitious people, who have a stable personal situation and clean habits. Make sure their ethics and principles and ideas are in harmony with yours — chemistry is important.
2. Make it clear what their job is and then let them have the freedom to do it their way. Make them accountable for achieving results for you; if they don't, don't keep them. Make sure they understand the way it is before they go to work.

3. Pay them well, better than your competitors pay, or better than their friends in the cleaning business are making, and don't give each a different bonus. If there is a commission or bonus, make it a firm percentage or dollar at the end of the period, so that there's absolutely no question about what they have coming, or it will backfire on you.

4. Work directly with the person for a while before turning him or her loose on your accounts and customers. It will only take you a day or two on the job to know if you've hired a rotten or fresh apple.

If you follow these four guidelines and follow them well, your growth points will never be critical. Timing *is* critical, though. Make sure you are taxed to the max and then some before delegating your duties to someone else. If you don't there will be too much slack with the new person and loss of profitability will result. Load yourself and other managers to the maximum before taking on anyone new.

Keep yourself on the productive payroll; earn by your personal production.

## The Third Critical Growth Point: Expansion

Bigger and better will always tug at your heartstrings, and simulating growth may even be a necessity to keep you and your employees satisfied. Expansion is another critical growth point that often upsets or topples a business. Some think of it as having too many irons in the fire. **Expansion will always be a strain.** When you move your office and phone out of your home to a town location, it's not only farther, it's about $2,000 a month in added overhead. Make sure you know where you are in sales to justify it.

Expansion is necessary and healthy, of course. How much and how many and how far is totally up to you, your needs, your emotional makeup and health. Remember, before you look to expand, make sure you are handling well the business that you already have, and that you have the resources available to handle the new work. Bigger isn't always better — sometimes bigger will bury you.

The biggest problem with **big** is, it demands precision management. When you're small you are doing lots (or most) of the work yourself and working closely with a crew. Even if you are an amateur manager or a bad one, you'll survive and conquer. When you're big you're relying on other people under you to manage, and few people can manage well. That will be your first and biggest business revelation, learning that other people seldom run things like you do. Trying to manage someone else's management will keep you out of the productive work line and cut into the revenue you were directly earning. This is one of the biggest reasons people or businesses fail when they expand. It isn't cash shortage, or lack of knowledge or skill, it's having to rely on others to manage. It always looks good on paper and sounds good in the planning, but seldom comes out in reality. When you do find employees who can manage well (and you eventually will) then go for it, pay them well, keep them with you and you'll succeed.

Remember, there is only one of you and you can only be in one place at a time. Be careful that your expansion plans don't dilute your service. You don't want to lose the accounts you now have because you're out looking for new business and not taking care of your customers.

## The Fourth Critical Growth Point: Cash Shortage

In a growing business, the first thing most people blame cash shortage on is growth (and bankers will agree!) But good growth produces cash fast in a janitorial business. Other businesses might take years to regain the benefit of it, but in ours, one month with a big profitable new building puts you cash ahead, not behind. Ninety percent of your cash shortage is simply that you're overspending for things you don't need, you aren't collecting accounts receivable, or you aren't making a true profit. If you haven't got money, you're simply not taking in more than you're putting out.

Often the cash shortage isn't the business's fault, it's yours. When people think they're making money they do real dumb things, like vehicle overkill. You can letter up a $3,000 late-model used van and it'll last for years. After all, all you do is drive it to a job and park it all day, then drive it five miles back home. You'll hardly put any miles on it, and it's all you need. It looks good and no one walking by will know it from a new one. But we decide to buy a $15,000 van, loaded with accessories, that calls for heavy insurance and heavy interest for five years. The payments aren't that big and business is still good. Then we get a new car for our wife and a riding lawnmower, a motorcycle, etc. There's $30,000-$40,000 cash gone, maybe not all at once, but within five years, so we borrow money and rush to the bank to cover the payroll.

All my vehicles have over 100,000 miles on them and I intend to get 200,000. They're good-looking, safe, don't keep me up nights wondering if they'll be stolen, and leave me lots of cash left over for life experiences and free time. I hate working for a bank!

If you hit a cash shortage, first find out why, then work your way out. Don't try to borrow your way out. Borrowing doesn't pay anything, it just moves the bill from one pile to another and stacks on other bills called interest.

Another cash mistake we make is thinking we're the town entrepreneur and beginning to invest in real estate, diamonds, etc. If you have a good productive business, you should have more faith in yourself and your business than any outside enterprise. For awhile, at least until you're really solid, let your house be your only real estate venture. I've managed to gain a large net worth and have never, ever, touched a stock or outside brokerage investment. I have more faith in myself controlling and investing my money than in some broker playing around with it.

Any service business has to have ready cash. Example: you owe $12,000 (payables) and on the books you have $42,000 owed to you (receivables). Logically you say, "Ah, I have $30,000 of my money in there (true) and one day all that $42,000 is going to come rolling in and I'll pay off the $12,000 payables and be rich with $30,000 (wrong!). It'll never happen. For every gross dollar of monthly sales you average, you need 65% of that in cash reserves on hand for payroll expenses, emergencies, good deals on used equipment when one comes along, etc.

Sometimes, in fact most of the time, a janitorial contractor is super-optimistic about all the opportunities, and thinks it will all just keep on going. Suddenly your biggest account, the one that generates almost all your good profits, leaves the city for a new location. You were doing good work and they loved you, but the factory or the bank or the building is closing. The profit and the overhead absorbed by that building is suddenly gone, and you have nothing to replace it. Goodbye business, goodbye reputation, goodbye everything. Be prepared for disaster. It happens!

Contingency planning is like taking in firewood before winter. If you don't use it, nothing is hurt, but if you need it, it'll save your life. It's not pessimism, but contingency planning. Keep a reserve of funds, and a place for you to jump in with your crew again. Never assume all will go well forever, always have ten contracts brewing and interested. In short, hunt when your stomach is full and not when it's empty. You have no strength when your stomach is empty and you'll perish.

## The Fifth Critical Growth Point: Diversification

Diversification is a stage that can unnerve and undo a business. Notice that doctors, lawyers, bank officers, even politicians, specialize instead of trying to tackle the whole spectrum of skills.

About the time most small cleaning businesses get good and profitable in walls, floors, windows, and carpet cleaning, instead of doing more walls, floors, windows, and carpets to increase profits, they get greedy for new pastures. They start a cleaning supply company, a pest control service, or a security business, usually areas they know nothing about (but have heard great things about). The learning and financing of a new venture strips time and money from existing businesses and *phhht* — both are gone, or you will struggle for ten years. More isn't always better. One thing at a time. Stick to what you know and what made you successful.

## The Sixth Critical Growth Point: "Over the Top and Down the Other Side"

In the process of life we get older, and not only our age changes, but also our needs for money, freedom, rest, etc. The time of being able to work on the job twenty hours a day at a dead run (with your wife running right in there beside you) will end. Your interests in life will change, and your health may deteriorate with time. All of this will come and it will affect your business.

## CHARACTERISTICS

**Decide beforehand** what you will do. I meet and talk with hundreds of people in the cleaning business, new and old, and see these common cleaning company characteristics.

### First-year Beginners

They are in love, on a high roll, and making money. They cherish the cleaning business and can see nothing but the positive and vow to do it forever. People always do well in the beginning, and why is easy to see. They are out on the job and doing all the work themselves; they have no one to manage but themselves. They earn their own wages, make a profit, and have no complaints because they did the work themselves — a bed of roses indeed. Production and profit, plus satisfaction and joy in the work.

### Second and Third Year Blues

Some of the roses have wilted. Their first success brought a wayward younger brother to live at the house, and they put him to work supervising the night crews. Unfortunately, he doesn't show the same concern the owners did. Complaint-handling is now a daily routine.

They have $20,000 receivables on the books, and they only owe $5,000, but never get the money in all at once so they're always sweating the bills. The equipment they bought when they were making money in the first year is worn out. The wife has had four kids and is pregnant again, and hasn't been able to help clean, so that $500 per month income is lost. It's a little discouraging, but they have faithful accounts and hang on.

## Fifth Year, or Maybe
## There's Something Easier

This is about the time most businesses face some major hurdles. Several of the critical growth points seem to pile up at about this stage, and it can present a challenge getting past them all at once. Suddenly, you're getting bigger and handing off more and more responsibility to subordinates. They don't handle things quite the same way you did, and you have complaints and unhappy customers. You lose a couple of key accounts. At the same time, you're fighting cash flow; receivables are growing ever larger, and you're struggling to pay expansion costs. You've borrowed to finance your growth, and the bankers are nosing into your business to make sure their investment is safe. They want monthly income statements and financial reports, and you're spending more time with your CPA than with your wife.

This is the point at which a lot of business owners hang it up, but there's hope. If you just hang in there and get past these major hurdles, you move on to a new plateau of prosperity. Once you get a good staff built up and delegate responsibility effectively, things will go more smoothly. You'll move into a new phase of business operation, having learned how to jump through all the financial and accounting hoops. You move into a new, more sophisticated stage of operation, ready for more controlled growth and progress. Then, when you reach that time of slowing down, and passing the business on to someone else, you'll have built something on which you can rely for financial security.

# WHERE DOES IT ALL END?

I don't know if there is "that great janitor closet in the sky" for all good cleaners, but I do know for sure that someday, maybe next week, or maybe in thirty years, there has to be an end to your janitor business. It can come voluntarily or it can come involuntarily, when you reach the point that you either want to or have to let go. We've all heard that famous whine, "If I'd known it would end up like this, I'd never have done it." People say that about marriage, hunting trips, buying a car, having an operation, and going into business. Now before you start conceiving a plan of where and when you might end, or what you might do at the end, don't shoot before you know what you're aiming at. Taking off in an airplane with no place in mind to land would be pretty dumb — about equal to starting and gutting your way through a fine cleaning business and not having some idea of where it's taking you and what you plan to do with it when you're through. And as sure as life and death, there will come a time when you are through with it. The best, most successful plans of mice and men (especially men who clean up after those mice) reach an end.

I'm not trying to make you paranoid that something bad is about to happen, there are good as well as bad reasons you reach an end. Just look at this list of events that could affect your business:

- you receive a disabling injury
- you go bankrupt
- you develop an allergy to soap
- the economy fails
- you move
- you get so rich you don't need any more money
- you get divorced
- you fall in love with someone who hates the cleaning business
- you get a lucrative offer to sell
- you lose interest
- you gain or lose a giant contract
- you're hit with a lawsuit
- you decide to retire
- you get too old to work
- you die

Don't panic, just expect change and prepare, so you can relax and cope. If you just wait and see what happens, it will happen to you and you'll have to take the consequences that come, instead of getting the consequence you want. Planning the end you desire will help to make it happen.

You start and run your own business for a reason — maybe money, maybe ego, maybe for security for your old age, maybe for all of those reasons, plus some more. I started mine to earn my way through school, and it ended up giving me much more than a ticket through college. I gained net worth, adventure, had a tremendous means to raise and educate a family, and could serve my government, community, and church. It kept me tough and physically active, and emotionally and physically healthy. But nothing is forever, jobs and businesses change; newer and better chances to grow come along, and you may wish to change course in your life and business.

I thought of this when I was going along and building my team of managers, and I've now been able to let others assume some of my responsibilities. Because I knew where I was going, I collected information, humor, stories, etc., along the way and now have the liberty to pursue my interests in writing and consulting while staying active in the cleaning field. All because I decided to stick it out and become the best pro cleaner I could be. My business has been good to me, and to my staff and friends and family. You have lots of choices. Should the change be occasioned by an emergency that causes you to have to cease your business pursuits, plan for it now, not later. Here are some options to kick around.

## THE HAND-OFF

Of those working with and for you, some will be outstanding; they will be loyal, ambitious, and will have treated your business like their own. They will know your operation, style, and customers. They will like the business and want to stay in it. They are indeed great candidates to sell, lease, or hand off your business to. Even with all the positives, this is still risky — isn't everything?

Leadership is a rare quality, which maybe you have and your general manager doesn't. He or she might be superior to you in many respects, in skill, discipline, etc., but if he or she isn't a leader, your business and accounts can fade and become worthless. You're taking a real chance here, so be careful and consider well. Most managers and supervisors in your business will grossly underestimate what you do and your value to the firm. Many times, when I was going eighteen hours a day to keep the work going,

I heard comments from the rank and file that I had it made, and was sitting back and raking in the dough. If you are making future plans to stop running the business yourself, and are expecting your faithful "Tontos" to run it while you move on to other things, do it slowly and carefully. Let the results be the proof of the pudding, especially before you hand over more.

Thousands of good, profitable cleaning businesses are piddled away by a successor manager's well-intentioned thrashing. Once it's gone you can do nothing except start all over again.

## FOR SALE

Lots of janitor companies are being bought and sold, more than ever before. There are even full-time consultants that will sell your company for you, or come in, counsel and direct you, and help you find a market. Be practical in your thinking when considering selling. If your business is really rolling and making tons of money, it's worth more, but then why do you want to sell it? If it's struggling and waning and you're desperately in debt, you'll have to look long and hard for a buyer and you won't get much when you do find one. For a business in good shape the average going price is about twice your monthly gross sales. This arrangement usually includes you keeping the existing receivables and payables, gives you a reasonable down payment and pays you out over three or four years (out of the profits). The names of professional business sales consultants can be found in the classifieds of cleaning management magazines, and in the Yellow Pages.

Whatever you do, I wouldn't make the payoff a long slow, drawn-out, "what if" process. If someone pays you out for years and years, you'll still be carrying the burden of the business. And if they foul up for any reason, you'll suffer. Get your money, all of it as fast as possible and get out — it will be best for both parties.

Make sure you sell only to those capable of handling your operation. Some nice guy with a half-million might come along and buy you out, which may seem like a great deal for you, but he may have no idea of what he's getting into. Most people outside of the cleaning business grossly underestimate the skill and endurance it takes to survive. He might pay you part down and run the business into the ground, and then he can't pay you anymore. Then you will have no business left and no money, either. I'd stick to proven competent companies and individuals you know have the capacity to succeed.

## MERGING

This is a good thing if you can stand to share the leadership after being top dog for so long. Some companies have a stronger name and position, and by hooking on with them, both will benefit. Just make sure your attitudes, ethics, and standards are the same. Some businesses operate close to the shady line; if you don't, and it makes you nervous, then stay away. Merging is a lot like getting married, there's a honeymoon during which some delicate balancing and merging of two separate (and perhaps quite different) entities is required, and it won't be all that easily accomplished.

Remember also, someone has to be king. Co-equal never works. Committee leadership in a cleaning business is "cancer of the contract." If you and someone else are half owners, one takes charge, or both pull back and let a third party be king in running it. I don't know of one successful cleaning operation that is co-operated well — that includes husband and wife deals too. One has to be king-pin, even if you take turns ("a year for you and a year for me").

## A GOOD WILL BEQUEATHMENT

Again, be careful. All the cautions regarding choice #1 apply here. This is a live operation, not a chunk of real estate or an office building or the like. The business will not sit there and do pushups while a new owner learns the ropes. Employees will leave, insurance rates may jump, and your young son-in-law or best friend will quickly begin to believe you gave him a can of rattlesnakes to tend. Dumping a janitor business on a family member is not, in my opinion, a good will bequeathment unless you're sure they're

equipped to run it. After they try to run it for a while, they may be out pouring ammonia and wax stripper on your grave.

## OFFSHOOTS

Be careful about slowing or cutting back — it's hard. Your mind and memories still will want to do what your muscle someday can't. When you've built a dynamic, fast-moving business, and you and your employees are used to you and the business moving at full speed, it's hard to slow down. If you try to slow down and still stay in control, you'll probably see the business slow down, too. Probably better to let it go forward full steam without you and find something else you can enjoy doing. It keeps you young and rewards you for your investment of effort! There are many offshoots of the cleaning business and they're all fun, productive, profitable, and rewarding.

Check one or two, or as I have, all of the below. Any of these can be a great end-plan for a professional cleaning career.

- Training
- Teaching
- Counseling
- Consulting
- Inventing
- Working for a professional organization
- Selling cleaning products
- Selling cleaning services
- Serving as a spokesperson
- Speaking
- Doing endorsements (TV shows/radio)
- Writing (a cleaning column, popular books on cleaning or cleaning texts)

When you start getting the career-changing blues, or are just doing your start-up plan and trying to foresee where you're going to end up, don't be afraid to call some of us who have been in the business awhile. Or write and ask questions. We janitors are a brotherhood and will share ideas and advice.

# MOTIVATE AND RETAIN YOUR PEOPLE

## KEEP YOUR EMPLOYEES PERFORMING

You'll discover rather quickly in the cleaning business that you cannot do all the work yourself and that you need help – good help. We covered how to legally recruit and handle employees and some basic guidelines earlier in the book. Those items are all pretty mechanical, but because we are talking about human emotions, weaknesses, and strengths that all relate to the success of your business, it can't stop here. The skill of finding, hiring, training, and keeping good people is the key to your success in building a strong business.

There are secrets to finding and keeping good people. One of the biggest expenses to a cleaning business is the big "T": turnover. You spend hours or even days finding a person and getting them hired, then training them for weeks, introducing them to the accounts, and entering them in the books on payroll and other tax reports and records. You are not getting paid for all this time and effort. Then, if the person leaves, quits, or changes for any reason, good or bad, you are out all that time and expense, to say nothing of the mistakes and complaints that arise while you're getting the replacement trained. Lose enough employees and it's equal to dumping the profits of a $10,000 job. Because the expenses of employee turnover are hidden and seemingly unaccounted for in actual cash entries, too many bosses never realize the impact it has. Turnover will kill your business if it gets too extreme.

Another item to make you think about the value of retaining employees and keeping them loyal is their ability to sell more work. A happy, fulfilled employee is a missionary for more jobs for you, while a disgruntled, lethargic person will poison and alienate your customers and make them go looking for another contractor.

Cleaning workers generally have three gears of performance: willing, neutral, and unwilling. They are all on the job, getting paid your money, working around your customers, and all the while performing at one of these levels. Make "neutral" and "unwilling" unacceptable in your company. Set your sights on "willing"; invest in your employees to get it.

It's true that all employees hire cleaners from the same pool of people, but it's important to remember that if you hire them and they give their word, and you pay them good money, you should get top performance. It won't happen without real leadership and effort from you.

I remember a building in California, contracted out to ABC company. The manager of the building never could get the company to clean well, and for years he suffered from their poor service, attitude problems, and complaints from his tenants. With legal matters the way they are, the manager took one year of documenting and collecting evidence to fire the company and finally, one Friday, justifiably dismissed this cleaning thorn in his side. The manager was jubilant at being free of this poorly-run bunch of rubbish rascals and spent the weekend happily anxious to meet the reputable contractor coming in Monday morning. When he got to work on Monday, the new company was there. They had retained (rehired) all of the old company's people, including the supervisor of the building (after all, they were seasoned, knew the building, etc.). The building manager could do nothing except consider suicide. But things did change. The new owner knew how to treat people, and soon the crew evolved to a caring, productive group, who were polite and thorough in their cleaning work. It's all up to you — the owner, the leader. You are the one to find out how to treat your people well. Remember a key factor:

### HOW YOU TREAT YOUR EMPLOYEES IS EXACTLY HOW THEY TREAT YOUR CUSTOMERS

With the national sales of this book and fourteen others, and reports in the media, we get lots of calls for advice, help, bidding information, how to name a new company, and forty other items we cover in the book. Without doubt, the two biggest questions are:

1. How can I find good people (and where)?
2. How can I keep them?

I always chuckle and tell them if I knew the full answer and method for that, I would unquestionably own all the maintenance companies and accounts in America, perhaps in the world, as soon as I learned to say "toilet" in their language. Those questions rank equal with "what is the secret of life?" There are, however, good counsel and principles used by those most successful in obtaining and retaining. By the way, these two terms (obtaining and retaining) are self-complimentary,

if not self-feeding. When you retain a person satisfactorily, see what they do for you. Even more than a good job, they bring their friends and family aboard. Yes, they recruit new people for you. A double benefit!

## Little Things that Make a Big Difference

1. **Pay on time.** A few days late, a day late, even hours can really upset cleaning people, as most are working for extra money for a tight payment, and many have their payments timed to the minute of getting the check from you. Don't punish your people because you manage collections poorly. Be sure to honor your payday and time right to the hour, at any cost, even mortgaging your house for a loan. Whenever you are late, your people will be looking elsewhere, mentally at first, physically if you repeat it.

2. **Keep your promises.** Just because they are part-time, or "only cleaning people," or can't speak English well, there is no excuse for being lax about a promise you make, be it for a raise, a day off, a change in area, a promotion, or a new machine. If you say it, you'd better write it down so you won't forget it. Because if you do, they won't and, as the old saying goes, "a man is no better than his word!"

3. **If you lose a contract or an account, or things get slow, look out for your employees.** It's so easy just to let people go. Remember, you might want them back some day, and where they go can hurt you, especially if they are class cleaners and go to your competitor. I would direct and arrange for them to go to work for my competitor. They will love you forever and would come back to you at the drop of a squeegee. It isn't your worry to place them somewhere, but being considerate, caring, and concerned, and looking ahead with notice will help when the changes come. No one likes to be dropped suddenly. A slow, loving letdown gives them time to relocate. They won't forget it, and best of all, you'll feel good about it too!

4. **Make them a companion instead of a commodity.** I've been a scoutmaster for around ten years of my life (so far) and met with the boys once a week and every month or so did a hike or an outing and thought I knew my boys well. Then I took thirty-eight boys to an international jamboree, a three and one-half week trip where I was with them twenty-four hours a day. One of the scout executives told me something that really

proved surprising and true. He said, "Don, you will get to know these boys in three weeks better than you did in ten years." He was right. Since then I learned the value of intense one-on-one interaction for getting to know people. Someone can work for you for five years, and you know them cordially and well enough to say hello and as a name on the payroll records. But work with them on a project or job for just one full day, and your whole relationship will change. They will become a person to you and you to them. It's worth the investment. I guess the saddest part of building a company as large as ours is that slowly, with the thousands of employees, we as owners don't get to know and appreciate each one personally. Remember that when you are striving to be a corporate giant, it isn't all glory; you miss a few glorious friendships along the way.

5. **Go carefully on incentive programs.** Every contract cleaner, including the giants, has been grinding away trying to find the perfect incentive bonus program for their people. We all think the other one has a secret idea that will reward, motivate, and inspire people to work harder and stay longer. This isn't true. We and the others have had a dozen or more we've tried, all with good intentions, but most ending in someone finding an angle of incompatibility. The goof-off gets rewarded for goofing off if they happen to have a good area or work in a good group. Commissions, percentage of jobs, and fifty other methods have been used by all of us, and none of us today will brag about having the perfect plan. Another problem is that most of the plans require so much extra record-keeping that they are almost self-destructive. I still feel that generous salary and wages are the best incentives, and then give a discretionary bonus if things go well and you make money, thereby creating no false expectations. It might be a little arbitrary in your judgment, but if people are happy with their pay and then get something extra, especially as a surprise, they are delighted with you-know-who. You might come up with a master plan and have all of us pay to get your idea. It is worth working on one, but don't instigate too many or too much of a plan without careful thinking and testing. Getting out of a poorly-thought-out incentive program sometimes comes with high expenses, flaring tempers, angry spouses, and greedy lawyers.

6. **Promotions.** When you dangle a carrot, have a real carrot and never dangle in jest. You'll quickly be amazed when you are hiring and mentioning the starting wage will be $5.20. If they stay and are good, you say, in one year they get $5.80. If they rise to leadership and stay several years, they can go as high as $8.00. They remember only the $8.00 per hour and everything under that is below what they want. I've done that and then for a month tried to correct the employee's bad attitude, finally deciding to fire them. When I call them in for the event, they are smiling and actually think it is to get the $8.00 raise! If becoming president is possible in your company for them, I'd let them know, but I would *clearly,* in writing, give them the steps and requirements and abilities necessary. Then I'd make sure they were given the opportunity to get where you told them they could go. If you are clear and fair, the good will rise and the poor will weed themselves out. Remember, even the biggest stumblers you have working for you, or the worst troublemakers, all imagine themselves as someday being the boss or the supervisor. If the steps are clear-cut, they are seldom crushed when someone else gets the promotion. If all are living the illusion of the promise it is "them" next, you are going to have a mutiny on your hands!

7. **Recommend employees for special opportunities.** If one of your people came to the closet at the dark building at 9:00 and there was an envelope from you, telling them that you had recommended they handle the display in the cleaning booth at the home show, the person would be sure it was the greatest day of their life. "Would you come with me and sit in on a meeting with the salesmen?" "I am bidding the building, would you come over and walk it with me?" "We are getting a new vehicle, John; you'll be driving it. Would you drive out to the S and J, look at the white van, take it for a drive, and let me know what you think?" "There is a parade for homecoming, Patty. Would you mind heading up a cleaning float?" "The school Home Ec class asked me to lecture. I told them you would be better and could teach them stain removal. Would you like to do it? I'll pay regular hours for it, too. Thanks."

I found in building my business that including the people in the boss's matters worked miracles for both of us. They always did better than I realized they could, and they gained self-esteem and status with their peers for the effort.

8. **Side with them publicly.** Complaints are a part of this business. If you ever tell a client that you will cease all complaints, he'll know you are a liar or suffering delusions. If you instead told

him, "I'll cut the complaints in half," he'd probably hire you! Well, when these complaints come in, they are generally linked to someone (your employee) doing the work. Most of us have the tendency, in an attempt to quell the customer's anger, to agree with them and slap down the employee. Word gets around fast on this one. Cutting your people in public, even if they are guilty, is a real loser. Instead, say something like, "Gee, Harry has always done satisfactory work and is super careful. He'd be disappointed to know we displeased you. Let me talk with Harry and find out what happened and I'll get back to you." Even if Harry is guilty, when you come back you can counsel Harry and impress the customer. Stand up for your people every chance you get, even taking the blame yourself when needed (not near as bad as lying on hand a grenade to save your people in a foxhole).

9. **Furnish your people good tools and supplies.** Remember, we told you that supplies and equipment account for only around 6 percent of your gross dollar, but I can tell you that an employee having a nice, clean, well-kept, modern tool in hand is worth about 600 percent in attitude and pride. Look how you react to having a new suit, car, tool, toy, etc. It changes your whole motivation and approach to the day or the job. I'd let my people have a choice in choosing their tools. Another one of the big reasons for unmotivated people is: "these chemicals they gave me won't work. The windows streak, the vacuum won't suck, or the mopstrings snag on everything." This generally happens in big government or school cleaning crews, but it can happen in your company if you are not listening.

10. **Giving awards and recognition.** Make sure your altruistic intentions are fulfilled and you don't insult your people. The world is known for pen sets and gold watches at retirements and thirty-year anniversary parties and maybe an engraved "employee of the month" plaque for the rank and file. Trinkets, toasters, and prime rib can say "thanks" if done at the right time.

## TRAINING

With so much "cleaning material" out on the market, you'll have a tendency to fall into an attitude of complacency about making sure your people are trained and up to date on the newest in cleaning and conduct on the job. There are tons of films, stories, magazines, editorials, and seminars about cleaning, and you'll figure that you and your employees will absorb enough to be wise to the ways of the cleaning tides. Not so! Real leadership and changing habits will have to come from you, the owner, the leader. No matter how busy you get thrashing in the daily survival of the cleaning business, you have to stop and get your people together and teach them and share with them. You can do lots of that on the job, if you are working with them, but unfortunately, we procrastinate and soon months go by. Then years go by, and then your employees and your reputation go bye-bye! You'll get the feeling, once you get rolling in your business, that all your people are thinking the same as you; that they're inspired, consumed in building the business and cleaning up the world, but that isn't so. They work for a check until you give them something more. One area in which you can and will beat your 10,000 competitors is by taking the time to teach, inspire, and love your people. Sometimes the business just doesn't give them much positive attention and appreciation, and if you do and your competitors don't, then guess who'll have most of the good cleaning people around? You!

### Keep the Meeting Positive

Most of us wait until there is a crisis or until we lose a building or contract or until Mrs. Van Snoot's rug was shrunk ten inches, and then we call the gang in for a chewing out like we see in the movies. That is the quickest way to clean out your cleaning staff. Call the meeting when things are on a high or when there is occasion to reward or congratulate someone. That is the perfect environment to teach, ask, correct, and get positive results. If you do it right — the right time, the right content, the right setting — it will be your own "State of the Union" message and will spearhead higher production and morale. Here are some outlines and guidelines I've found to work:

**Setting:** Don't hold it in the shop or a drafty storage room. The place can say a lot. Sometimes, do it in your home or rent a room at the local motel (conference rooms are only $40 or so a day). Avoid restaurants and combining the meeting with a meal; you'll lose the focus. Just think of a private place with no distractions. Even some of your accounts will gladly let you use their conference rooms in exchange for a carpet cleaning, or in fact because they are enthused that you are training for their place.

**Keep it short:** Cover what you have to cover,

but keep the meeting short. You can cover a lot in thirty to ninety minutes and no one gets restless. Remember, good cleaners are not good sitters. If you are going to have longer training, or a guest, make it two hours. Just don't drag the meeting out or the employees will begin to anticipate meetings as a negative and dread their coming, which is a poor frame of mind for learning.

**Curtail any negativism:** Whatever you do, allow no moaning and groaning, crying and complaining. Once one person starts whining, all the others will join in like sheep and do their best to out-complain each other. Janitors and maids love to complain. It's probably a psychological retaliation for all the whining and complaining they hear every day. Don't let any of them even whimper. Keep the emphasis positive so all are aware of it and they correct each other when one begins to bawl about something.

**Guest speakers:** Be careful to screen the person first, but if you find someone who has a short, interesting message, even a supplies salesman with an introduction of a new method or product, invite him to the meeting and let him speak to your people. You can even give your message to the other person and have them tell your employees. Outsiders are new and fresh and remember, sometimes seeing your people every day, you become like a parent to them, and you know how kids believe their uncle or a stranger before they will their parents. Well, the same is true here. The guest can be speaking of cleaning or not, and if you just ask, you'll be surprised at how many guests will come freely and graciously!

**Participation:** Don't make this a lecture meeting. Let them talk and tell their experiences of what they have found to work. It is even wise to approach one or two of the people and say, "Harry, we have a meeting coming up and lots of the people are still confused about handling the Haitian cotton upholstery. Could you take a few minutes and show us how you do it? You have done a great job and are the one to teach it." Do you realize what that will do for Harry and the others? Magic!

**Tangible blessing:** Always have something for them to take home, in their hands, in their minds, and in their stomachs. Copy helpful information out of trade magazines or books, or pick up some safety or technical materials from your insurance carrier or sanitary suppliers. Not too much, just a few items they will read and enjoy and keep. Cleaners generally get very little information, so they will treasure the beneficial stuff you put in their hands.

If the occasion is right, a few exhibits are nice. Lay out some pictures of recent jobs, and even print some extras for your people. One picture of them hanging from the scaffolding to take home and show to the family will do more to bind them to you than two hours of lectures.

## Outline for a Successful Meeting

**Open/welcome and greeting:** You should conduct the meeting, and introduce each person by having them stand and give their name and where they work, and if you are on the ball you can say something nice about each one right as they finish.

**Report the good news:** Those letters, calls about honesty, compliments from customers, and birthdays, too — take time to read them out loud in front of everyone! Also report any promotions or changing responsibilities, new contracts, and so on.

**Humorous cleaning story:** Have it pre-assigned and always take turns. Have an employee stand and tell the story; they will love it.

**A time for challenges:** People love contests — a game, puzzle, or competition concerning cleaning. Get all of them working and get their brains going. Even a song might be the thing.

**Program and business:** Invite a speaker, watch a video, demonstrate a new machine, plan a party, take a trip or tour. There are hundreds of exciting things you can do here.

**Questions and answers:** Let all of them speak, and remember, cut short the moaning and complaining questions.

**Refreshments:** How about a toilet punch bowl?

**Distribute the material:** Time for handout stuff and any final prizes or surprises.

## RETAINING: THE FINAL MAGIC OF A PRO CLEANER'S SUCCESS!

Sustaining your cleaning business is exactly like sustaining your marriage, health, garden, friendships, hobbies, or spirituality. It is a simple law of the universe. If you don't take care of it and enhance it, it will fail. Remember, there is about a 96 percent failure rate in the cleaning business, and the failure rate for marriage is only 55 percent. So your chances for losing all you have built and invested in your cleaning business are a harsh reality. I would say that most of your competitors are spending their time right now in retaining and recovery efforts for some customer or account that they did not take care of. Remember, we told you that word of mouth is the best way to grow and to get business. Well, word of mouth is also the most effective way of getting rid of business. Word of mouth carries both good and bad news equally, and in cleaning especially, you can be lulled into a false sense of security, thinking that once you have built the best, the most reputable business in town, you have it made and can run on cruise control for a while. Keeping contracts and customers is not "luck." Trying to get a lost contract or customer back is not fun or free. It can break your back and your bank account. Remember there are 4,000 competitors (and some might be good, new, determined ones) out there knocking on the doors of your customers fifteen minutes after you finish cleaning their place. And they never let up. Success is never final; it's not a destination, it's a journey.

Let's go about this using rust as an example. When you see a rust spot appear, you sand, re-prime, and paint while it's still very small. You've stopped it and it cost you very little time or money. If you let it go a while because the metal is thick anyway, then sand, prime, and paint it, you still save it, using some of your time. If you let it go until it rusts through and breaks, and then fix it, people lose confidence in you. It costs like crazy and you lose lots of time. So you say, "You're right, I'll do the first one." Wrong. The secret is not to let it rust, keep it well painted (well covered), and you'll never get any rust at all and that is the way to look at your now-sharp business. Just think of all the time you spend obtaining and, if you spend little time retaining, how much will be spent on recovery! Here are ten commandments of retainment:

1. **Inspect:** Go back and read pages 119 to 128 again and believe it. Inspections force you to a performance and exposure level with the customer that makes it hard to procrastinate and fail.

2. **Initiate:** This is the simple principle of not having to be asked to do something that needs to be done for the customer. It is human nature to notice, analyze, appraise, and give suggestions, but it is rare for someone to see the problems and just go take care of it, without being beaten, threatened, asked, coaxed, or bribed. One thing you want to keep your customer convinced of is that you are the Pro and that you know your business. The best way to do that is not by taking them to dinner or flashy resorts, but simply ferreting out their problems and taking care of them before they have to call you in and ask. Ninety percent of your competitors are going to sit around and wait for the phone to ring with a request. You should be out and about, searching for something to help clean and care for the customer. You could send a note or drop by the manager's office and say, "Mr. Williams, I noticed the weather forecast says snow next Thursday. I moved the mat out of the basement for the day people so it would be ready to go. I'll tell them to put it out at the first sign of snow, so no one will slip and fall on that slick entry floor." Or you could say, "Mr. Williams, I noticed the brass on the second story sign is pretty badly oxidized. I know we don't clean your sign, but we would be glad to take care of it for you. It would probably only take a few hours and cost under $60. Let me know."

Think of how you respond, how your confidence level soars, when someone finds and takes care of problems. There are a million people saying, "call me if there is anything I can do" and only a few saying "here, I did this." You are the pro in the cleaning business. It's up to you not to only do the assigned work, but to seek out and do the other work needing to be done. If you see a construction problem in the building during remodeling, don't go whining to the building manager about the drywall mud on the toilet set; he or she is already up to the ears with problems. You just figure out a way to correct it and clean it up and then go tell the manager what you did. If he doesn't faint, he'll never forget you, and you leave with a shield of service that any competitor will have a hard time penetrating, regardless of their price or policies.

3. **Watch winners.** There are people out there who have their act together in life and in the cleaning business. Because you cannot be all things for all seasons, you need to watch and chart and study the winners. I daily collect cleaning ideas within and without my company and from my competitors, and then get to thinking that nothing is left

out there to learn. There is a maid in a North Dakota motel who does some magic cleaning or public relations trick that amazes me. Contain yourself from being jealous or envious of those who are superior to you in something. Learn to love and respect them and befriend them and guess what? They'll teach you, and there is a possibility they'll help make you better than they are. Nothing is worse in the cleaning business than developing a thick forehead, so be flexible. If a competitor takes away your best account and is seemingly now doing a better job than you did, find out how he did it and you'll not lose another one the same way. By the way, this is a good habit to have, not only for cleaning, but in marriage and family, too.

4. **Heap on the health.** If anything should be related to success in making things clean and nice, then having and maintaining a healthy body should. Everything in the success of your cleaning business depends on you: how you look, how you feel, and the physical energy and strength you have as an individual. Cleaning is one job for which you have to be strong, in shape, and able to endure tough hours, physical and mental strain, and stress. For some jobs you can be half in tune and get by, but not in the cleaning business. You'll lift, reach, trot, run, drive, carry, counsel, and stay up nights more than almost any profession going. All of it is pretty exciting, too, if you endure! Remember, to be successful in cleaning, you aren't going to stand around with a clipboard and have the coolies do all the work. That might come in twenty years, but not starting out. You are going to have to get in there and do the work. If you don't look and feel well, you seldom perform well. People don't like being around you or even working for you when you're not fit. Poor physical fitness really hurts your leadership abilities, and leadership will be your number one asset in the business, even with only a few employees. Being overweight, smoking, or using drugs will project you as the opposite of clean, which makes selling your service and yourself rather difficult. The bottom line is that you have to be vibrant twenty-four hours a day!

5. **Stay on the job.** I don't know where the public gets the illusion that a businessman puts all the people to work, then sits in a big office and scoops in the money, while he delegates all the problems and blame. I'll tell you a big truth about the cleaning business. If you aren't out there scooping up the dirt, you won't be scooping up any of the money. In the cleaning business, especially in the beginning and building stages, you have to be out on the job, possibly every day, getting there first and leaving last. You have to learn all the skills, customer needs, chemicals, equipment, how to mix and fix. If there is a substitute for this, I do not know of it. You'll find (if you haven't already noticed) that you seem to get more done than anyone else on the job. That means you are making money. Even though you might not be taking a paycheck, the equity and worth you gain are astounding. You'll generate from $10 to $25 per hour income, when you are working, plus being with your people. You'll inspire, motivate, train, and anchor their loyalty. It will take a long time or a mighty good supervisor before you can turn loose and stay home to count the money and bid jobs. I'm convinced that if you ever make it big and good, you have to have solid seasoning on the job with your head in the toilet and your hand in the garbage can. I've seen a few cleaning people who did well early on and seemed to have a system that produced them fat profits while they stayed in the office and took friends to dinner. Eventually, however, their lack of seasoning showed and they lost it. Another benefit of being on the job is that the customer gets to know you and you get to know them, instead of them just knowing your people (who then can and will, on occasion, steal your contracts and accounts). There is a lot of security in working on the job. Don't worry, the time for you to be an executive will come, when you are ripe for it.

6. **Use time fragments.** Our fast-paced society doesn't give us full days anymore, or full weeks or months. Finding full hours to get something done is rare anymore, but we do have lots of spare minutes bouncing around, before, after, and during our jobs and free time. You have to learn to use them. If the customer is not there to unlock the door, do you sit and wait? Something breaks and is getting fixed. Free time? Never! These three and five minute fragments of time have to be used, because you, the entrepreneur, don't get paid a salary for just being around during a certain time. You get paid for doing something, producing something. A five-minute repair will probably save you a five-hour fixup later on (while a three-man crew sits around watching and getting paid). "I'll do this when I get a few minutes," is the

famous statement we make during the few minutes we have. You don't manage or save time, as the experts say, you only use time. Keep a list of recalls, contacts, calls, jobs, etc., that is always right there ready to go when a cancellation or conflict comes along. I know lots of pictures show (and you have seen) janitors kind of lagging around at a go-to-sleep pace. They are working for someone (maybe the government). But it's a lot different from you and your own business. You have to move fast, thinking, scheming, hunting, panting, reasoning, and snatching up all the chunks of time you find, always doing something to upgrade you, your accounts, or your employees.

7. **Keep equipment/supplies in prime shape.** Slippage, the act of letting something good deteriorate until it is raunchy, is the worst of all sins for a cleaning contractor. Here you are, trying and claiming to clean up their place, and your equipment, ladders, trucks, etc., are worn and chipped and dirty. Almost without exception, no matter how rich or poor, successful or loved cleaning people get, they get careless about the machines and tools they use for their living. I think that is worse than even a dentist's tools getting caked and dirty. I fight it in my own business constantly. People are tired when the job is over; it is late and the vacuum, still with soft crud hanging on it, is stored away. Next day the crud is cement hard, but the vacuum works fine and after all, getting the job done is the most important thing, so the mangy thing is thrust back and forth in the customers' and clients' eyes, saying with each pass, "we don't care, we don't care, we don't care." Some of our equipment is so wounded it is almost unidentifiable, and yet we lug it into a fine $300,000 home to do a $500 cleaning job when $20 and a few minutes cleaning and painting would have shaped it up fine. The bottom line is: the biggest value of clean is appearance, how things look when you are finished, both the building and the machine. There is built-in invaluable training when you make your people keep their equipment up. It is a principle that once they learn and practice it, they begin to think, "neat," "clean," "snappy," "right," etc. Another item here is to keep the stuff labeled and your name on it. Your stuff will eventually get left behind, fall out of the back of the truck, or get borrowed, and the recipient of the newly lost item has no idea who to call

and return it to. Brand it, then tend it. A little item, but it will pay big dividends.

8. **Deal with losing one or two.** I've been at this business for thirty-five years, ABM has been at it fifty years, Servicemaster and others a lot of years, too. Last year my company lost over one hundred accounts, and in most of them we were doing a good job. It doesn't seem fair, but it is part of the cleaning business. You can be underbid (by bad competitors), the manager can suddenly decide to hire his worthless brother-in-law, the company can go bankrupt, there are numerous (besides lousy workmanship) reasons we lose contracts. Any are unfortunate, but your first one will be devastating to you emotionally, even more so if it is the majority of your income. Many people are so set back by this that they just quit and give up. After all that work and investment, and learning the cleaning business, to surrender it all because you lose one of the rounds. It's not good for your pocketbook or your self-esteem. I've had contracts taken away so unfairly on equality bids, by jerk managers, etc., that it would make a full-grown man just bawl. I still bawl, for five minutes, then I practice a philosophy you should learn. The first impulse is to say "well, if I'm going out, I'm going to get my pound of flesh and a little revenge." And you can cut hours during the notice period, rape the building, slack off, and get one fat month. That is the shortest reward you'll ever get and a one-way ticket out of the business. Do good to those who despitefully use you. I now put extra effort into the account that gets cancelled. We're determined to leave it so good the competitor cannot keep it that way and the manager won't forget us. Blessed are the peacemakers, for they shall again get the building. And that will happen someday. Nothing is nicer than to go back into a building or an account you lost (for any reason, even your fault). So when you get notice you are going, go and make peace and make tracks, and go in the last day when you clean out your equipment and point out to the manager how good you left the building. Thank them and leave a card. If you did something wrong, then correct it, and if you got underbid, find out how they did it. Sometimes losing contracts can be a real educational experience and beneficial in the long run. Just don't get discouraged and think you are the only one ever to lose one.

# SOME FINAL SECRETS FROM THE PROS

WET FLOORS

## PROGRAM TO PROFESSIONAL

About the time you get serious about starting your cleaning company, or as you first begin, you'll notice there are cleaning companies all over the place. Thousands of them will seem to sprout out of nowhere. Even your relations, whom you've known for years, will spout "Oh yes, Mergatroid, we've been cleaning three banks for the last fifteen years — didn't you know that? That's how we got our motorhome and how we sent the kids through college."

You'll see scraggly buffers in the backs of station wagons in every town you drive through at 6 A.M. Janitorial supply stores will appear to be on every corner. TV ads for cleaning products will suddenly look ridiculous. Sloppy, careless people will irritate you more. Yes, all of this was going on long before you decided to throw your hat in the ring, but you were not tuned in to it. There have always been thousands of cleaning businesses in this country, so it's nothing new. Cleaning is the oldest profession in the world and also the largest — over 10,000,000 are doing it.

On my last trip to Los Angeles I found out that the Chamber of Commerce lists over 7,500 cleaning companies in their vicinity. Yet, I'll bet you there are hundreds more they're not aware of. How do they all survive? Look around you — you can always find a mess. There's an infinity of cleaning work available and there always will be. It is a wonderful business.

But we, you and I, don't want to be one of those who just survive in the business. Survival isn't fun, it isn't profitable, and it's not at all motivating. Of your competitors (millions of 'em) 20% are survivors: "just-enough-to-get-by'ers," slugging out an existence in life, taking what they can get with the least amount of effort expended. Seventy-eight percent are just average, putting out average effort, making average income, doing average work for average customers. They have an average training program, work an average day, keep their books and equipment up to average snuff. They have average employees that they keep around for an average number of years.

Now, if you are going to make the effort to start and run a business, do you want to be a slug, or one of the averages? Or do you want to be one of the remaining 2% in the cleaning field, and be TOP NOTCH? It takes a bit more effort, but it can double your profits and double the pleasure you get from your job, not to mention your company's value. It is thrilling to be in the top 2% of the industry, and it takes no magic, just a tiny bit more effort and at the heart of that effort, desire!

## SECRETS

Here are the parting "secrets" that I'd like to share with you.

### How Can I Serve?

Before you actually open your business, take several days. Take a pencil and a notebook and go to the very best restaurants, stores, service stations, medical centers, fast food chains, parks — high traffic areas — and sit and watch. Just watch the movement, the people at work, the operation. Watch the service, attitudes, neatness, promptness, employee morale. Watch how they treat customers, their facility, their fellow workers. This exercise will beat any university course on "how to succeed in your own business." After two days of watching and jotting down notes, spend a day watching the losers, the low-end stores, the barely-making-it joints. Then go home and go to work! It is easy to see why successful people are successful in a business: they serve. You are going into a service business; the only asset and product you have is service. You can learn skills and products and methods in minutes, but service — the pure, selfless attitude that makes your customer feel his needs are your number one priority — that is paramount to making you a success.

You have made the commitment to serve when you become a cleaner. Other things like the weather, how big a job is, how messy it is, or how much it's worth are irrelevant. Follow the successful businesses you observed and make your goal "How can I serve?" Instantly you'll be ahead of 98% of your competitors.

### A Sacred Trust

Ownership is not power, it's a sacred trust! The day you start cleaning, even small window jobs and trash cans, you've taken possession of other people's lives and facilities. You are the director of lives and places, not the ruler — don't ever get them mixed up.

### Clean Up Your Life

Spend your first weeks in business fixing up your own home, cars, possessions, and life in general. You lead and manage by example. What you are will be 90% more influential over others than the title or position you hold. De-junk your life of the garbage and habits that for years you've wanted to be rid of. Lose the weight, cut out the mild drugs (tobacco, alcohol), improve your grooming, make the choices you've put off, etc. Take an hour a day to read about and keep current in the industry. Mend the fences of bad relationships — you won't have time for grudges, family feuds, etc. Simplify your money matters so you can concentrate your energy on cleaning up the earth's surface without financial worries.

### The Little Extras

Give more than you promise on every job — an extra couch cleaned, an extra coat applied, an extra few minutes spent will be remembered longer than the entire five-day job. People remember how you make them feel over what you do for them. Doing more than the customer asks will give you more referrals than forty sales calls, a weekly mailer, or a colorful brochure. The little extras like fixing some little thing, an extra service, or a follow-up card or gift — do them graciously. You'll feel great about it, and you'll endear yourself to the customer. They'll be your best advertisement.

### The Customer's Always Right

Disputes and arguments with dissatisfied customers (and they happen even to the very best) can only harm you and your company. Even if you're right and they are over-demanding, listen to them (a common courtesy they will appreciate) and make an adjustment in their favor. Ask them how they want you to handle the situation, then give more than they ask. Generally you'll absorb little cost, but a lot of pride. By yielding to a customer you keep your principles and most likely keep them as a customer forever (it becomes an advertisement as they tell their friends how good you were to them.)

## Give Fair Warning

All the jobs you take on will not be ideal. Sometimes the house or building is a real stink bomb ready to explode when you get there. Four German shepherds have visited one corner of the house for years, the paint is forty-two years old; the couch that you are to clean is threadbare and has a grease spot where the master lays to guzzle beer in front of the TV; the floor tiles are the cheapest on the market and their pit bull keeps biting your employees and eating their sponges. You cannot, however, point out these liabilities and criticize their abode, "Boy, is this a hole. Don't expect much, we'll be lucky if we don't lose two employees to staph infection." Instead take a professional approach and point out possible problems before you even accept the job. If you discuss your concerns the customer will take on reasonable expectations. People expect miracles from professional cleaners, because they think you know everything, that you can make new velour grow on the back of the couch with a magic shampoo. If they're told up front, they know what to expect. For example, stare at the couch with wonderment and say, "These were certainly hearty pieces of furniture. We can clean them Mr. Creaky, however, there is damage and wear. Like here on the seats the velour is gone and the piping has worn completely off. Cleaning the pieces won't really restore their appearance. Perhaps it might pay to consider reupholstering, and apply the twenty-nine dollars we'd charge toward that." You've given fair warning, plus your professional opinion. The ball is in their court. Tread lightly when criticizing sloppy paint jobs and construction — it was probably done by one of the family, and your unsolicited opinion will lose a job and friends.

## Don't Lend or Rent

Your equipment, ladders, scaffolding, machines, and paraphernalia will fascinate your neighbors, friends, and family — and all the organizations in the county, who, when they need a little something done, will think of your equipment and want to "rent" it from you. They really don't want to "rent" it, they just want to borrow it, and if you do charge them for it, they'll be put out. If they break it, what are you going to do? Make them pay? Never! You'd just have to take it on the chin (and out of your pocket). Keep all your professional equipment, including vehicles, under tight control. Don't lend or rent, it only leads to problems. Just tell them "My liability carrier won't let me loan or rent equipment — it is out of my hands." That will keep them thinking for a while.

## The Expert

Live your "cleaning" like a religion. Now that you are a cleaner, act like one. Become the expert at home and abroad: always carry with you some notes on cleaning and some anecdotes in case you're asked to speak, a stain chart or two to hand out, a cleaning item to demo or use in case of a spill. After all, you're the expert and like a doctor carrying his bag, you too should carry the tools of the trade so you can perform in an emergency. Have your own cleaning library, subscribe to cleaning trade magazines, ask questions and give information about cleaning; no matter where you are people will open up and do the same.

## Thank You's

If someone gives you a good reference or is responsible for getting you another job (from a friend or associate) be sure to write or call that person and thank them graciously, even send some little gift (such as an Aslett book!) as a thank-you gesture. Too often, totally from someone else's effort, we land an $800 carpet job, making $300 profit, then we take our spouse to lunch, forgetting to take five minutes to thank the person responsible for our good fortune.

## Establish Effective Communications

Establish effective communications. In a service business you must be accessible and easy to find. Emergencies in our business are a double-edged sword. If they happen and you get there, your client loves you more and the extra work is extra profitable, because people are willing to pay more for immediate service. On the other hand, if you are unreachable the client becomes unnerved and will call someone else or do it themselves. Both have the potential to eliminate you from their call roster. This doesn't mean you are sitting poised by the phone or on the customer's door step twenty-four hours a day, it means you leave information of your whereabouts while you work, play, go to church, etc.

## Politics

I've never believed in the old political stand-by, "It's who you know, not what you know that counts." Until you owned a cleaning company, you always thought that all the politicians and crooks were in Washington. Wrong again. A whole new world of opportunity for dealing with political situations emerges as you begin to clean up after people. You'll not only be aware of "political deals" going on, but many will come your way. A chance for you to make special considerations or "courtesies," as they are called. And you get certain advantages later on called "payoffs," or "favors." They are so little and innocent at first, like someone asking you to loan or smuggle out some of the company equipment without telling anyone. Or doing a little job for them personally at no charge, burying the cost in the big job you're doing for their company. Or doing an extra job and billing it to another department as a favor, or padding a billing to add in other work that wasn't approved. On my second job, the mayor of the town asked me to double the bill to the insurance company and he would split it with me. (I didn't, but it was tempting.) Remember how you and others, when reading about a politician, a public figure, a famous athlete, a smart Wall Street businessman who is a million dollars in trouble, would ask, "how could they ever do that, be that stupid?" Well, they are smart and often good people and not stupid. They just made a misjudgment in some way at some time, and then repeated it a few times and soon they were buried in "beholding to" other people. Don't confuse favors with service, for every time you think you have found an easy street it will end up a dead-end road. It generates a lot of embarrassment and sometimes costs you all your hard-earned business and good reputation. Don't get "obligated" to anyone for any reason.

## The Job for You

Another big question we get here at the Cleaning Center from all of you owning or starting your own janitorial company is: "Which is best, big or little jobs?" Size isn't always a key to profitability. For example, you get a $300 floor stripping job, spend all day on it, and make $30 profit. Or you might do a $50 window job, spend one hour, and net the same $30. I know lots of contractors who have a $1000 per month cleaning contract and make 4 percent; that's $400 for the whole month of risk, fighting problems, and employee turnover. Another contractor who lives next door shampoos carpets and mats a few days a month and makes $800 profit. There are two factors at work here: (1) selecting the work that nets the most profit for the shortest time; and (2) selecting the work that you enjoy doing. I never liked or could make money cleaning grocery stores. I have a friend who makes $150,000 a year at it and loves every minute, thinks it's a piece of cake. I hate routine and love extra work. Some people love steady, sure work with guaranteed results. I guess my ultimate answer is to select the work you really enjoy doing, get good at it, and then you'll make money and be happy while doing it. I couldn't be an accountant in L.A. for a million dollars a day, but there are accountants in L.A. who wouldn't live on a farm in Idaho and be a janitor for two million dollars a day, yet both of us are happy.

## Being Your Own Boss

You might think we are overkilling the counseling to be really sure that being on your own is what you want and expect. Ninety percent of people, jobless or job rich, all tell me: "I want to have my own business, I want to be on my own." I can sure understand that, as I have been on my own entirely since age sixteen and I love it. I love risk, I love pressure, and I love survival. I love being entirely responsible for my own welfare and problems, but not everyone feels that way. In fact, I find that only a small percentage of people who want their own businesses, to be their own boss, really have any idea what it means. They have seen an illusion of the "boss" and think just changing their position will change them and their life. We have lots and lots of people working for us who, after watching us and visiting our homes and families, etc., decided they were going into their own business and broke off from our company into one of their own. Almost every one of them failed, not because they were bad people or poor workers or didn't know the business. They all were sharp, good cleaners and producers. The problem was, they didn't realize there was suddenly no one to turn to for sympathy, money, answers. They were the end of the line. If a job went bad, they and their kids went hungry, not the employees. If something was stolen or broken on the job, they paid for it, not the company. They were the company.

This is a big surprise and a big adjustment. I had a top employee cleaning a local area. I got $1500 a month for the area and then, in the '60s, was paying him a handsome $1300 a month to do it. With my payroll tax, it was costing me $1500 to clean, but worth it because of the key area. The man knew I was getting $1500 and he only $1300. He figured if he had it all, he'd be $200 a month richer, so he cleverly stole the contract for $1450. At the end of the first month, by the time he paid the little business things, self-employment tax, his own insurance, uniforms, and twenty other items, he had $900–$300 less than before. I don't think he has figured it out yet! I taught a Facility Care Course for would-be professional cleaners at a college. All of them were in the class because they had decided to be "professional cleaners," all baring their souls that that was the profession for them, and they would learn and pursue it with much gusto. On the second day of class I brought in fake $1,000,000 checks and presented them to each student and gave them fifteen minutes to list on paper what they would now do with their life and the money. Not one single person said they would use it for a cleaning company or gear. Every one of them (forty) was going to buy the truck for hauling, the ranch for farming, the boat for touring, the flower shop, the restaurant. Really, not one of them wanted to be or was converted to being a cleaner. They were there to find something they might like to do, which is the initiation for failure in this business. I had another couple of twenty-five year olds, who read my books and, watching my success, came in the office tough, willing, and able, wanting to have their own company. They were sure! After they had signed in blood testimony their commitment to their own business, all of a sudden I said, "I have two $80,000 jobs waiting for managers working under me." They both jumped at the offer. I knew then they were not entrepreneurs, destined right now for their own business. You have to be willing and able emotionally and physically to take any risk and failure and have more faith in your own wit than a secure guaranteed job. This business is not an eight-to-five job. It is a midnight-to-midnight job of which you chisel your time off backwards. It will make you sharper and better than any business person in town, it will educate you, in fact you'll become a great person from it and that is worth everything. Just make sure right now that is what you want and that you are willing to pay the price.

## Lose the Blues

Lose the "I feel sorry for myself — I work Saturdays" blues. You knew when you decided to come into this business that your prime-time work hours are those when everybody else isn't working. Meaning, of course, nights and weekends. This really bothers people who are geared around "play-days." Personally I think working Saturdays and off-hours are to my advantage. You miss the traffic jams, crowds, noise, lines, etc. It didn't take me long in life to figure out that on holidays and Saturdays, vacation spots are full of pushing masses, drunk drivers, and lines. By working on Saturdays, Veterans Day, Labor Day, etc., and taking my family on outings the day after, it's really living — we have the world to ourselves. I don't work Sundays for two reasons: first, it's the Sabbath, ordained for man to rest, second, for all the others who think like I do, who don't like businesses operating on Sunday. I won't be a customer for those who stay open.

Well, there you have it, the summation of my experience in the cleaning industry. I hope you enjoy your own cleaning business as much as I have, and get the same kind of growth and fulfillment. This last section of the book will give you some places to look for resources and ongoing training material.

## RESOURCES

Between this book and your own initiative, you can learn anything you need, and somewhere, if you have the hustle, you can find a source for any other information you may need. There is always a place, a person, a seminar, a book or brochure to help you. Just make sure the information and sources you tap are good ones. Lots of people who fail in running their own janitorial business, or who've only been in it for a year or two, are giving information, but it's only partial information and it can lead you into thinking that running a business is a simple and mechanical operation. Being really successful at running a business is mostly heart, commitment, and desire. You want to accomplish, to make something of yourself, and provide things for your family. Very few businesspeople are greedy or stingy so if you want good solid information, go to the people who are doing it, not those who are just going around telling others how to do it. I don't agree with every piece of information in all the sources

I'm giving you. I think, though, that you're smart enough to sort out a lot of it for yourself. New innovations come along all the time. I put a lot of information in my book *Is There Life After Housework?* It has more good technical knowledge and information than any book of its type in print, and has sold over half a million copies since it was published. After we put out the first edition I realized that there were little things about wood floors and carpets, for example, which I, a professional, figured everyone would know, so my publisher and I spent a lot of time and money and we upgraded and revised it, adding 50 more pages of good solid information. You ought to have this book before any other. It contains thirty years of my experience and know-how and professional shortcuts to help you do things right and fast.

Remember, you can always pick up the phone and call and ask people when you're in doubt. Write and exchange ideas and stories and share. This will be one of the nicest experiences you've ever had.

The most important requirement for a good successful cleaning business, aside from some basic financial knowledge, is a burning commitment and desire to "MAKE IT." With these virtues YOU CAN DO IT, even if you know nothing about cleaning. You can learn cleaning skills! But bear in mind that when we talk about cleaning and maintenance, it seems that EVERYONE is an expert. They all seem to have their secret remedy, hint, or tip, yet never has anyone solved the basic CLEANING problems. Never has there been one single place or source where one could go to get the information, direction, and inspiration to do the whole job.

But there are places and people who know a lot about cleaning, and how to make it go more efficiently. It often only takes a call or a letter, or getting a subscription to the right professional journal in the field. There are classes, seminars, videos, cassette tapes, and other programs. Many of these are available at little or sometimes no cost.

You don't have to suffer through trial and error. What you can't handle yourself, you can get help to do. You don't have to rely on old wives' tales or so-called magic formulas. (And doing the job right and more quickly means a better life and job for you, your associates, and your family.)

The final section (appendix) lists references and resources which will be valuable in your future self-education. These lists are by no means complete, but they will provide you with detailed information about many aspects of a small service business.

These resources are one key to self-improvement. Once you know where to find what you need, and put forth the effort to get ahead, you are on the road to success. The future is your hands. Good luck. I've done all I can — the rest is up to you.

# Appendix

For career or class research and more information here are some professional associations and producers who can help you with cleaning and maintenance education and improvement.

## PROFESSIONAL ASSOCIATIONS

American Hospital Association
840 North Lake Shore Drive
Chicago, IL 60611
(312) 280-6000

American Hotel & Motel Association
1201 New York Avenue
Suite 6000
Washington, DC 20005-2031
(202) 289-3100

Building Service Contractors Association
    International
10201 Lee Highway, Suite 225
Fairfax, VA 22030
(800) 368-3414

Chemical Specialties Manufacturers
    Association, Inc.
1913 I Street NW
Washington, DC 20006
(202) 872-8110

Cleaning Management Institute
13 Century Hill Drive
Latham, NY 12110-2197
(518) 783-1281

Hoover Home Institute
101 East Maple Street
North Canton, OH 44720
(216) 499-9200

International Sanitary Supply Association
7373 N Lincoln Avenue
Lincolnwood, IL 60646
(800) 225-4772

International Window Cleaning Association
P.O. Box 48426
Niels, IL 60648
(708) 295-7700

National Executive Housekeepers Association
1001 Eastwind Drive, Suite 301
Westerville, OH 43081

National Sanitation Foundation
P.O. Box 1468
Ann Arbor, MI 48106
(313) 769-8010

New York Rug Cleaners Institute
301 Norman Avenue
Brooklyn, NY 11222
(718) 389-9129

Proctor & Gamble Co. Educational Services
P.O. Box 14009
Cincinatti, OH 45250
(513) 983-2029

The Soap & Detergent Association
475 Park Avenue South
New York, NY 10016
(212) 725-1262

## BOOKS ON MANAGEMENT AND SUPERVISION

Aslett, Don A. *How to Upgrade and Motivate Your Cleaning Crews.* Pocatello: Article 1 Publishing, 1986. A detailed program for motivating and inspiring your service personnel.

Blanchard, Kenneth, and Johnson, Spencer. *The One-Minute Manager.* New York: Berkeley Publishing Co., 1983.

Dible, Donald M. *Up Your Own Organization.* Fairfield: The Entrepreneur Press, 1974. An enthusiastic guide to starting a business.

Drucker, Peter E. *Management: Tasks, Responsibilities, Practices.* New York: Harper and Row, 1974.

Drucker, Peter E. *Managing for Results.* New York: Harper and Row, 1964. Drucker writes sophisticated, philosophical books on business and management.

Greene, Gardiner G. *How to Start and Manage Your Own Business.* New York: New American Library, 1975. A good survey.

Nicholas, Ted. *How to Form Your Own Corporation Without a Lawyer for Under $50.00.* Wilmington: Enterprise Publishing Company, 1972. A step-by-step guide to incorporation complete with tear-out forms.

Peters, Thomas and Waterman, Robert. *In Search of Excellence.* New York: Warner Books, 1984.

Revel, Chase. *The Truth About Small Business Profits.* Santa Monica: Baronbrook Publishing Company, 1979. An enthusiastic book with many ideas for small businesses.

## BOOKS ON CLEANING

Aslett, Don A. *Is There Life After Housework?* Step-by-step instructions and diagrams show you how to clean every area of your home — and cut out up to 75% of your cleaning time!

Aslett, Don A. *Do I Dust or Vacuum First?* One hundred most-asked questions on cleaning with detailed answers.

Aslett, Don A. *Clutter's Last Stand.* It's time to dejunk your home and your life! Aslett provides all the inspiration, ideas, and encouragement you need in this fun-packed, eye-opening book.

Aslett, Don A. *Who Says It's a Woman's Job to Clean?* Aslett dares to tackle a new cause: getting men to do their share of the work around the house!

Aslett, Don A. *Make Your House Do the Housework.* Could there be such a thing as a maintenance free house? Aslett tackles that problem and also how to cut maintenance from the work place.

Aslett, Don A. *Pet Clean-Up Made Easy.* All the information you need to clean up pet messes — including what tools and products to use and where to find them. Plus everything you need to know to "petproof" your home and prevent messes from happening.

Aslett, Don A. *How Do I Clean the Moosehead? And 99 More Tough Questions about Housecleaning.* Those questions just keep coming! Detailed answers about how to clean a personal computer and which disinfectant is truly the best.

Aslett, Don A. *Clean It and Mean It + Lesson Plans.* A maintenance development course. Graphic, basic cleaning lessons with ability test for each chapter. Teacher's manual and answer key (for home and commercial).

Bishop, L.J. Jr. *Answers! Volume I — The Product.* More answers than you have questions about carpeting. Covers construction, fibers, yarns, dyes, wear factors, backing, pads, color restoration, defects. Geared to professional carpet cleaners who want to understand their product.

Bishop, L.J. Jr. *Answers! Volume II — The Procedures.* A comprehensive guide to carpet cleaning procedures. Covers basic installation, soiling, carpet fundamentals, chemistry, specialty chemicals, methods, pre-cleaning inspections, crew procedures, drying.

Bishop, L.J. Jr. *Specialized Carpet Spotting.* An 85-page illustrated book covering definitions, fiber and construction, identification, removal methods, equipment, basic chemicals, special agents, mystery discolorations.

Bishop, L.J. Jr. *Upholstery and Drapery Cleaning.* A comprehensive guide. Covers fibers, fabrics, fundamentals, chemicals, methods, including charts, illustrations, fabric samples.

Bishop, L.J. Jr. *Comprehensive Deodorization.* A complete book on professional deodorization by the industry's recognized expert. Includes basic procedures, concepts, chemicals and equipment for structure, contents, ductwork, automobiles.

Bishop, L.J. Jr. *Flood-Damage Restoration — Part I.* Organizing, managing, and marketing a flood-restoration service business. Covers selection of equipment and supplies, marketing, pricing the service, forms, paperwork.

Bishop, L.J. Jr. *Flood-Damage Restoration — Part II.* Specific, detailed technical procedures for dealing with flood damage in a variety of situations. The how-to-do-it on the job part.

Books by Don Aslett are available from: P.O. Box 1682, Pocatello, ID 83204. (208) 232-6212.

Books by L.J. Bishop are available from: Clean Care, 605 N. Oates Street, Dothan, AL 36302.

## MAGAZINES AND NEWSLETTERS ON CLEANING

*American Window Cleaner.* Bimonthly publication promoting "communication, safety and professionalism in window cleaning." 27 Oak Creek Road, El Sobrante, CA 94803. (415) 222-7080. FAX (415) 223-7080.

*Building Operating Management.* Monthly magazine covering a variety of topics for building managers. P.O. Box 694, Milwaukee, WI 53201-0694. (414) 228-7701. FAX (414) 228-1134.

*Cleaning Digest.* A bimonthly publication for professional cleaners, carpet manufacturers, department stores, building maintenance authorities, carpet sales, janitorial services, dry cleaners and laundries. 3940 N Keystone Avenue, Indianapolis, IN 46205. (317) 546-5448.

*Cleaning Management Magazine.* A monthly "how-to educational reference for the building cleaning maintenance industry." 13 Century Hill Drive, Latham, NY 12110-2197. (518) 783-1281. FAX (518) 783-1386.

*EHT Executive Housekeeping Today.* Monthly NEHA publication features "articles on problem-solving, training, new products and association news." 1001 Eastwind Drive, Suite 301, Westerville, OH 43081. (614) 895-7166. FAX (614) 895-1248.

*Installation & Cleaning Specialist.* "Published monthly for the nation's resilient floor covering installers, workrooms, contractors, installing retailers, cleaning and maintenance and distributors." 17835 Ventura Blvd., Encino, CA 91316. (818) 345-3550. FAX (818) 344-9647.

*Maintenance Supplies.* "A monthly magazine for sanitary supply distributors and manufacturer's agents." P.T.N. Publication Co., 445 Broad Hollow Road, Suite 21, Melville, NY 11747. (516) 845-2700.

*New York Rug Cleaners Institute Newsletter.* 301 Norman Avenue, Brooklyn, NY 11222. (718) 389-9129.

*Professional Cleaning Journal.* P.O. Box 810195, Dallas, TX 75381. (214) 484-4474. FAX (214) 484-4280.

*Professional Sanitation Management.* "A magazine about industrial sanitation published six times a year by the Environmental Management Association." 255 Detroit Street, Suite 200, Denver, CO 80206. (303) 320-7855. FAX (303) 393-0770.

*Sanitary Maintenance.* "The business journal for owner/executives of firms involved in distribution, building service contracting and manufacturing." P.O. Box 694, Milwaukee, WI 53201-0694. (414) 228-7701. FAX (414) 228-1134.

*Service Business Magazine.* Published for the self-employed professional cleaner nine times a year. P.O. Box 1273, Seattle, WA 98111. (206) 682-9748. FAX (206) 622-6876.

*Services.* The magazine of the Building Service Contractors Association International. 10201 Lee Highway, Suite 225, Fairfax, VA 22030. (800) 368-3414 (outside Virginia). FAX (703) 352-0493.

## BROCHURES AND BOOKLETS

Aslett, Don A., *Check Up.* A basic format for effective inspection and quality control. P.O. Box 1682, Pocatello, ID 83204. (208) 232-6212.

Aslett, Don A., *Ten Steps to Proper Telephone Building Maintenance.* Introduction and special needs when cleaning around special equipment. P.O. Box 1682, Pocatello, ID 83204. (208) 232-6212.

*Cooperative Extension Service Publications.* These valuable books, many about specific service techniques, are available from the Cooperative Extension Service office in each state. Stop by your local office.

*Dartnell Bulletins.* Useful bulletins about business supervision and management. 4660 North Ravenswood Avenue, Chicago, IL 60640. (312) 561-4000.

*The Tax Advisor* or *The Business Advisor.* Up-to-date tax and business information. 20271 Goldenrod Lane, Germantown, MD 20874. (301) 428-1040.

## UNITED STATES GOVERNMENT PUBLICATIONS

All of the following publications are available from the Superintendent of Documents, U.S. Government Printing Office, Washington, DC 20402. These are only a sample of the vast number of government publications useful to you. Write to the above address for an index to government publications, or contact the U.S. Government Printing Office Book Store in a city near you.

*Franchising and Business Opportunities.* Federal Trade Commission.

*A Guide to Basic Law and Procedures under the National Labor Relations Act.* National Labor Relations Board.

*Handy Reference Guide to the Fair Labor Standards Act.* U.S. Department of Labor.

*How to Write Positive Descriptions.* U.S. Civil Service Commission.

*Internal Revenue Service Publications.* These useful tax guides are available at all regional IRS offices.

*Personnel Testing and Equal Employment Opportunity.* Equal Employment Opportunity Commission.

*Small Business Administration Publications.* These valuable guides to all aspects of a small business are available free from all field offices of the Small Business Administration. Write to the U.S. Printing Office for a bibliography of these numerous publications.

*Urban Business Profile: Building Service Contracting.* This and other useful booklets are researched by the Department of Commerce, Economic Development Administration.

## SEMINARS AND TRAINING PROGRAMS

*American Management Associations.* A variety of management classes (as well as videos, tapes, and publications) offered throughout the U.S. and Canada. 135 West 50th Street, New York, NY 10020. (212) 586-8100.

*Building Service Contractors Association International.* 10201 Lee Highway, Suite 225, Fairfax, VA 22030. (800) 368-3414.

*Bureau of Business Practice.* Training manuals and other aids for managers, supervisors, and sales personnel. 24 Rope Ferry Road, Waterford, CT 06386. (203) 442-4365.

*Cleaning Consultant Services, Inc.* Offers seminars and training programs in supervision, management, and cleaning techniques. P.O. Box 1273, Seattle, WA 98111. (206) 682-9748.

*System 1 Seminars and Consulting.* Don Aslett's in-house training programs for you, your staff, your clients — you'll also see Don at industry conventions and the janitor rodeo! P.O. Box 1682, Pocatello, ID 83204. (208) 232-6212.

## TRAINING AIDS

The following companies provide various books, films, slide/sound and videocassette programs to aid in training custodians and supervisors.

AMS Distributors, Inc. P.O. Box 457, Roswell, GA 30077. (404) 442-1945. Training videos covering a wide range of general cleaning topics.

Cleaning Management Institute. 15550-D Rockfield Blvd., Irvine, CA 92718. (714) 770-5008. Maintenance Supervision Home Study Course, various books and articles on maintenance and supervision.

Management Dynamics. P.O. Box 15811, Boise, ID 83715. (203) 377-4461.

*Restroom Maintenance and Sanitation.* P.O. Box 15811, Boise, ID 83715. (208) 377-4461. Training video on restroom maintenance with accompanying text that includes quizzes.

Service Engineering Associates. P.O. Box 10095, Atlanta, GA 30319-0095. (404) 261-2050. Books and slide/sound programs dealing with various aspects of general and specialized cleaning, as well as supervision.

The Cleaning Center. 311 South Fifth Avenue, Pocatello, ID 83204. (208) 232-6212. Don Aslett's hilarious and helpful 90-minute video on how to clean a home the easy way — using professional products and equipment.

In addition to the above, many manufacturers of maintenance chemicals and equipment provide training programs which cover different aspects of cleaning and maintenance. Information on these can be obtained from janitorial-supply stores.

# Reproducible Blank Forms

# Detailed Contract Work Schedule

For

Days of Service _____

Time Service is performed _____

Building Representative _____

## Work to be Performed

| GENERAL CLEANING | TIMES PER WEEK | TIMES PER MONTH | TIMES PER YEAR |
|---|---|---|---|
| Empty and Damp-wipe AshTrays & Urns | | | |
| Empty Wastebaskets | | | |
| Dust Tops of Desks, Furniture, Counters | | | |
| Dust Telephones | | | |
| Dust Tops of Cabinets, Picture Frames | | | |
| Dust Partitions and Ledges | | | |
| Spot-clean or Damp-wipe Desk Tops | | | |
| Spot-clean Doors, Light Switches | | | |
| Spot-clean Walls, Partitions | | | |
| | | | |
| Clean Drinking Fountains | | | |
| Clean Sinks | | | |
| Damp-wipe Furniture in Eating Areas | | | |
| Dry clean Chalkboards (if erased) | | | |
| | | | |
| **PERIODIC GENERAL CLEANING** | | | |
| High Dusting | | | |
| Dust Venetian Blinds | | | |
| Polish or clean Kick Plates and Handrails | | | |
| Replace Burned-Out Bulbs and Lamps | | | |
| Dust or clean Vents and Grills | | | |
| Vacuum Window Draperies | | | |
| | | | |
| **FLOOR MAINTENANCE** | | | |
| Vacuum Carpeting - General Offices | | | |
| Vacuum Carpeting - Executive Offices | | | |
| Vacuum Carpeting - Lobbies and Hallways | | | |
| Vacuum Mats and Runners | | | |
| Dust-mop or sweep Hard Surface Floors | | | |
| Dust-mop or sweep Stairs & Landings | | | |
| Damp-mop or spot-mop Floors | | | |
| Spot-clean Carpet | | | |
| Buff or spray-buff Resilient Floors - Offices | | | |
| Buff or spray-buff Resilient Floors - Hallways | | | |
| Buff or spray-buff Resilient Floors - Entrance | | | |
| Surface Scrub Carpet | | | |
| | | | |
| Scrub and Wax Resilient Floors | | | |
| Strip, Seal, and Wax Resilient Floors | | | |
| Shampoo and/or Extract Carpeting | | | |
| | | | |

## Detailed Contract Work Schedule (Continued)

| Work to be Performed | TIMES PER WEEK | TIMES PER MONTH | TIMES PER YEAR |
|---|---|---|---|
| **REST ROOM CLEANING** | | | |
| Empty Trash and Waste Containers | | | |
| Re-fill Dispensers (Paper, Soap, Etc.) | | | |
| Clean Mirrors and Bright Work | | | |
| Clean and Sanitize Sink and Fixtures | | | |
| Clean and Sanitize Toilets and Urinals | | | |
| Dust Partitions and Furnishings | | | |
| Spot Clean Partitions and Walls | | | |
| Sweep and damp-mop Floors | | | |
| | | | |
| **MECHANICAL EQUIPMENT AND POWER ROOMS** | | | |
| Sweep Floors | | | |
| Change Filters | | | |
| Dust Low Flat Surfaces (Wall Fixtures, Etc.) | | | |
| Dust upper Cable Racks | | | |
| Dust Tops of Equipment | | | |
| Wax Floors | | | |
| | | | |
| **EXTERIOR MAINTENANCE** | | | |
| Sweep Walks | | | |
| Sweep Entranceway | | | |
| Police Grounds for Trash and Debris | | | |
| Cut and Trim Lawns | | | |
| Remove Weeds | | | |
| Water Lawns | | | |
| Sweep Parking Lot | | | |
| Remove Snow from Walks | | | |
| | | | |
| **GARAGE AREA** | | | |
| Remove Grease Spots | | | |
| Sweep Floor Area | | | |
| Hose Down Floor Area | | | |
| Low Dust Wall Fixtures | | | |
| | | | |
| **WINDOW CLEANING** | | | |
| Exterior Windows | | | |
| Interior Windows | | | |
| Lobby Glass | | | |
| | | | |
| **CLOSING INSTRUCTIONS** | | | |
| Arrange Furniture | | | |
| Clean Janitor Closet | | | |
| Report any Damage or unusual Circumstances | | | |
| Secure Exterior Doors and Windows | | | |
| Turn off Lights | | | |
| Turn on Night Lights | | | |

| EQUIPMENT AND SUPPLIES | FURNISHED BY CONTRACTOR | FURNISHED BY OWNER |
|---|---|---|
| Buffers - Vacuums | | |
| Cleaning Equipment (Carts, Buckets, Pails) | | |
| Restroom Soap, Paper, Napkins | | |
| Cleaning Chemicals and Compounds | | |
| Light Bulbs and Fluorescent Lamps | | |
| Dust Mops | | |
| Cleaning Rags - Cloths | | |
| Plastic Bags | | |

# Building Survey

SURVEYED BY: _____ DATE: _____

ACCOUNT: _____  CONTACT: _____

ADDRESS: _____  ZIP: _____ PHONE: _____

FREQUENCY: _____ WORK DAYS: _____ WORK TIME: _____ ALARM: _____

FLOORS: _____ CARPETS: _____ WINDOWS: _____ BLINDS: _____

LIGHTS: _____ SUPPLIES: _____ DENSITY: _____

PRESENT CONDITION: _____ INITIAL: _____

EQUIPMENT: _____ DISTANCE: _____

OVERALL DIMENSIONS: _____  GROSS SQ. FOOTAGE: _____

EXTERIOR MAINTENANCE: _____

| AREA | DIMENSIONS | FLOOR TYPE | NUMBER UNITS | | ESTIMATED TIME | WINDOWS @ _____ | BLINDS @ _____ | OTHER _____ |
|------|-----------|-----------|-------------|---|---------------|------------------|-----------------|---------------|
|  |  |  |  |  |  |  |  |  |
|  |  |  |  |  |  |  |  |  |
|  |  |  |  |  |  |  |  |  |
|  |  |  |  |  |  |  |  |  |
|  |  |  |  |  |  |  |  |  |
|  |  |  |  |  |  |  |  |  |
|  |  |  |  |  |  |  |  |  |
|  |  |  |  |  |  |  |  |  |
|  |  |  |  |  |  |  |  |  |
|  |  |  |  |  |  |  |  |  |
|  |  |  |  |  |  |  |  |  |
|  |  |  |  |  |  |  |  |  |
|  |  |  |  |  |  |  |  |  |
|  |  |  |  |  |  |  |  |  |
|  |  |  |  |  |  |  |  |  |
|  |  |  |  | TOTALS |  |  |  |  |

KEY: CC=COMMERCIAL CARPET; SC=SHAG CARPET;
R=RESILIENT FLOORING; CT=CERAMIC TILE; T=TERAZZO; CT=CONCRETE; W=WOOD

# Building Survey (cont.)

| AREA | DIMENSIONS | FLOOR TYPE | NUMBER UNITS | @ UNITS | ESTIMATED TIME | WINDOWS @ _____ | BLINDS @ _____ | OTHER _____ |
|---|---|---|---|---|---|---|---|---|
|  |  |  |  |  |  |  |  |  |
|  |  |  |  |  |  |  |  |  |
|  |  |  |  |  |  |  |  |  |
|  |  |  |  |  |  |  |  |  |
|  |  |  |  |  |  |  |  |  |
|  |  |  |  |  |  |  |  |  |
|  |  |  |  |  |  |  |  |  |
|  |  |  |  |  |  |  |  |  |
|  |  |  |  |  |  |  |  |  |
|  |  |  |  |  |  |  |  |  |
|  |  |  |  |  |  |  |  |  |
|  |  |  |  |  |  |  |  |  |
|  |  |  |  |  |  |  |  |  |
|  |  |  |  |  |  |  |  |  |
|  |  |  |  |  |  |  |  |  |
|  |  |  |  |  |  |  |  |  |
|  |  |  |  |  |  |  |  |  |
|  |  |  |  |  |  |  |  |  |
|  |  |  |  |  |  |  |  |  |
|  |  |  |  |  |  |  |  |  |
|  |  |  |  |  |  |  |  |  |
|  |  |  |  |  |  |  |  |  |
|  |  |  |  |  |  |  |  |  |
|  |  |  |  |  |  |  |  |  |
|  |  |  |  |  |  |  |  |  |
|  |  |  |  |  |  |  |  |  |
|  |  |  |  |  |  |  |  |  |
|  |  |  |  |  |  |  |  |  |
|  |  |  |  |  |  |  |  |  |
|  |  |  |  | TOTALS |  |  |  |  |

# Bid Work Sheet

Account Name:_____

Bid by:_____ Date:_____

| Daily Work | | | | | | | | |
|---|---|---|---|---|---|---|---|---|
| Area/Type | Square Footage | ÷ | Sq. Ft. Per Hour | = | Daily Hours | x | Days Per Mo. (21.1) | = | Hours Per Mo. |
| General Offices | | ÷ | | = | | x | | = | |
| Executive Offices | | ÷ | | = | | x | | = | |
| Corridors | | ÷ | | = | | x | | = | |
| Lobbies | | ÷ | | = | | x | | = | |
| Elevators | | ÷ | | = | | x | | = | |
| Cafeteria | | ÷ | | = | | x | | = | |
| Restrooms | | ÷ | | = | | x | | = | |
| Mechanical Rms. | | ÷ | | = | | x | | = | |
| Auditorium | | ÷ | | = | | x | | = | |
| Conference Rm. | | ÷ | | = | | x | | = | |
| | | | | | | | | |
| | | | | | | | | |
| **Totals** | | * | | | | ** | | |

**Total Daily Work Hours/Mo.**

* Does this agree with overall sq. footage estimate from survey?

** Does this agree with estimated time on survey sheet?

| Periodic Work | | | | | | |
|---|---|---|---|---|---|---|
| Area/Type | Task | Frequency | Unit | Unit Rate | Task Time | Hours*** Per Mo. |
| Resilient Floors | Strip & W | | | | | |
| Resilient Floors | Scrub & W | | | | | |
| Carpeting | Surf. Cln. | | | | | |
| Carpeting | Shampoo | | | | | |
| Carpeting | Extract | | | | | |
| Windows | Interior | | | | | |
| Windows | Exterior | | | | | |
| Parking Area | Police | | | | | |
| Parking Area | Sweep | | | | | |
| Stairs | Sweep | | | | | |
| Blinds | Dust | | | | | |
| Lights | | | | | | |
| | | | | | | |

***Weekly tasks x 4.33; Quarterly tasks ÷ 3; Annual tasks ÷ 12

**Total Periodic Work Hours/Mo.**

**Total Hours/Mo.**

## Bid Work Sheet cont.

| Work Loading | | | | | |
|---|---|---|---|---|---|
| Labor Type | Hours Per Month | x | Rate Per Hour | = | Labor Cost Per Month |
| Supervision | | x | | = | $ |
| General Cleaning | | x | | = | |
| Floor Work | | x | | = | |
| Utility | | x | | = | |
| Matron/Porter | | x | | = | |
| Trash | | x | | = | |
| Vacuum | | x | | = | |
| Restrooms | | x | | = | |
| | | x | | = | |
| | | x | | = | |

**Total Hours/Month** [_____]          **Total Labor**          $ [_____]

Payroll Costs:
F.I.C.A. _____ %
S.U.T. _____ %
F.U.T. _____ %
W/CI _____ %
PL/PD _____ %

TOTAL _____ %

Total Labor                 $ _____
Payroll Costs               _____
Supplies                    _____
Equipment Amortization      _____
Uniforms                    _____
Dust Mops, etc.             _____
_____            _____
_____            _____
Total Direct Cost           $ _____

Markup or Overhead          _____
Profit                      _____

Total Monthly Price         $ [_____]

Total sq. ft. _____ ÷ Total hours/mo. _____ = _____ Overall Production Rate

Total Monthly Price $_____ ÷ Sq. ft. _____ = $_____ Per sq. ft.

# Employment Application

**EQUAL EMPLOYMENT OPPORTUNITY POLICY**
Applicants are considered for all positions without regard to race, color, religion, sex, national origin, age, marital or veteran status, or the presence of a non-job related medical condition or handicap.

Date of Application ———————————

Position Applied For ————————————————————————————

Name In Full (last, middle, first) ——————————————————————

S.S.N. ————————————————————   Phone ————————

Home Address ——————————— City ———— State ———— Zip ————

Are you over eighteen years of age?   ❑ yes   ❑ no

Highest Education Level Completed ——————————————————

Do you have any physical condition that may limit your ability to perform the job for which you have applied?   ❑ yes   ❑ no

If yes, please explain ——————————————————————————
——————————————————————————————————————

Does heat, standing on your feet, or lifting cause you any difficulties? ————————————

## WORK HISTORY
*(Start with present or last job)*

| Date Employed | Employer | Position | Supervisor | Reason For Leaving |
|---|---|---|---|---|
| FROM | NAME | | | |
| TO | ADDRESS | | | |
| FOR OFFICE USE ONLY | | | | |
| | | | | |
| | | | | |
| FOR OFFICE USE ONLY | | | | |
| | | | | |
| | | | | |
| FOR OFFICE USE ONLY | | | | |
| | | | | |
| | | | | |
| | | | | |

Indicate languages you speak: _____ read: _____ write: _____

## REFERENCES:
(Name 3 persons other than relatives, former employers, or persons whose identity might
reveal or suggest religious or ethnic affiliation.  Include address and phone numbers.)

NAME                                    ADDRESS                                    PHONE

_____

_____

_____

What kind of work can you do? _____

_____

_____

Do you have reliable transportation? _____

HAVE YOU EVER BEEN CONVICTED OF A CRIME OTHER THAN MINOR TRAFFIC VIOLATIONS?   ❑ yes   ❑ no

If yes, explain fully.  A criminal conviction will not necessarily be a bar
to employment.  Any relevent factors such as age at time of the offense,
seriousness and nature of the violation, and rehabilitation will be taken
into account.

_____

I AUTHORIZE INVESTIGATION OF ALL STATEMENTS CONTAINED IN THE ATTACHED APPLICATION. I UNDER-
STAND THAT MISREPRESENTATION OR OMISSION OF FACTS CALLED FOR IS CAUSE FOR DISMISSAL.

Signature _____

Date _____

# Employee Reference Checklist

NAME _____SSN_____

CHECKED  BY  _____DATE _____

PERSON TALKED TO _____ PHONE _____

COMPANY_____ DEPT. _____

EMPLOYMENT VERIFICATION:

Employed  from  _____to  _____ Dept. _____

Position  _____  Supervisor  _____

**Could you please rate the employee on a scale of 1 to 10 for the following traits, 10 being best:**

Reliable   (dependable)                                                  _____

Punctual (showed up for work on time, etc.)                  _____

Trustworthy  (honest)                                                   _____

Job Skills (accomplishment of assigned job)                 _____

What  did  you  like  about  this  employee?_____

_____

Did you notice any problems or weaknesses which might cause

difficulties  in  the  new  job?_____

Would  you  re-hire  this  employee?_____

Any  other  comments?  _____

_____

_____

# YOU MUST READ FIRST

Please fill out time card completely. They must be signed by employee and supervisor before processing. Time cards must be in the office by the 15th and 30th of each month. Employees are responsible for their own time cards. All overtime prior to working must be approved by manager. Late time cards will be held and processed in the next pay period.

NAME OF BUILDING _____

MONTH _____

NAME _____

ADDRESS _____

CITY _____ STATE _____

ZIP _____ PHONE _____

SOCIAL SECURITY NUMBER _____

"I CERTIFY THAT THIS RECORD WHICH HAS BEEN MAINTAINED BY ME IS COMPLETE AND ACCURATE. I FURTHER ACKNOWLEDGE THAT I WAS GIVEN AN OPPORTUNITY TO MAKE CORRECTIONS."

_____
EMPLOYEE SIGNATURE          DATE

**Do Not Write in This Space**

EMPLOYEE NO. _____

| BLDG | HOURS | O.T. | RATE | TOTAL |
|---|---|---|---|---|
| | | | | |
| | | | | |
| | | | | |
| | | | | |
| | | | | |
| | | | | |

MILEAGE _____ OTHER _____

_____
SUPERVISOR

| DAY | DATE | NAME OF BUILDING BLDG. # | NAME OF BUILDING BLDG. # | NAME OF BUILDING BLDG. # | NAME OF BUILDING BLDG. # | NAME OF BUILDING BLDG. # | TOTAL |
|---|---|---|---|---|---|---|---|
| M | | | | | | | |
| T | | | | | | | |
| W | | | | | | | |
| TH | | | | | | | |
| FRI | | | | | | | |
| SAT | | | | | | | |
| SUN | | | | | | | |
| TOTAL | | | | | | | |
| M | | | | | | | |
| T | | | | | | | |
| W | | | | | | | |
| TH | | | | | | | |
| FRI | | | | | | | |
| SAT | | | | | | | |
| SUN | | | | | | | |
| TOTAL | | | | | | | |
| M | | | | | | | |
| T | | | | | | | |
| W | | | | | | | |
| TH | | | | | | | |
| FRI | | | | | | | |
| SAT | | | | | | | |
| SUN | | | | | | | |
| TOTAL | | | | | | | |
| M | | | | | | | |
| T | | | | | | | |
| W | | | | | | | |
| TH | | | | | | | |
| FRI | | | | | | | |
| SAT | | | | | | | |
| SUN | | | | | | | |
| TOTAL | | | | | | | |
| M | | | | | | | |
| T | | | | | | | |
| W | | | | | | | |
| TH | | | | | | | |
| FRI | | | | | | | |
| SAT | | | | | | | |
| SUN | | | | | | | |
| TOTAL | | | | | | | |
| M | | | | | | | |
| T | | | | | | | |
| W | | | | | | | |
| REG. HOURS | | | | | | | |
| O.T. HOURS | | | | | | | |
| TOTAL HOURS WORKED | | | | | | | |

# Employment Contract

THIS AGREEMENT made and entered into the date and place hereinbelow identified, by and between _____ _____ (hereinafter the "Company"), an_____ corporation, and _____ _____ (hereinafter "Employee").

## Introduction

The Company is engaged in the business of providing janitorial maintenance and related services, especially to large enterprises. Company desires to employ Employee for the period specified herein in accordance with the terms and conditions hereof and Employee desires to be so employed.

NOW, THEREFORE, IN CONSIDERATION OF THE MUTUAL PROMISES CONTAINED HEREIN, COMPANY AND EMPLOYEE AGREE AS FOLLOWS:

1.   **Retention of Employee.** Company hereby employs Employee to perform the duties hereinafter set forth and Employee hereby accepts said employment and agrees to perform said duties during the term of this agreement.

2.   **Duties.** Employee agrees to perform whatever duties may be required of him by the Company, including, but not necessarily limited to, the following:

and to otherwise assist in the successful operation of the Company's business as it is now or may hereafter be constituted. Employee shall discharge such specific responsibilities as the Company shall from time to time assign to him.

3.   **Term.** The term of employment under this contract shall commence _____, 19____, and shall continue thereafter until December 31 of the same year, and shall be renewed automatically each calendar year until terminated under the provisions of this contract.

4.   **Compensation.** Company agrees to pay Employee for all services rendered pursuant to the provisions of this Contract, and the Employee agrees to accept as full compensation, a salary of $_____, per _____, to be paid [(1) during the first week of each month] or [(2) in semimonthly installments] for the previous month's service. Said salary shall be reviewed at regular intervals by the Company and may be increased as the Company may direct.

Payment of salary is contingent upon Employee filing with the Company such report forms as the Company may direct, documenting Employee's activities for the week.

5.   **Exclusive Service.** Employee promises to work [(1) exclusively] or [(2) part time] for the Company during the term of this contract and to devote his entire time, attention and energies during his working hours to the business of the Company, and shall not be connected with or have any interest in any business similar to or competitive with that of the Company.

6.   **Incentive Compensation.** As additional compensation provided as an incentive for Employee to excel in his assigned duties, Company promises to pay Employee a portion of the Company's profits according to the following plan:

7.   **Fringe Benefits.** The Employee shall be entitled to participate in the following fringe benefit programs of the Company:

8.    **Vacation and Sick Leave.** After one year's continuous Employment, the Employee shall be entitled each year to a vacation of _____ weeks, during which time his compensation shall be paid in full. After several years employment with the Company, this agreement may be renegotiated to increase the amount of vacation time. In no case does vacation time accumulate beyond one (1) year.

9.    Restrictive Covenants.

9.1    **Confidential Information.** The Employee acknowledges that Company possesses certain proprietary information including but not limited to customer lists, service or personnel requirements, pricing of services or contracts, Company procedures, methods and processes; Company financial position or activities; and other privileged information. Employee promises that he will not at any time or in any direct or indirect manner divulge or communicate to any person, firm, or corporation any proprietary matters relating to the business of Company, Employee and Company stipulating that as between them, such information is important and gravely affects the successful conduct of Company's business and goodwill, and that any breach of the terms of this section shall be a material breach of this Agreement.

9.2    **Noncompetition.** The parties recognize that Employee will perform services of a unique, unusual and extraordinary character by reason of his training and abilities. Employee therefore agrees that he will not, either during the term of this agreement or for a period of one (1) year thereafter, engage directly or indirectly for himself or as a representative or employee of others, in the janitorial maintenance business or other business activity which is in competition with that of the Company, within an area of fifty (50) miles of Employee's principal place of business under this contract. Employee further agrees that he will not, during such period, directly or indirectly, for himself or for any other employer, solicit or divert or attempt to solicit or attempt to divert the patronage of any Company customers.

9.3    **Remedies.** In the event of a breach or threatened breach by the Employee of the provisions of this section, Company shall be entitled to an injunction restraining Employee from any breach by whole or in part, of the provisions of this section. Nothing herein shall be construed as prohibiting Company from pursuing any other remedies available to it for such breach or threatened breach, including the recovery of damages from the employee.

10.    **Termination.** The term of Employee's employment as set forth herein at Section 3 shall be subject to the Following:

(a)    Without cause, either party may terminate this agreement at any time upon giving thirty (30) days' written notice to the other party, and in that event, Company shall be under no obligation to Employee except to pay such compensation as Employee may be entitled to receive up to the date of termination.

(b)    Company reserves the right to terminate this agreement without advance notice for gross insubordination, repeated drunkeness, addiction, theft or embezzlement, fraud, disclosing of confidential or private Company information, aiding a competitor of the Company, violation by Employee of any of the provisions of this agreement, or failure or refusal to perform the services referred to herein.

(c)    Company shall be entitled to terminate this agreement in the event Employee dies or is permanently disabled from substantially performing his duty as assigned, in which event Employee shall be entitled to receive his salary computed to _____ days after termination and such other Employee benefits under the plans of the Company to which Employee is properly entitled only to the date of termination.

(d)    Company shall be entitled to terminate this agreement in the event Employee is temporarily disabled (whether by one or a series of events) so that he is unable to perform his duties during sixty (60) business days (whether or not consecutive) during any period of six calendar months.

11.    **Assignment.**

(a)    By the Company. This agreement shall be binding upon and shall insure to the benefit of the transferees, successors and assigns of the Company.

(b)    By Employee. Because this agreement is based upon the unique abilities and personal confidence in Employee, he shall have no right to assign this agreement or any of his right hereunder without the prior written consent of the Company.

12.    **Waiver.** A waiver of any term hereof shall not be construed as a general waiver by the Company, and the Company shall be free to reinstate any such term or condition without notice to Employee.

192   CLEANING UP FOR A LIVING

13.   **Company Policies.** Employee hereby acknowledges receipt of a company EMPLOYEE'S HANDBOOK which contains policies and guidelines for all levels of employees. Employee agrees to abide by said policies personally and to direct their compliance by employees under his supervision. Special note should be taken of the sections titled "Code of Conduct,' "Safety," and "Security," in this regard. Employee further agrees to abide by and enforce company policies contained in the company Policies and Procedures Manual, which may be added to or deleted from time to time. Employee agrees to take a lie detector test when and if requested to do so by the Company to verify the compliance of Employee with the terms of the above named policies. Employee further understands and agrees that his failure to pass said lie detector test or refusal to take said lie detector test may result in his immediate termination under this Employment Contract.

14.   **Severability.** The provisions of this contract are subject to compliance with state and federal laws and regulations governing such employment where applicable. The finding of any court of law that any portion of this contract is void or inoperable as a matter of law or equity shall have no effect as to the remaining parts and provisions of this contract.

15.   **Attorney's Fees.** In the event of any breach of this contract, the defaulting party shall pay any and all costs incurred by the other party for a reasonable attorney's fee or for arbitration in settling the claim or a controversy.

16.   **Integration.** This instrument contains the entire understanding of the parties with respect to the subject matter hereof. It may be amended or cancelled only by a written instrument signed by the party against whom enforcement of such amendment or cancellation is sought.

17.   **Prior Contracts.** This agreement voids any prior contracts between Employee and Company.

IN WITNESS WHEREOF, Employee has executed this agreement and Company has caused this agreement to be executed by a duly authorized employment officer, this _____ day of _____, 19____, in the city of _____, state of _____.

_____
Employee

By _____
Duly Authorized Employment Officer

# Inspection Form

P F G E

**ENTRANCE**

☐☐☐☐ Matt, Carpet
☐☐☐☐ Glass, Metal Surfaces
☐☐☐☐ Corners
☐☐☐☐ Floor

**LOBBIES**

☐☐☐☐ Dusting
☐☐☐☐ Floor Appearance
☐☐☐☐ Sweeping, Vacuuming
☐☐☐☐ Spot Cleaning
☐☐☐☐ Fixtures
☐☐☐☐ Water Fountains

**ELEVATORS**

☐☐☐☐ Treads
☐☐☐☐ Lights
☐☐☐☐ Walls, Doors
☐☐☐☐ Floor, Carpet

**CORRIDORS**

☐☐☐☐ Sweeping, Vacuuming
☐☐☐☐ Floor Appearance
☐☐☐☐ Baseboards
☐☐☐☐ Spot Cleaning
☐☐☐☐ Water Fountains

**STAIRWELLS**

☐☐☐☐ Rails, Walls
☐☐☐☐ Steps, Landings

**REST ROOMS**

☐☐☐☐ Dispensers, Hardware
☐☐☐☐ Basins
☐☐☐☐ Floors
☐☐☐☐ Mirrors
☐☐☐☐ Partitions
☐☐☐☐ Toilets, Urinals
☐☐☐☐ Waste Cans
☐☐☐☐ Walls, Doors

**OFFICE-EQUIPMENT AREAS**

☐☐☐☐ Ash Trays
☐☐☐☐ Furniture Equipment
☐☐☐☐ Doorkick Plates
☐☐☐☐ Phones, Lamps
☐☐☐☐ Walls, Doors, Spot Cleaning
☐☐☐☐ Waste Baskets
☐☐☐☐ Partitions
☐☐☐☐ Low Dusting
☐☐☐☐ High Dusting
☐☐☐☐ Floor Appearance
☐☐☐☐ Sweeping, Vacuuming
☐☐☐☐ Baseboards
☐☐☐☐ Corners

**WINDOWS**

☐☐☐☐ Glass
☐☐☐☐ Sills, Frames
☐☐☐☐ Blinds

**EXTERIOR & GROUNDS**

☐☐☐☐ Policing
☐☐☐☐ Sidewalks
☐☐☐☐ Entrance Area
☐☐☐☐ Stairwell, Equipment Drop
☐☐☐☐ Lawn Area
☐☐☐☐ Parking Area
☐☐☐☐ Trash Area

**JANITOR CLOSETS**

☐☐☐☐ Cleanliness, Organization
☐☐☐☐ Supplies, Equipment

**MISCELLANEOUS**

☐☐☐☐ Air Vents
☐☐☐☐ Exit Lights
☐☐☐☐ Carpet Spotting
☐☐☐☐ Cafeteria
☐☐☐☐ Phone Booth
☐☐☐☐ Storage Areas
☐☐☐☐ Other _____

Building_____ Floor _____ City_____

Inspected By _____ Employee_____ Date _____

| Classification | Poor | Fair | Good | Ex'llnt | Quality Value |
|---|---|---|---|---|---|
| Entrance | 3.5 | 5 | 6.5 | 8 | |
| Lobbies | 3.5 | 5 | 6.5 | 8 | |
| Elevators | 3 | 4 | 5 | 6 | |
| Corridors | 3 | 4 | 5 | 6 | |
| Stairwells | 1 | 2 | 3 | 4 | |
| Restrooms | 6 | 9 | 12 | 16 | |
| Office - Equipment Areas | 12 | 18 | 24 | 30 | |
| Windows | 1 | 2 | 3 | 4 | |
| Exterior & Grounds | 3 | 4 | 5 | 6 | |
| Janitor Closets | 3 | 4 | 5 | 6 | |
| Miscellaneous | 3 | 4 | 5 | 6 | |

Quality Index [        ]

Comments:

_____
_____
_____
_____
_____
_____
_____
_____
_____
_____
_____
_____
_____
_____
_____
_____
_____
_____

# Frequency Work Schedule

Month _____

| Account | Job | 1st Week | 2nd Week | 3rd Week | 4th Week | 5th Week |
|---------|-----|----------|----------|----------|----------|----------|
| | | | | | | |
| | | | | | | |
| | | | | | | |
| | | | | | | |
| | | | | | | |
| | | | | | | |
| | | | | | | |
| | | | | | | |
| | | | | | | |
| | | | | | | |
| | | | | | | |
| | | | | | | |
| | | | | | | |
| **EXAMPLE:** Mt. Bell - 5th. | F C | | STP B | | | |

**WINDOWS** (W) **FLOORS** (F) spray buff (B) scrub & wax (STP)
**CARPET** (C) spotclean (SC) deep extraction (EX) surface clean (B) bonnet **OTHER** _____

To be checked and reviewed at weekly staff meetings.

# Extra Work Job Sheet

ORDERED BY: _____  BILL TO:_____

_____ DATE _____  _____

_____ PHONE _____  _____

| DESCRIPTION OF WORK COMPLETED | UNIT COST | COST |
|---|---|---|
| LOCATION | | |
| | | |

JOB SHEET No. _____  TOTAL BILLING

DATE WORK COMPLETED | SIGNED:

## EXTRA WORK JOB SHEET

NUMBER_____

| FOR OFFICE USE ONLY | | | | FOR FIELD USE | | |
|---|---|---|---|---|---|---|
| CHECKED BY | DATE | POSTED & BILLED BY | DATE | PAY COMMISSION TO | AMOUNT | |

TOTALS

| LABOR EXPENSE | RATE | •••••• DATE •••••• | | | | | TOTAL HOURS | TOTAL COSTS |
|---|---|---|---|---|---|---|---|---|
| BOSS | | | | | | | | |
| | | | | | | | | |
| | | | | | | | | |
| | | | | | | | | |
| | | | | | | | | |
| | | | | | | | | |
| | | | | | | | | |
| | | | | | | | | |

TOTAL BILLING

TOTAL LABOR EXPENSE
PAYROLL EXPENSE 15%

OVERHEAD
(20% OF JOB COST)

TOTAL LABOR

### GENERAL EXPENSES

| GENERAL EXPENSES | | | | | | | | |
|---|---|---|---|---|---|---|---|---|
| VEHICLE | .18/mi | | | | | | | |
| PHONE | | | | | | | | |
| EQUIP. RENTAL | | | | | | | | |
| | | | | | | | | |
| | | | | | | | | |
| SOAP & CLEANERS | | | | | | | | |
| WAXES & FINISHES | | | | | | | | |
| TOWELS | .10 ea | | | | | | | |
| | | | | | | | | |
| PAINT | | | | | | | | |
| THINNER | | | | | | | | |
| OTHER PAINT EXP. | | | | | | | | |

PAYROLL EXPENSE 15%

GENERAL EXPENSES

TOTAL COSTS

PROFIT OR LOSS

BID BY: _____

WRITE RECOMMENDATION ON BACK | TOTAL GENERAL EXPENSE

PROFIT OR LOSS

# Disciplinary Action Report

Date_____ Location_____

_____, an employee of                    is hereby cited for

the following violation of company policy or procedure:_____

_____

_____

_____

_____

(continue on back if necessary)

This is the   ☐ first   ☐ second   ☐   third citation to this employee for this specific violation.

The following disciplinary action has been taken:_____

_____

_____

I have discussed this violation with my supervisor, and have received a copy of this citation.

Signed: _____ Date_____    _____ Date_____
                    employee                                                    supervisor

- - - - - - - - - - - - - - - - - - - - - - - - - - - - - - - - - - - - - - - - - - - - -

# Disciplinary Action Report

Date_____ Location_____

_____, an employee of                    is hereby cited for

the following violation of company policy or procedure:_____

_____

_____

_____

_____

(continue on back if necessary)

This is the   ☐ first   ☐ second   ☐   third citation to this employee for this specific violation.

The following disciplinary action has been taken:_____

_____

_____

I have discussed this violation with my supervisor, and have received a copy of this citation.

Signed: _____ Date_____    _____ Date_____
                    employee                                                    supervisor

# Maintenance Service Agreement

THIS AGREEMENT entered into on _____ between _____ whose address is _____, hereinafter referred to as "Company", and                              whose address is _____;

hereinafter referred to as "Contractor", for services to be provided at _____; Contractor shall, in accordance with the conditions and specifications set forth in this Agreement, furnish to Company building maintenance, supplies and services as specified in the attached Detailed Contract Work Schedule which is made a part hereof and by reference incorporated herein, for a period of _____ months beginning _____, 19 ____ In consideration of the above, Company agrees to pay to Contractor $_____ per month for services as outlined in the attached Detailed Contract Work Schedule, together with any other costs incurred for additional services as specified in the Cost Schedule hereto attached and by reference incorporated herein. Said sum shall be due and payable by the tenth day of each month, beginning _____ 10, 19 ____, and on the tenth day of each month thereafter.

IT IS MUTUALLY AGREED:

1. All work shall be performed by Contractor in a good and workmanlike manner, and Contractor shall provide regular inspections by the Contractor's supervisory personnel of all premises on which services are provided.

2. Company shall have no right to direct or instruct persons employed or hired by Contractor in the performance of services herein enumerated.

3. All supplies, equipment and property brought on to the premises by Contractor shall remain the property of Contractor and shall not be subject to any lien or encumbrance resulting from any action of or against Company. Contractor may remove such property during Company's normal business hours at Contractor's convenience.

4. Contractor shall carry worker's compensation insurance as required by state statute. Contractor shall carry liability insurance for personal and property damage in the amount specified in the Certificate of Insurance specimen hereto attached and by reference incorporated herein.

5. Company shall pay a service charge on any past due amounts, to be calculated at the rate of 18% per annum. Company shall pay any costs, including reasonable attorney's fees to enforce the provisions of this Agreement.

6. Company agrees to indemnify and hold Contractor harmless from any personal and/or property damage claims in excess the amounts specified in the Certificate of Insurance hereto attached and by reference incorporated herein.

7. Either party shall have the privilege, with or without cause, to terminate this Agreement at any time upon 30 days written notice to the other party as hereinafter specified.

8. In case of default by the Company of any of its agreements contained herein, Contractor shall have the right, at its option, to declare this contract null and void. Contractor may declare immediately due and payable all amounts due hereunder, including monthly payments for services not yet rendered.

9. In the event that Contractor continues to provide services on this contract beyond the initial term of this agreement, it is agreed that this contract will continue in effect until 30 days after written notice of termination is given by either party.

10. Notice to the parties, as herein required, shall be given in writing, by certified mail, at the above listed addresses.

11. Modifications to this agreement may be made by mutual consent of the parties, which consent must be in writing and signed by both parties.

12. Company may, at its option, request Contractor to perform additional services beyond those listed on the attached Detailed Contract Work Schedule and Cost Schedule. However, Company agrees that any additional work will be performed at a price mutually agreed upon by the parties as of the time of performance. Such additional services shall be performed in accordance with the terms of this agreement.

13. Company may not assign its right under this agreement without prior written consent of Contractor.

14. No services shall be performed by Contractor, its employees or subcontractors which, in Contractor's sole opinion, pose a safety hazard.

15. During the course of this Agreement or in the event of its termination for any cause, Company shall not solicit employment of any employees or subcontractors of Contractor for a period of _____ months.

16. This agreement shall be governed by the laws of the State of _____

17. Additional terms:

COMPANY:

By _____
       Authorized Signature

CONTRACTOR:

By _____
       Authorized Signature

# Index